THE EARTH, THE STARS, AND THE BIBLE

Paul Steidl

PRESBYTERIAN AND REFORMED PUBLISHING COMPANY

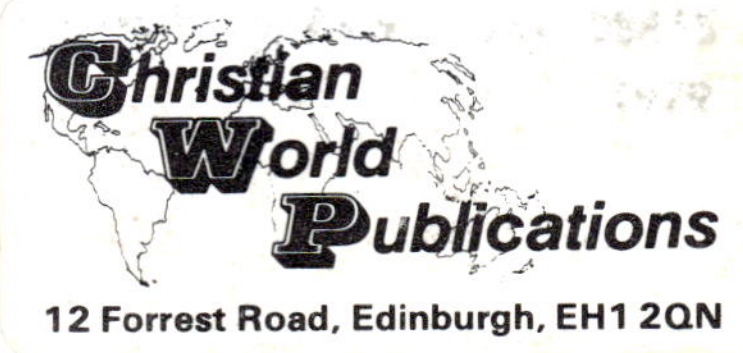

Printed in the United States of America

To Joanne

CONTENTS

PREFACE vii
1. ASTRONOMY AND THE CHRISTIAN 1
2. SOME FUNDAMENTALS 9
3. THE EARTH 18
4. THE SOLAR SYSTEM 31
5. THE MOON 62
6. THE SUN 80
7. THE FORMATION OF THE SOLAR SYSTEM 97
8. STARS 124
9. GALAXIES 161
10. COSMOLOGY 188
11. OF GALAXIES, QUASARS, AND REDSHIFTS 211
12. PROBLEMS OF TIME 219
13. LIFE 225
APPENDIX 239
INDEX 241

PREFACE

Ever since I started studying astronomy in school I have felt that this science in particular had more to say about the wonders of God's creation than almost any other. Perhaps each Christian who has studied a science feels the same way about his own, and that is as it should be. Everything that God has created praises His name (Phil. 2:9, 10).

This book represents my efforts to discern the hand of God in the heavens. It has not always been easy to divorce the facts from the evolutionary framework in which they are usually presented; often a closer examination of a "fact" reveals that it is really only an interpretation after all. Hopefully no one will find fault with any of the facts presented here. But there will certainly be some who disagree with my interpretation, perhaps violently. This is bound to be the case when someone presents an interpretation contrary to the prevailing views, and especially when it has a bearing on man's relationship to God. For these people, I hope that this book will at least bring to their attention the legitimacy of applying a Christian point of view to the study of astronomy. For those who, like me, feel that every aspect of God's creation can be studied profitably in the light of His inerrant word, I hope that this book gives a deeper understanding of and appreciation for the marvels of His creation in the heavens.

Paul M. Steidl
December 6, 1978

1 ASTRONOMY AND THE CHRISTIAN

For the invisible things of him from the creation of the world are clearly seen, being understood by the things that are made, even his eternal power and Godhead; so that they are without excuse (Rom. 1:20).

Astronomy is unique among the sciences. In scope it includes the entire physical universe, including much of the earth itself. It is also the most limited of sciences in the sense that it can perform no experiments—it can only observe. Astronomy is possibly the most intriguing of all the sciences. Our imaginations are easily carried away to the blowing desert sands of Mars, or the icy surface of one of Jupiter's moons, or to a distant star which no man will ever visit. The sheer inaccessibility of the stars is both frustrating and fascinating. When we add to this the fact that now, in our generation, we are just beginning to visit other planets for the first time in human history, it is apparent that astronomy is a dynamic science with something of interest for everyone.

LOOKING AT THE HEAVENS

What does astronomy have to do with the Christian? Does a Christian see anything different through a telescope than the non-Christian? In a way, yes. Thousands of years ago David wrote, "The heavens declare the glory of God; and the firmament sheweth his handiwork. Day unto day uttereth speech, and night unto night sheweth knowledge. There is no speech nor language, where their voice is not heard" (Ps. 19:1-3). David saw God's glory in the heavens; they spoke to him in a language understandable to all. However, most astronomy textbooks do not devote any space to the glory of God. Clearly most astronomers have missed something—they see something different in the sky than David did. This book is intended to show what the astronomers missed, including, of course, much of what they did not miss. For even though most astronomers have been blind to the glory of God in the heavens, they have enabled us to see it much better. The invention of the telescope about four centuries ago expanded the visible universe by thousands of times. Today's modern equipment has expanded it thousands of times more. Christians are indebted to astronomers for helping them see the heavens far better than David ever could, and thus to hear their language far more clearly. Modern discoveries play a large part in making astronomy relevant to the Christian.

How can one read the language of the heavens? The apostle Paul wrote, "For the invisible things of him from the creation of the world are clearly seen, being understood by the things that are made, even his eternal power and Godhead." What one sees when he looks at nature, and especially when he gazes into the heavens, is that it must have taken an infinitely powerful and wise God to do this. In addition, he sees the beauty there, the glory of God in the immeasurable outpouring of starlight, the delicate colors of a reflection nebula, the almost toylike perfection of a spiral galaxy. All this is the work of God's hands and a reflection of His mind. The heavens are a show of infinite variety and endless energy. The psalmist, in his necessarily limited way, must have had this in mind.

Filling mankind with awe, however, is not the only way the heavens speak. The Bible makes some definite statements which have astronomical implications. If observations show these to be true, then the heavens have confirmed the truth of the word of God. This I believe to be their major function. Some of these statements are about the earth. The other statements concern the Biblical account of creation.

THE AGE OF THE UNIVERSE

We are told in the first chapter of Genesis that God created the heavens and the earth, and finished them all within a period of six days. Now the Bible is not filled with deception—this is not the nature of God. Certainly if we must be like a child to enter the kingdom of God, we may also, with childlike faith, believe that what God has said about creation is true. There are certainly many fine Christians who, for a variety of reasons, prefer to accept scientists' statements that the universe is many billions of years old. But it is much better to accept the word of God that He created it in six days. And as this book will show, this is not as unreasonable as some believe.

There is also enough information given in the genealogies of the Bible to indicate that this six-day creation did not take place billions of years ago but thousands. Following the Genesis figures, as did Bishop Ussher, gives a date for the creation of about 4004 B.C. This may not be altogether correct since, for instance, the figures vary among different manuscripts. But it does show that there is no room for the millions of years during which the world is supposed to have evolved. The word of God says that creation took place in six days (Ex. 20:11) and that it was only a few thousand years ago (from the genealogies in Gen. chaps. 5 and 10, and Luke 3, for example). This is the view that has always been accepted by most conservative Christians and it is the view adopted in this book. I hope to show that this is also what the heavens are proclaiming in every speech and language.

Evolutionist Assumptions

Since astronomers are limited in that they cannot perform actual experiments with what they are observing,* astronomy tends to take on the aspects of philosophy as well as science. In order to develop a theory to explain some observed facts, a scientist must make some assumptions. These assumptions usually deal with the nature of the physical universe and concern laws and principles, such as the law of gravity. Never having been to distant galaxies, astronomers can only assume that the same laws of gravity work there as here; hence the applicability of the law of gravity on a universal scale is an assumption. One assumption that is always made, though usually not explicitly, is that the universe is very old. This idea is derived primarily from the areas of geology and evolution, which, over the last two centuries, have demanded more and more time for their slow

* Only now is this beginning to change in the area of planetary astronomy.

processes to develop the earth into what it is. The great age is not based upon astronomical evidence initially but upon the theory of evolution which many Christians, correctly we feel, believe not to be true. If the theory of evolution is disregarded, there is far less reason to begin with the assumption that the universe is old. The evidence can be examined more objectively.

Evolution itself is more a philosophy than a science. It begins with the implicit assumption that God did not create the universe. Astronomy is like a philosophy since hidden deep within astronomy's foundational presuppositions are the philosophical assumptions about the nonexistence of God which have been gradually infiltrating all the sciences for centuries. Some areas of astronomy are naturally more affected by this than others, for example, stellar evolution and cosmology. When scientists make observations, they automatically try to fit what they see into the framework of their assumptions. Thus they build an entire system for interpreting evidence upon their assumptions, some of which may be more philosophical than scientific. If it should turn out that in fact the observations do not fit their theories, it speaks poorly for their assumptions. Part of the scientific method is to revise theories and assumptions on the basis of how well the predictions fit the evidence, and this is a necessary part of any science. If it is shown that modern theories are not in accord with the evidence, or are untenable for other reasons, it indicates that there is a flaw somewhere in their assumptions.

Christian Assumptions

As Christians we also have a philosophy with assumptions concerning the time and nature of creation. This book will try to fit them into the framework of a Christian philosophy. No excuses need be made for this, for assumptions are necessary before one can proceed. The word of God indicates that our Christian assumptions are more valid than those of modern evolutionary science.

It is impossible that incorrect assumptions will constantly produce correct conclusions or predictions. Thus much of the current astronomical theory, if it is indeed based upon false assumptions, will run up against observations for which it cannot account, but which can be accounted for within Christian presuppositions. One role the Christian can play in astronomy is to start with the correct set of presuppositions, fit observations into the framework of these assumptions, and consequently obtain correct results and predictions.

At present such results and predictions are necessarily limited since very little time has been devoted to this type of astronomy.

Throughout this book I shall be dealing with such elements of Christian participation in astronomy as the wonder, beauty, and grandeur of creation as evidence of God's power and Godhead, the confirmation of Biblical statements pertinent to astronomy, and the far larger task of fitting observations into a Christian philosophical framework. The last-mentioned takes in far more ground than the first two as it involves all observations. This process will consist primarily of three elements: (1) using astronomical evidence to show that the universe is much younger than astronomers think, thus confirming the Biblical statements about a recent creation, (2) showing that man-made theories and philosophies do not fit the observations, and that only by God's revelation can we hope to understand our universe, and (3) giving whatever predictions can be made at present.

The "Christian assumptions" used in this book need to be stated explicitly. They are, I believe, based upon sound Biblical exegesis. First, there is an all-powerful and omniscient God who created the universe. Second, in spite of differing opinions among the Christian community, He did it recently. For lack of a precise number, I shall simply say about ten thousand years ago. Third, God did not create haphazardly but for a purpose, and with wisdom and organization. Thus it is proper and even obligatory to ask not only when God created, but also, why He created as He did.

Before proceeding, there are two matters which I wish to discuss in the light of the Christian viewpoint as applied to astronomy. The first is a point often raised by those who can accept God as the Creator but cannot accept Him as a personal God. The arguments usually state that because the universe is so very large and we, by comparison, are so small, God cannot really be concerned about us. Surely a God who can create all that has better things to do than occupy Himself primarily with our little earth. He must, in fact, have created millions of civilizations besides ours to amuse Himself or keep Himself busy. However, those who say this are limiting God, not in power but in compassion. They grant Him power but deny Him the love which He promises for each individual human. Thus they rob Him of His Godhead, for God is Love. In fact, the size of the universe is not so much a statement of His power as it is of His love for us. His love is shown by the fact that a God who *can* create all that He *has in fact* created, loved us enough to concern Himself solely with us and to let His Son die for us. The size of the universe is awesome and reveals the power of God. But only in His word can we find the truth concerning His relationship to us.

Christians must also reject the notion that disproof of geocentricity shows that we are, after all, nothing special in God's sight. The church of the Middle Ages insisted that the earth was the center of the universe, physically as well as spiritually. The universe was thought to be geocentric or earth-centered with the sun, moon, and stars revolving around the earth. Galileo was threatened with death by burning at the stake unless he retracted his statements that the earth actually moved. Later, when it was demonstrated that the earth does move around the sun, it was considered not only a blow to the church's views of the physical universe, but to its views of God as well. Since then it has additionally been shown that the sun is not at the center of the universe, as some tried to maintain. The sun is not even the center of our galaxy, the Milky Way. Neither is the Milky Way galaxy the largest galaxy in the universe, or the most central one, as some have proposed in order to save the outdated dogmas of the church. The sun occupies an average place in an average galaxy in an average cluster of galaxies. Some astronomy books, in presenting the history of man's changing view of his place in the universe, imply that a belief in God, or in God's concern for man, is as outdated as the medieval church's belief that the earth was the center of the universe.

While proof that the universe is indeed geocentric might be strong evidence of God's concern for the earth alone, disproof of geocentricity does not demonstrate a lack of God's concern. The truths of God's word and the work of Jesus Christ in no way depend upon our position. This is adequately demonstrated in Romans 5:8: "But God commendeth his love toward us, in that, while we were yet sinners, Christ died for us." If anything, our lack of a unique position in the natural universe is only an illustration of the natural man's lack of a unique position before God. God does not love us because of what we are or where we are. We have nothing to present to Him which could justify us in His sight (Ps. 49:7). It is only because of what God has done for us, reconciling us to Himself through the blood of Jesus, that we have any standing at all. In this sense we are His special concern, but we should not expect the natural universe to know anything of it by putting us at the center any more than we can expect the natural man to understand the gifts of the

Spirit of God. It may be, perhaps, that in the new creation when God makes a new heaven and a new earth, our unique position in Christ will be reflected by a central position in the physical heavens. But for now we have no reason to expect it. The disproof of geocentricity, instead of dismaying the church, should cause us to reflect on God's love and grace.

Viewing astronomy from a Christian point of view consists basically of fitting astronomical evidence into the framework of Christian presuppositions as derived from Biblical statements and principles. This will be applied differently in different areas of astronomy. The Bible has much to say about the earth, comparatively little about the stars, and nothing about galaxies or cosmology. Observations of the earth fit into the Biblical framework by directly corroborating its statements. At the solar system level there are no Biblical statements to corroborate, but there are evidences for the age of the solar system. Expanding to the level of the galaxy, we may find age evidences as well as objects of great beauty or power which illustrate God's nature or power. As we go farther into space, other galaxies can also indicate ages, but with far less certainty than does the solar system. Here also one can begin to see how man's theories fail to explain the universe, and that only by a revelation by the Maker of the universe can man expect to gain any insight into it. Each area has its own contribution to make to our understanding of that revelation, and each area is different.

Not all age indicators point conveniently to a few thousand years. There are many evidences for great age in the universe. Some of these depend entirely upon the philosophical framework within which scientists have chosen to work and are thus not important. Some are only upper limits, the maximum age that the universe could be. It could, of course, always be younger than these limits. Other estimates do point to millions or billions of years. We cannot dismiss these as simply the results of atheistic philosophies, for while they fit nicely into these philosophies, they can also stand alone. The Christian must face these squarely, realizing that they may have something to say to him one way or another, perhaps only that further evaluation is necessary. We will often have suggestions as to how these might be interpreted, but there will always be questions which, for now at least, must go unanswered.

It is also true that one cannot examine every age estimate in astronomy—there are far too many. Every astronomical object is assigned an age. Some estimates are on sounder ground than others. We shall try to pick out those examples which are most important, either because they are strongly for us or against us, or because of special interest. We believe that a strong case has been made for the viability of the Christian interpretation of astronomy.

2 SOME FUNDAMENTALS

This is not intended to be a textbook on astronomy, but there are still a few points that must be explained to enable the reader to understand the discussion to follow. We begin by giving a description of the immense size of our universe, a greatness that most people do not realize. Then we explain two of the most basic tools of the astronomer—spectral lines and the Doppler shift. In this chapter and throughout the book we will be using scientific notation to express extremely large or extremely small numbers. For those who need a refresher on scientific notation, there is an explanation in the appendix.

THE IMMENSITY OF THE UNIVERSE

To begin with, we shall look not at the very large, but at the very small. Nearly the smallest thing known is the nucleus of an atom, the concentration of mass at the atom's center. If we pick the meter (about one yard) for the standard of length, the nucleus of an atom is about 10^{-15} meter in diameter. (Much easier than saying one millionth of a billionth of a meter.) A line made of one billion of these would still be too short to see. The atom itself is much larger, about 10^{-10} meter. (It is apparent that an atom is mostly empty space!) Yet it would still take tens of thousands of them to make a line the eye could see.

Another jump to the size of a human cell places us at about 10^{-6} meter. Another step to the human body gives a size of two meters. Even before reaching the size of a man we have passed a fantastic range in size, and an even greater increase in complexity.

The next jump is to the size of the earth, which is over 10^7 meters, ten million times the height of a man. While this appears large to a man upon its surface, the earth is completely dwarfed by the distance to the earth's nearest neighbor in space—the moon. The distance to the moon is 4×10^8 on our scale, or forty times the earth's diameter. The earth and the moon orbit the sun together at a distance of 10^{11} meters, a further increase of 100 times. The diameter of the whole solar system, which is the diameter of the orbit of Pluto, the most distant known planet, is 10^{13} meters.

If the whole solar system were reduced to the size of a football field with the sun on the fifty yard line, the planet Pluto would be on the goal line at one end. The sun would be the size of a marble, and the earth would be a small grain of sand four feet away. Though the earth may seem small in comparison with the vast size of the solar system, the solar system itself is our own back yard in comparison with our galaxy, and is invisible from the nearest star, except for the sun itself. The nearest stars are 10^{17} meters away. Using the football field model, the nearest star is another marble four hundred miles away. If our football field were in San Francisco, the nearest star might be in San Diego.

Stars are organized into much larger systems called galaxies. We live in the Milky Way galaxy. The Milky Way is 10^{21} meters in diameter, or about one hundred thousand times the distance to the nearest star, and contains 10^{11} stars. We begin to run out of comparisons at this point. Already, compared to the size of the galaxy, the earth is so small as to be entirely insignificant in influencing the physical universe. Insignificant it would be, did we not know that it is with the earth that God concerns Himself. But we are far from finished exploring the size of the universe. There are millions and billions of known galaxies, and they continue to increase in number as telescopes probe further and further into space. Galaxies appear to be organized into clusters of galaxies, and those clusters may also be organized into clusters of clusters, known as super clusters. The cluster to which our galaxy belongs is known as the Local Group. As clusters of galaxies go, it is fairly small, but on our scale it is 10^{22} meters. We have finally reached the size where astronomers use the word *local.*

Is the Galaxy also a member of a supercluster? Many astronomers think so and it has been called the local supercluster. On our scale it comes to 10^{24} meters. How many superclusters are there? Are there clusters of superclusters? These questions haven't been answered yet. This leaves the next jump in size to be the final one, the universe itself. I cannot give the exact size of the universe; telescopes are able to see only so far and no farther, and as yet astronomers have not seen the edge. They do not even know if there is an edge. A rough estimate of the size of the universe which they are able to see is 10^{26} meters. However, astronomers still discuss whether the universe is finite or infinite, and whether it is flat or curved, and how. These questions belong to the subject of cosmology.

We should indeed be truly awed by what we see in creation, both in the ranges of size and complexity. From the atom, to man, to the universe, we see the power, wisdom, and even imagination of the Creator always manifest. And we should realize that to show this very thing is part of God's reason for creating the universe as it is.

SPECTRAL LINES

A great deal of information about stars and other heavenly bodies comes to us in the form of lines in their spectra. This deserves further explanation. Normal white light as from the sun can be broken up into colors by means of a prism. Visible light is part of the electromagnetic spectrum. The light we can see, the visible spectrum, is only a small portion of the entire spectrum of radiation. Other portions of the spectrum are known by different names, such as x-rays, radio waves, infra-red, and so on. All these forms are basically the same; they differ only in the amount of energy they possess. A complete spectrum, say of the sun, would range from radio waves at the low energy end through infra-red, visible, ultra-violet, x-rays, and gamma rays at the high energy end. Any hot object gives off some electromagnetic radiation of all energies. The hotter an object is, the more energy it radiates at all wavelengths.

Electromagnetic radiation can be described by either its wavelength or its frequency. One might think of light as a wave (waving electric and magnetic fields). The wavelength, as shown in figure 1, is the distance between two crests of the wave, and the frequency is the number of times it "waves" per second. The energy is proportional to the frequency. The higher the frequency of a light wave, the higher its energy, and, as it turns out, the shorter the wavelength. By using

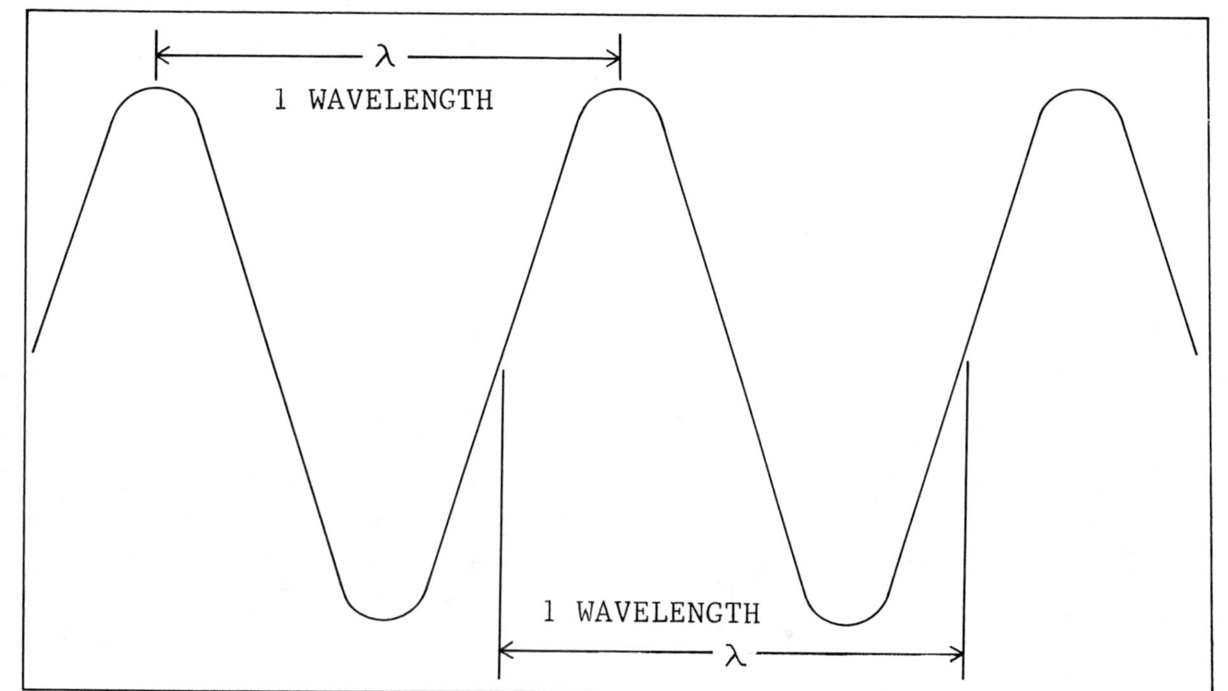

FIGURE 1.—The wavelength of a wave is the distance between corresponding points on successive waves.

a spectroscope, the fancy equivalent of the prism, an astronomer at a telescope can break down the light from a star or a galaxy into its spectrum.

Figure 2 shows a portion of a negative of the spectrum of a star. The many light lines are the spectral lines. From our previous discussion it can be seen that each line corresponds to a particular energy of light that is missing. To see how this comes about we have to delve into the structure of the atom. Most people are familiar with the fact that an atom consists of a fairly heavy nucleus around which the atom's electrons orbit. The nucleus of the atom consists of two types of particles, the protons which are positively charged, and the equally weighty neutrons which have no charge. The electrons, which are negatively charged and weigh only about one two-thousandth as much as the protons and neutrons, whip about in a sort of orbit around the nucleus, somewhat as the planets orbit the sun.

The type of element to which an atom belongs is determined by the number of protons in the nucleus. Hydrogen atoms, the lightest, have one proton, helium has two, lithium three, and so on. The number of neutrons may vary, but is usually about the same as the number of protons. If an atom is to have no electric charge, it must have the same number of electrons as it does protons so that the equal numbers of positive and negative charges will cancel. The situation can be otherwise, however. If something gives one of the electrons enough of a kick, it may be dislodged from the atom entirely. The remaining atom is then positively charged and is called an ion.

In the case of the solar system an object is allowed to orbit the sun in just about any orbit it pleases. This is not so with atoms. An electron in an atom is restricted in the number of orbits it may occupy. A hydrogen atom is shown schematically in figure 3 with some of the orbits allowed for its electron. The fundamental difference between the different orbits is the energy which the electron must have to occupy them. An electron in the innermost orbit has the least total amount of energy. The energy increases progressively with increasing orbit size. What supplies the energy for the electron to jump from one orbit to another? Light.

For this purpose we must think of light as little bundles of energy. If the light's energy is absorbed by the electron upon which it falls, it will be kicked into a higher, more energetic orbit. But since there are only certain allowable orbits, there are only certain allowable energies. Our photon of light must have just the right energy to kick

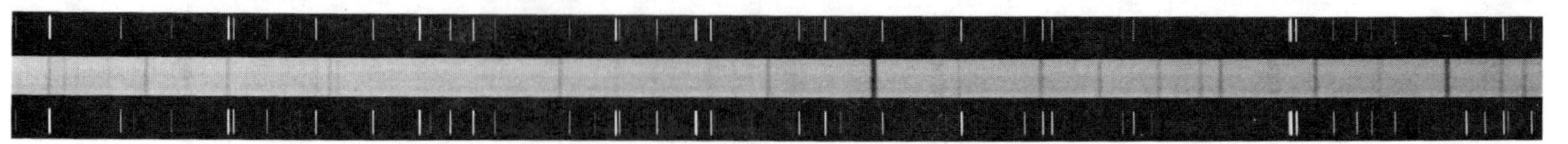

FIGURE 2.—The spectrum of the star α Lyra. Lick Observatory Photograph.

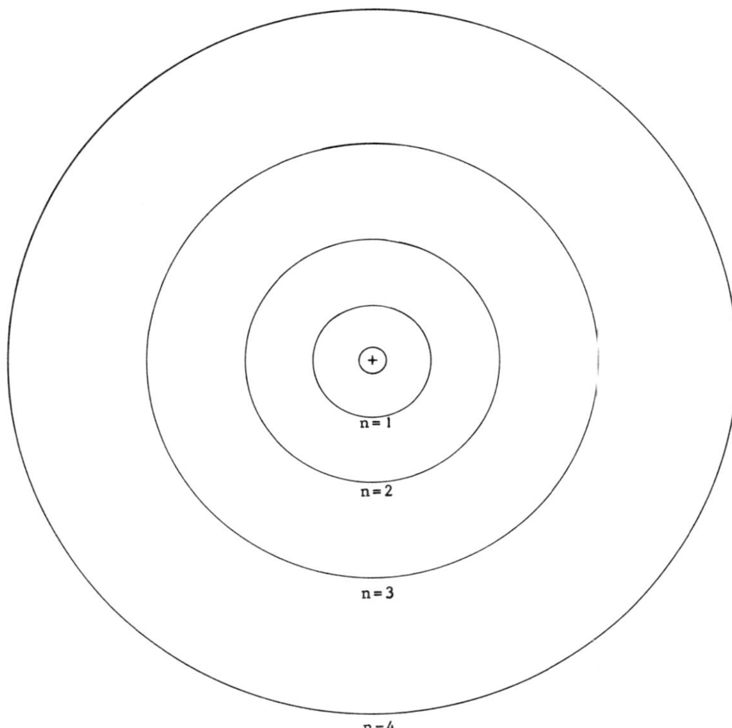

FIGURE 3.—Diagram of some of the orbitals in a hydrogen atom.

the electron into the higher orbit if it is to be absorbed. If it has too much energy the electron ignores it. If it does not have enough energy, it will not be able to supply the energy the electron needs to move upward. If our hydrogen atoms are in the atmosphere of a star, and the starlight, which contains photons of all energies, is passing through the hydrogen, the electrons of the hydrogen atoms will be able to absorb only those photons which have the right energies to move them from one orbit to another. The rest of the photons will be left alone. An observer on earth looking at the spectrum of the star sees that photons of certain energies are missing; they were absorbed by the atoms in the star. Remember that light can be described either by its wavelength or its energy. The prism, or spectroscope, separates light according to its wavelength and thus also according to its energy. In the visible portion of the spectrum we see different wavelengths of light as different colors. Thus in the spectrum there is a continuous range of color except where they have been removed by the absorbing atoms.

The second important point is that each type of atom has a different set of permitted orbits or energy levels. Thus astronomers can determine which types of atoms are present in the star from which colors are missing (the positions of the lines). This is how astronomers tell what a star is made of. It should be obvious that the more absorbing atoms there are in a star, the darker will be the spectral lines. Thus astronomers can tell not only which elements are present in a star, but also approximately how abundant they are. In reality, things are considerably more complicated than I have described them here. But this has its advantages also, for detailed analysis of spectral lines can tell an astronomer what the surface temperature of a star is, whether or not it is spinning, how big its magnetic field is, and a host of other wonderful things. And this is the way we learn about stars. All that can be known about any heavenly object is through similar analysis of the light we receive from it.

THE DOPPLER SHIFT

The final tool I shall discuss is the Doppler shift, named after the man who discovered it. The Doppler shift is the change in wavelength (or energy or frequency) of a wave when the object which emits the wave is moving. Everyone is familiar with the fact that a train whistle or an automobile horn has a different pitch when it is moving towards us than when it is moving away. At the moment the object passes a distinct change in the pitch can be heard. This is the Doppler shift, and it applies in principle to anything which acts like a wave, including light. If an object which emits light, such as a star, is moving towards us, we perceive the light at a slightly higher frequency or energy than we would if the object were standing still. A normally "white" star might look a little bluer when it is moving quickly towards us. Actually, though, it is not the apparent color change which is measured, for the change is usually too small to see. It is the position of the spectral lines which shift. A line which normally appears in the red portion of the spectrum might appear in the blue when it is moving with sufficient speed towards us. Thus any light-emitting object moving towards the earth is said to be blue-shifted.

Correspondingly, an object moving away from us is said to be red-shifted.

For example, quasars are objects moving so quickly away from us that spectral lines which normally appear in the ultra-violet portion of the spectrum are shifted into the visible. The unfamiliar appearance of the lines prevented them from being identified readily. When it was realized at last that the unfamiliar lines were actually familiar ones which had been red-shifted by a large amount, it created quite a sensation. If the Doppler interpretation of quasar redshifts is correct, it means that some quasars are moving away from the earth at speeds which are substantial fractions of the speed of light.

These phenomena have been explained in only enough detail to enable the reader to understand the discussion in the following chapters. Those interested in more information can find it easily in many introductory astronomy texts. But even with the brief explanation given here, the reader has gained enough insight into these physical processes to understand quite a bit about the work of astronomers and the nature of the universe.

3 THE EARTH

For the earth shall be filled with the knowledge of the glory of the Lord, as the waters cover the sea (Hab. 2:14).

If the knowledge of the glory of the Lord will not fill the earth until Christ's reign, it is not because His glory isn't here already. It is manifest in the things which He has made. There is nothing on earth or in heaven which does not by its very existence cry out that it has been made by an all-wise God. The complexity of the simplest living creatures is still beyond man's ability to understand. The beauty which is a snow-capped mountain range or a single flower speaks eloquently of a beautiful Creator. We cry out with David, "I will praise thee; for I am fearfully and wonderfully made; marvelous are thy works; and that my soul knoweth right well" (Ps. 139:14).

What do all these things have to do with astronomy? They are all a part of our earth, and any study of astronomy must begin with an understanding of the position in the universe of this most familiar of planets. The earth is an astronomical object in orbit about a star. It is one of the solar system's nine known planets, and, as it is the one we know best, it is the one whose language we can understand best when it tells of the glory of God. Not only can the statements about it found in the Bible be studied, but we can pick up pieces of the earth and examine them. We can read in its rocky bones what it tells of its own history. Because this is so, it would fill many volumes to properly cover the subject. Instead I shall leave this primarily to the earthbound disciplines of geology, biology, and so forth, and choose only those aspects which deal most nearly with the earth as a planet.

SHAPE AND POSITION

The most obvious characteristic of the earth is its shape. That the earth is a sphere is common knowledge now, and it can easily be proven by photographs taken from space by the astronauts. However it was about 2,700 years ago that Isaiah said, "It is he [God] that sitteth upon the circle of the earth" (Isa. 40:22). Of course, Columbus was not the first to suspect that the earth is round. The ancient Greeks knew it. In fact, in the third century B.C., the Greek Eratosthenes was the first to measure the circumference of the earth, and his result was correct to within two percent! Isaiah, however, predates Eratosthenes by five centuries.

Even earlier than Isaiah, probably by hundreds of years, is the book of Job. Job, a man of great knowledge, said, "He has inscribed a circle on the surface of the waters, at the boundary of light and darkness" (Job 26:10, NASB). If a light is directed at a globe of the earth, the boundary between the light and the dark sides is a circle. The same effect can easily be seen on the moon as its phases change from day to day. This may even be the clue that gave some of the ancients the idea that the earth also is round. The line that divides the light from the dark sides is called the terminator. The earth's terminator can easily be seen on a photograph of the earth from space. The only shape that the earth could be which would give the earth a circular terminator as it spins on its axis is a sphere. Job, by describing the terminator as circular, proved thousands of years ago that he knew the earth to be spherical, a fact which the Bible teaches. A modern photograph from the moon is graphic proof of the truth of the word of God.

The Bible even tells us where the earth is. It is also Job who says, "He stretcheth out the north over the empty place, and hangeth the earth upon nothing" (Job 26:7). Most ancients had a concept of the earth as being set upon some other object, like Atlas' shoulders or the back of a giant turtle. This in turn was set upon something else and on and on. They simply could not conceive of an earth which did not rest upon something. Not until the days of Newton and his theory of gravitation did man come to understand that the earth is hung upon nothing except the slenderest of invisible threads, gravity.

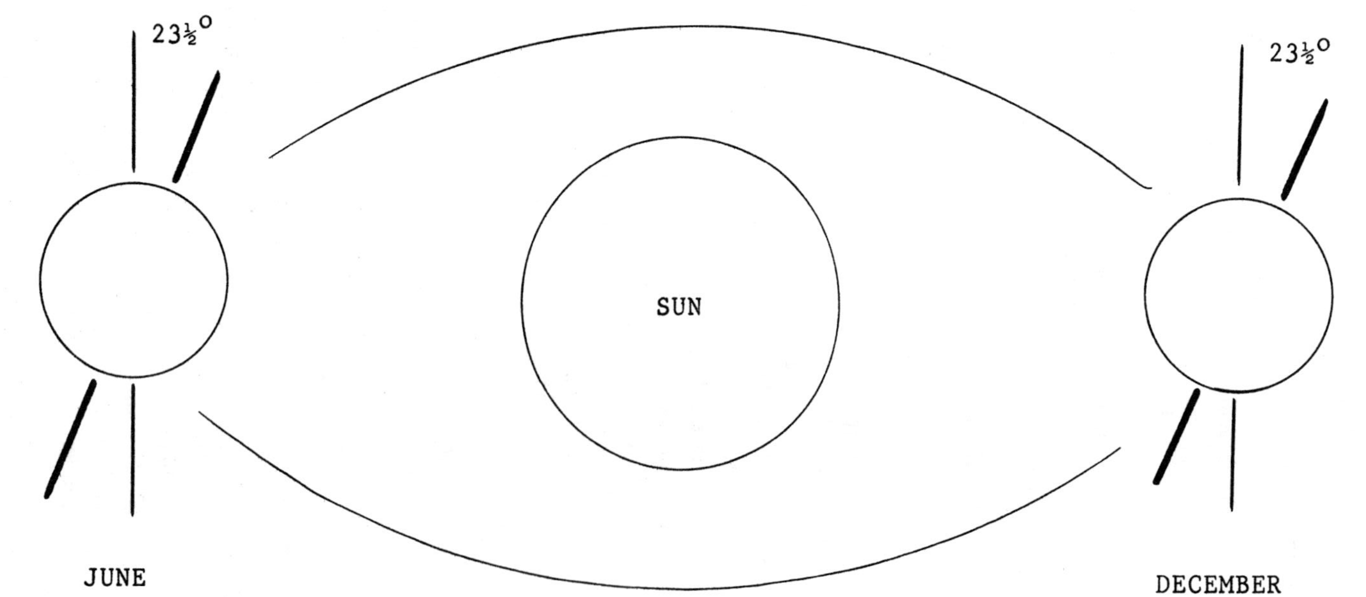

FIGURE 4.—The earth's axis is tilted 23½ degrees with respect to the ecliptic.

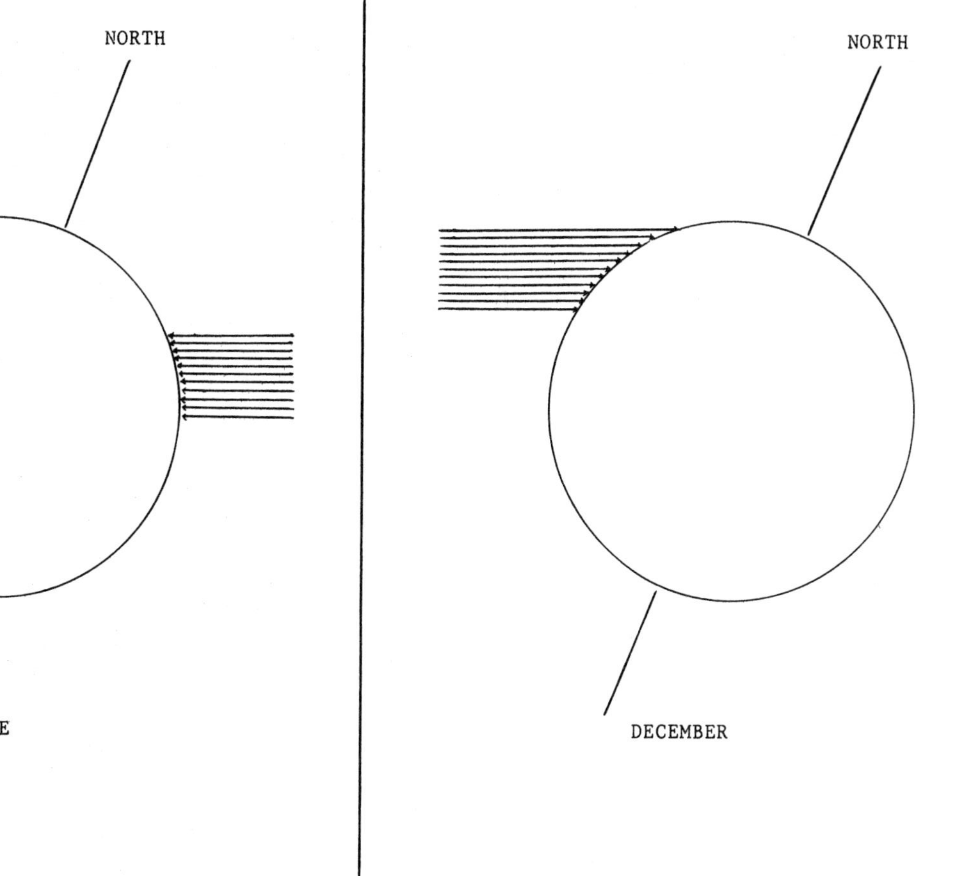

FIGURE 5.—Sunlight strikes North America at different angles during the summer and winter.

Moving outward from the earth so that it can be viewed as the astronomical object that it is, we see that as far as planets go it is medium sized and revolving in an orbit about the sun, being the third planet from it. There are four planets smaller than the earth (Mercury, Venus, Mars, and Pluto) and four larger (Jupiter, Saturn, Uranus, and Neptune). Earth's distance from the sun averages 92,956,-000 miles. This distance is called an astronomical unit. Sometimes the earth is slightly closer and sometimes slightly farther from the sun. This is due to the fact that the earth's orbit is in the shape of an ellipse, which is like a flattened circle. The plane in which this orbit falls is called the ecliptic plane. The orbits of all the planets fall close to being in this same plane. Thus the orbits of the planets, instead of circling the sun in all directions like bees buzzing around a hive, are more to be compared with the flatness of a phonograph record.

The earth's axis, the imaginary line about which it spins, is not perpendicular to the ecliptic, but is tilted at 23½ degrees as shown in figure 4. The direction toward which it tilts is the same throughout the year, pointing approximately at the North Star. It is this tilt that causes the seasons, since, as can be seen from the diagram, the northern hemisphere can be said to point toward the sun in the summer, and away from it in the winter. Figure 5 shows that it is really the angle at which the sunlight strikes the earth that causes our seasonal differences. In Part A a shaft of light strikes an area in the northern hemisphere in the summer. Part B shows a similar shaft of light striking the same location in the winter. Notice that in the winter the same amount of light is spread over a much larger area. This means that each location receives less light in the winter and hence is colder. The coolness of the winter is not due to the earth's being farther away, for, although the earth's distance from the sun changes throughout the year, the earth is actually closer to the sun when it is winter in the northern hemisphere. The difference in temperature is due entirely to the tilt of the earth.

When the Apostle Paul was preaching in Lystra, he knew that the people there were unfamiliar with his message, so he began with a subject with which they were all familiar. "Nevertheless he left not himself without witness, in that he did good, and gave us rain from heaven, and fruitful seasons, filling our hearts with food and gladness" (Acts 14:17). Paul knew that nature showed the power of God, and to him the seasons were one of the most easily perceived examples.

Here is one of the most direct applications of Romans 1:20, with an example from astronomy bearing witness to the goodness of God.

And surely it is fitting that the resurrection of Jesus Christ from the dead took place in the spring. The awakening of dormant life and the beginning of new have been a type of Christ's resurrection from the beginning. It is a reminder to us even now that "that which thou sowest is not quickened except it die. . . . It is sown in corruption; it is raised in incorruption," as Paul's beautiful example in I Corinthians 15 tells us. As surely as Israel's sacrificial system pointed to the death of Christ, God created the seasons from the beginning to point to Christ's resurrection. The regular passing of the seasons is one of the most easily seen manifestations of God's glory in the heavens.

MEASURING THE EARTH'S AGE

The earth tells us of its own history. What does it tell concerning its age? There have been many methods used over the centuries to tell the age of the earth. In general, all tell different stories. One method was to measure the rate at which salt is being taken to the sea by rivers and streams and then to figure how long it would take for all the salt in the oceans to accumulate there at that rate. This, of course, makes the assumption that this process has been going on at the same rate throughout all history. This is what is called uniformitarianism—the concept that all present geological processes have continued at the same rate for all history. The present is said to be the key to the past. All catastrophic events, short periods of large change, are dismissed from their thinking to begin with, including creation. In the case of the oceans, however, this calculation gives a maximum age of 50 to 90 million years. In actuality, the rate would have had to be higher at first since there would have been more salt in the earth, and the maximum age of the oceans is correspondingly reduced. However, biologists believe that life evolved in the sea, billions of years ago. Since scientists had already made up their minds that 90 million years was too little time, they dismissed the ocean-salt method as unreliable.

Radiometric Methods

The most familiar methods are those which use radioactive elements to determine the age of the earth. One method is to measure the relative amounts of thorium and helium in a rock sample. Thorium is a radioactive element, which means that as time goes by it changes from thorium to another element by means of radioactive decay. As it decays, thorium releases a number of helium atoms one at a time. With each helium atom that it sheds, thorium changes to a different type of element. Since we know the rate at which this process occurs, the earth's age can be discerned by measuring the amounts of helium and thorium. Scientists can compute how long this process must have been going on to produce the amount of helium measured from the amount of decayed thorium, or really, lead, that is found. The result is about 12,000 years.[1] This, of course, is far too low for scientists, and this method was also pronounced unreliable. Assumptions made by scientists before the experiments were ever performed caused them to reject perfectly valid evidence for the youth of the earth.

Other radiometric methods are similar to the thorium-helium method discussed above. In a rock that is to be dated there is a radioactive parent element and its daughter elements, those into which some of the parent has decayed. It is reasoned that by knowing the amount of the original radioactive element and the amount of its daughter elements one can determine how long the process has been going on, using the decay rate determined in the laboratory. This reasoning embodies a number of assumptions: (1) the decay rates have been constant in the past, (2) it can be determined how much of the daughter elements is a result of the radioactive decay of the parent and how much is not, and (3) none of the parent or daughter elements have been added or removed during the whole time. We shall look at these one by one.

One of the most firmly held tenets of nuclear physics is that no physical influences can change the rate of decay of radioactive elements. Experiments in which radioactive elements have been subjected to heat, pressure, electric and magnetic fields, and other stresses were thought to show that this is so. However, more recent experiments have shown that some decay rates can be altered by external influences.[2,3] The changes noted so far have been small, but they serve to show that the first assumption is not entirely correct.

The second assumption has to do with the determination of the origi-

---

1. Donald Patton, *A Symposium on Creation* (Grand Rapids: Baker Book House, 1970), p. 71.

2. H. M. Morris and J. C. Whitcomb, *The Genesis Flood* (Philadelphia: Presbyterian and Reformed Publishing Co.), p. 346.

3. Emery, *Annual Review of Nuclear Science* 22 (1972).

nal chemical composition of the sample rock. It is likely that some amounts of the daughter element are not the result of the decay of the parent element, but were there to begin with. If this original amount of daughter element is also attributed to the decay of the parent element, it will look as if the parent element had been decaying for a longer time than it actually had. In practice this is a difficult determination to make, and often different samples from the same location will give different ages. However, the large ages obtained are not surprising. It is only reasonable to assume that when God created the elements He created all of them. Why would He create uranium but no lead? It is reasonable to believe that God created everything at the same time, and that if scientists prefer to interpret the presence of lead as proof of great age, they have simply misunderstood.

Leaching is a process whereby minerals may be removed from or added to rocks by moving water. Assumption number three is violated if leaching has occurred. It has been shown that leaching by a mild acid can remove as much as ninety percent of the uranium from a mineral.[4] A removal of uranium or an addition of lead would increase apparent age of the rocks.

All of the above point out possible uncertainties in the dating methods and tend to cast doubt on these methods. But, to use a cliché, the proof of the pudding is in the eating. If one could find rocks whose age is known exactly, the accuracy of the radiometric dating methods could be tested. In 1968 Naughton and Funkhouser attempted to use the potassium-argon method to measure the age of some lava which had come from the eruption of the volcano Hualalai in Hawaii. The eruption had occurred in 1801, making the rocks 167 years old. The two scientists, using the radioactive method, arrived at an age of between 60 million and 160 million years.[5] This makes the age too high by a factor of between 350,000 and one million. Assuming a creation model age of 10,000 years, this error factor would give a 10,000-year-old rock an apparent age of 3.5 and 10 billion years. Coincidence? I think not.

A more astronomical application of radiometric dating concerns the dating of moonrocks and meteorites.* We are told that the ages of these rocks confirm the age of the earth rocks. The supposed

---

4. Morris and Whitcomb, *Genesis Flood,* p. 336.
5. Bible Science Newsletter, vol. 14, no. 2.
* For an excellent treatment of this topic, see *The Genesis Flood,* by Morris and Whitcomb.

agreement among rocks from all these sources assures scientists that the earth and the rest of the solar system are about the same age—4 to 5 billion years. On the surface these consistent ages seem to confirm the concept of an old solar system. And since the leaching process and other external influences are absent in moonrocks and meteorites, and those influences which might affect decay rates would not be expected to be the same at these different locations, their agreement would seem to be extremely significant. However, the criticisms which applied to the first two assumptions here on earth also apply to space rocks. Further, agreement among ages for different rocks is not as good as is sometimes reported. Ages for meteorites range from 60 million to 7 billion years.[6] Yet some theories indicate these all came from the same source.

Continental Drifts

An old theory that has been revived in recent years concerning the structure of the earth is that of plate tectonics, or continental drift. It has been noted many times in the past that, if all the continents were brought together, they would fit like pieces of a puzzle. South America and Africa fit amazingly well. This strongly implies that the continents were once together and have since spread apart. According to the usual method of interpreting geological processes with uniformitarian suppositions, it is now believed that this spreading has been going on at the same slow, steady rate for millions of years, and that the Atlantic Ocean is growing in width at about one inch per year.

The theory of sea-floor spreading is of interest to Christians for a number of reasons. One is the problem of the redistribution of living things after the flood. It has often been asserted that Noah could not have collected animals from the world over, since they could not have crossed the oceans. Further, after their emergence from the ark the animals could not have reached such continents as Australia, since they would not be able to cross the oceans. If, however, the continents were not separated at the time of the flood, life could have easily traveled over all the land areas of the world. A subsequent continental drift would have separated the continents and islands into the positions they occupy today. This idea apparently occurred to P. Placet, for in 1668 he wrote a piece called "The corruption of the great and little world, where it is shown that before the

6. Morris and Whitcomb, *Genesis Flood,* p. 381.

deluge, America was not separated from the other parts of the world."[7]

This hypothesis, while it might account for the present distribution of animal types, seems far-fetched and imaginative without corroborating evidence. It is significant, therefore, that in some very old maps, called maps of the ancient sea kings, Antarctica is shown very much closer to Australia than it is now. The map of Arontius Phinneus shows a 16-degree separation between Australia and Antarctica, while at present the separation is more like 25 degrees.[8] Clearly, within only the last few thousand years a great deal of movement has occurred in the land masses, and the rate of separation is much greater than allowed by modern scientists. The separation of continents as described by scientists agrees with such a Biblical interpretation except for the time scale. And, as we have seen, the time scale is open to doubt.

Something else this says is that there must have been large-scale motions going on beneath the crust of the earth to propel the continents around. Evidence from seismographs, which measure shock waves produced by earthquakes, has shown that under the crust of the earth there is a semi-liquid layer of rock called magma. This appears to be thousands of miles thick. At the center of the earth there may actually be a solid core. It is hypothesized that the continental drift is brought about by currents in this molten magma. Though it is only a theory at the present time, it is thought that these currents are also responsible for the earth's magnetic field.

Magnetic Fields

The earth's magnetic field is important, not just because it enables us to tell directions with a compass; it is actually vital to our existence. Space is filled with a number of things less visible than stars and planets. Among them are cosmic rays, which are charged particles traveling at speeds near that of light. Many strike the surface of the earth, and many strike atoms in the upper atmosphere causing cascades of energetic charged particles to shower down on us. However, the magnetic field of the earth has an influence upon these particles, causing many of them to be trapped high above the atmosphere of the earth in the Van Allen radiation belts. Without this protective

7. Scientific American, *Continents Adrift* (San Francisco: W. H. Freeman and Co., 1972), p. 57.
8. C. Hapgood, *Maps of the Ancient Sea Kings* (New York: Chilton Books, 1966).

magnetic field, many more cosmic rays would penetrate to our level, and they could do much damage to life by destroying cells in our bodies. Thus, by creating the earth with a molten center God accomplished two purposes. He separated the continents and brought about the magnetic field which protects us from cosmic radiation.

The magnetic field of the earth is really one of the most convincing indicators of the youth of the earth. The strength of the earth's field at present is about one half of a gauss. By contrast, some toy magnets can be many times stronger. While this may not sound impressive, what is impressive is the tremendous amount of energy involved in this field, which fills billions of cubic miles of space. But the strength of the earth's field is decreasing. It is decreasing so rapidly that the change which has taken place in only the last 130 years is quite impressive.

Dr. Thomas Barnes has made an extensive study of this phenomenon and also of the source of the field, and has come to some amazing conclusions. He agrees with the generally accepted belief that the earth's magnetic field does not arise simply from magnetized rocks. The surface rocks do not possess enough magnetism of their own to produce the earth's field, and rocks deeper in the earth are too hot to hold a field permanently. The only alternative is that the field is due to electric currents within the earth.

For an electric current to have been flowing within the earth for many years shows that the earth's interior must be a relatively good conductor. But because any conductor possesses a certain amount of resistance, a current cannot flow indefinitely without some source, such as a battery, to keep it going. Thus there are only two possible reasons that there is still a current flowing inside the earth. Either there is some mechanism adding energy to keep the current flowing, or the current has been decreasing steadily due to the earth's electrical resistance since the time of creation. In the former case the earth's magnetic field might be able to maintain itself for an indefinite period of time. In the latter case the field must be continually decreasing and eventually will disappear.

This is why the dynamo theory was invented. Scientists realized that if they wanted the earth to be 4.5 billion years old, they would have to find some mechanism to keep the earth's magnetic field relatively constant over that period of time. This is not to say, however, that scientists believe the earth's field has remained unchanged for billions of years. They acknowledge the observed variations in the field's strength, and even say that the field has completely reversed itself a number of times. The latter assumption is based upon the magnetic fields which they measure in rocks. Thus scientists believe that the magnetic field is self-generating, variable, and occasionally reversible.

Dr. Barnes examines these statements in some detail in his paper, *Origin and Destiny of the Earth's Magnetic Field.* Can a dynamo-like mechanism really account for the existence of the necessary electrical currents within the earth? Scientists themselves have done calculations which show that while it is possible for some such mechanism to produce a field of sorts, the motions were extremely improbable. And in fact it has been proven mathematically that a dynamo-generated current cannot produce a magnetic field with axial symmetry like the dipole field of the earth.[9] This proof is quite a blow to scientists who had been hoping to explain the earth's magnetic field on this basis, but they are still trying.

Magnetic reversals, if they really occurred, would tend to indicate that there is some kind of a self-generating current in the earth, for if the field had reversed, it must at some point have disappeared. And if the field could have regenerated itself after decreasing to zero, it must have the ability to create and sustain itself. Now the magnetic reversals are believed to have happened because rocks in different locations, or at different levels at the same location, have some permanent magnetism, and these magnetic fields are oriented at different angles. It is thought that each rock retains some remnant of the earth's field as it existed at the time of that rock's formation. The varying orientations of these remnant fields implies to scientists that the earth's field was different at the time each rock was formed.

If that were the only way the rocks could have remnant magnetism with different orientations, the theory of a self-sustaining magnetic field might have some basis. However, Dr. Barnes states that there are at least four chemical and physical processes that can also bring about these "remnant" fields in the rocks.[10] There is no evidence that these differences were caused by the earth's field in the past rather than by one or more of the other possible processes. Hence one of the strongest evidences for a dynamo theory is really no evidence at all.

Since it is impossible for a dynamo mechanism to produce a field

---

9. T. G. Barnes, *Origin and Destiny of the Earth's Magnetic Field* (San Diego: Creation Life Publishers, 1973), p. 44.

10. Ibid., p. 27.

like the earth's, the only other alternative is that the currents producing the earth's field now are the remnants of whatever current was placed within the earth at the time of its creation. If this is so, this current must have been gradually decaying in the thousands of years since the earth's creation. This brings us back to the measurable decay which has taken place over about the last century. The earth's magnetic field was first measured in 1835 by the famous Karl Gauss. In the following 130 years the earth's field decayed by over six percent, quite a substantial amount.[11] At this rate, .046 percent per year, the earth's field would have been about four and a half times stronger at creation 10,000 years ago than it is now. But 4.5 billion years ago it would have been 200 million times stronger than now! This is stronger than all but the most intense magnetic fields in the universe, those in neutron stars, and is impossible to maintain on earth.

But in reality, even this is too generous, for this calculation assumes that the field has been decaying at a constant rate. In nature all decay rates are exponential. This means that the stronger a field is, the faster it decays. Thus the field increases more quickly into the past than the simple, steady increase assumed above. Dr. Barnes has calculated from the data that the half-life of the earth's field is 1400 years.[12] This means that 1400 years ago the field was twice the strength that it is now, and twice again as strong 1400 years before that. In 6000 B.C., 2,000 years before Bishop Ussher's creation date, the field was 35 gauss, high but not unreasonable. In 10,000 B.C. it was 240 gauss, very strong. But if the earth is billions of years old, the strength becomes absurd. At only 1,000,000 B.C. it would have been 10^{219} gauss, which is totally unthinkable. This demonstrates conclusively that the earth is not billions or even millions of years old, but only thousands.

This argument cannot be used to derive an exact age for the earth, since we do not know what the field was to begin with. What is known is that the earth could not possibly sustain the field it would need to if the earth were as old as evolutionists say. The earth itself is evidence that it is young. Scientists may continue to formulate theories, but in the end they will have to face up to the evidence and reveal the shortcomings of their theories if they have taken a stand contrary to the word of God.

---

11. Ibid., p. vii.
12. Ibid., p. 36.

4 THE SOLAR SYSTEM

Try to imagine how the heavens appeared to the ancients, long before man began to understand what a solar system or a galaxy is. Your vision would not have been colored with the facts we know today. In the sky you could see two great lights—the sun and the moon—and innumerable smaller lights. If you paid attention to constellations, you would notice that in different times of the year different constellations were visible, and that after one year the cycle would start over. You would also notice that the moon appears to move quite quickly against the background stars, and that after about one month it returns to the same position among the stars that it held before. In the same amount of time it completes a cycle of waxing and waning.

It would take only moderate powers of observation to notice that there is a second class of "stars" which appear to move among the background stars, some faster and some slower. They all seem to follow the same path (which we called the ecliptic in an earlier chapter). Along with all this you would have undoubtedly seen, at one time or another, a "shooting star," a bright streak of light visible for only a moment, or perhaps a very bright one visible for a few seconds. And finally, if you happened to be at the right place at the right time, you might see a comet, a bright fuzzy object with a hazy tail, or even many tails, which could stretch across the whole sky.

Every object just described in which a visible change took place is a member of the solar system. It took thousands of years before man was able to put all this into an orderly form as it is known today. How could the ancients have known that the stars are millions of times farther away than planets, or that most of these motions were due to the paths followed by these objects as they sped around the sun or the earth, held only by gravity? This is why there are no references to the solar system as such in the Bible, though these objects are mentioned individually.

REFERENCES IN SCRIPTURE

References to the sun and moon fill the Bible; they are important as light-givers, symbols, and timetables. The moving stars, of course, are the planets, which move in the sky as they orbit the sun. This might be what Jude called "wandering stars" in the thirteenth verse of his short book. Shooting stars, or meteors, might be the image referred to as the stars cast down from heaven by the dragon in Revelation 12:4, but considering the symbolic nature of this book, I cannot be sure if this is the best interpretation. Some people try to find comets in the Bible. For example, in II Samuel the destroying angel is sent to Israel because of David's disobedience in numbering the people. Some say that the angel which David saw standing over Jerusalem was really just a comet. But one cannot interpret the Bible in this way. When the Bible says there was an angel, it is dangerous to say that it was not an angel. David was there; the interpreters were not.

The ancients believed there were seven planets, but they included the sun and the moon in this number. That left only five known planets other than the earth. They were Mercury, Venus, Mars, Jupiter, and Saturn. All these seem to be mentioned in the Bible, though some references are uncertain. Mercury, the planet nearest the sun, is not specifically mentioned in the Bible, but the word *Nebo* occurs in Isaiah 46:1. Nebo was the Babylonian god of literature and science, and his planet was Mercury. His name is found in the name Nebuchadnezzar.

Venus is the morning star, and the day star of the New Testament. As such it is used as a symbol for Jesus Christ. It is possible that Venus is mentioned in the Old Testament also, in Isaiah 65:11, along with Jupiter. Here *fortune* and *destiny* (NASB) are the translations of *Gad* and *Meni* respectively, which seem to be the names for Jupiter and Venus. Nergal was the Babylonian god of the underworld, and also of plague and fever. In his later days he was associated with the planet Mars. He is mentioned in II Kings 17:30.

Saturn is the most certain identification of any planet. In Amos 5:25, 26 it says, "Have ye offered unto me sacrifices and offerings in the wilderness forty years, O house of Israel? But ye have borne the tabernacle of your Moloch and Chiun your images, the star of your god, which ye made to yourselves." Both Moloch and Chiun (or Rephan, as Stephen puts it in Acts 7:43) appear to be associated with Saturn.

None of these references have any astronomical significance. Instead, they are all associated with false religion (except for the morning star), usually stemming from Babylon. Stars were studied in Babylon thousands of years before Christ, but it was for the purpose of predicting the future and promoting their false religions. That this had much attraction for the Israelites of the Old Testament times is as certain as that it has much attraction for the superstitious of our own day. Millions read daily horoscopes and govern their lives by the positions of the planets. All these people are partners with those mentioned in II Kings 23:5: "And he put down the idolatrous priests . . . ; them also that burned incense unto Baal, to the sun, and to the moon, and to the planets, and to all the host of heaven." All those who seek guidance by such means are in rebellion against the true God (II Kings 1:6). The Bible tells us that astrology is totally powerless and false (Dan. 2:27) and must be avoided by the believer.

THE MAKE-UP OF THE SOLAR SYSTEM

Now it is known that the solar system consists of the sun, its nine planets, together with the moons of those planets, as well as asteroids, comets, and more minor members. If we go back to our football-field-sized solar system, with the sun as a marble on the 50-yard line, Mercury is an all but invisible speck of dust eighteen inches away, Venus is a small grain of sand on the 49-yard line, the earth is another grain of sand on the 48½-yard line, Mars is a dust speck on the 48-yard line, the asteroid belt is a few atoms on the 46-yard line, Jupiter is a large grain of sand (1/25 inch) on the 44-yard line, Saturn is another large grain on the 38, Uranus is a smaller grain at the 26, Neptune is another at the twelve, and Pluto is another dust speck at the goal line. Planets are packed fairly close together near the sun. But as one journeys outward, distances between planets increase quickly until, by the time we reach Pluto, it is lonely indeed. A spectator in the stands above the football solar system would not even be able to tell that it existed. Nothing is known to exist in the solar system beyond Pluto.

Planets are divided into two types, the terrestrial and the Jovian planets. The four terrestrial planets are so named because they resemble the earth in that they are about the same size and they are solid bodies. They include Mercury, Venus, the earth, and Mars. The Jovian planets, or the giant planets, are named after the largest one of all—Jupiter. They are very much larger than the terrestrial planets and appear to be made of gases, with no solid surfaces. These include Jupiter, Saturn, Uranus, and Neptune. It is interesting that not only do these fall into two groups according to their characteristics, they are also naturally divided according to the distances at which they lie from the sun. The four terrestrial planets are the four nearest the sun, and the Jovian planets are the next four. Pluto is so far away, and so little is known about it, that it is not classified for certain as either type.

Mercury

Mercury, the planet nearest the sun, was veiled in relative obscurity before the voyage of Mariner 10. It is so close to the sun and so small that almost nothing on its surface can be seen from the earth. Mercury is the smallest planet. Jupiter and Saturn both have moons larger than Mercury. Its diameter is only about 3,000 miles, and its orbit keeps it about 36 million miles or .39 astronomical units from the sun. The reason why it never appears far from the sun is illustrated in figure 6. Even when it appears at its farthest point from the sun, its greatest elongation, it is only 28 degrees away, or about 56 solar diameters. When it is closer, it is lost in the solar glare.

Mercury, like Venus, can appear as either a morning star or an evening star. Figure 6 shows the solar system from the "top" (above the earth's north pole). The arrow on the earth shows its rotation from west to east. When Mercury is in position A, it appears above the horizon before the sun and is a morning star. When it is on the opposite side of the sun, the sun appears to fall below the horizon before Mercury, and it is seen as an evening star.

Mercury takes 88 days to revolve around the sun and 60 days to turn on its axis. This means that a complete day on Mercury takes 172 earth days. It has a mass of about five percent of the earth's,

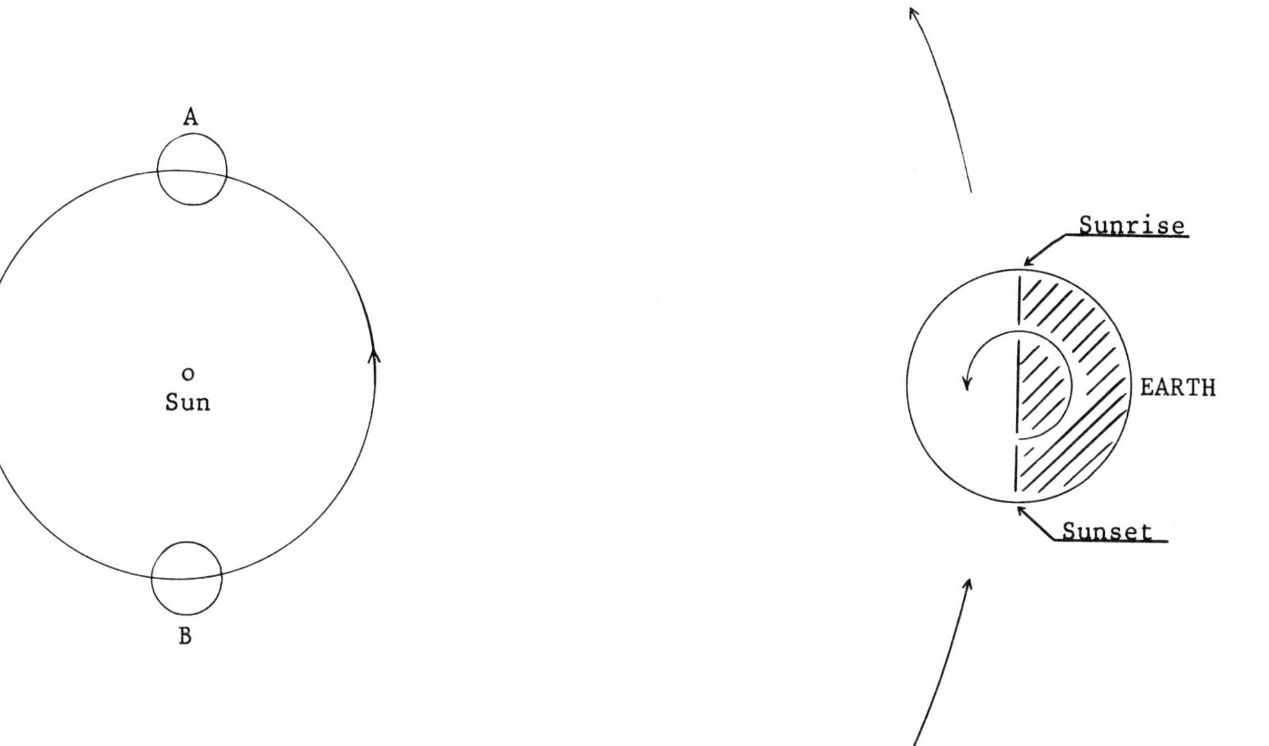

FIGURE 6.—Mercury, an inferior planet, never gets more than 28 degrees from the sun as seen from the earth.

and in its flight around the sun reaches speeds of 35 miles per second. Until Mariner 10, this was the basic information known about Mercury. Then in March of 1974, after flying by Venus, Mariner 10 became the first spacecraft to fly by Mercury. The data it sent back were amazing. Temperatures range from 800° F. on the sunlit side to 200° below zero on the dark side. The first pictures seen by man revealed a planet which looked much like the moon, covered with craters and maria (large smooth areas overlain by lava flows). This was a surprise because Mercury, being as dense as the earth, was not thought to have such light materials on its surface as the moon does. If the surface is made of such light materials, the core must be very large and made of heavy materials to give the planet its overall high density. The core would have to take up to three quarters of the planet's diameter. Another unexpected feature was a thin atmosphere. Because Mercury was known to be quite hot, it was thought not to have any atmosphere; in such heat it should all boil away into space—at least it should if the planet is billions of years old. The fact that any atmosphere remains at all might be an indication that the planet is younger than the expected age. However, it is also a real possibility that some of these gases are replenished by the solar wind, a thin wind of hot gas which pervades the whole solar system. Mercury's atmosphere is only one-hundred-billionth as dense as the earth's and is made up mostly of the noble gases helium, argon, neon, and xenon, relatively heavy gases which take quite a while to boil away, but still not as long as the supposed age of the solar system.

Another great surprise was that Mercury has a magnetic field, like the earth. Mercury's, however, is only one-thousandth as strong. As mentioned earlier, one theory of the origin of the earth's magnetic field is that there is an internal dynamo, or large convection currents of hot magma within the earth which produce the magnetic field as a result of electrical currents within the magma. On the planet Mercury, however, the rotation is so slow that no such current is expected to exist. If this is true, it may mean that Mercury's magnetic field is "frozen in" just as in a bar magnet.

At this time there are more data on Mercury than investigators know what to do with. It will be years before these data can all be digested and fit together into a coherent picture of the nature of the smallest planet. Nevertheless, they have already threatened to cause the rewriting of the textbooks on planetary formation and the history of the solar system.

Venus

In the Bible every heavenly object but the sun and moon is called a star. Only one of these is bright enough to be seen in the daytime, and hence is sometimes called the day star. This is the planet Venus. Venus is the second planet from the sun and thus is also inside the earth's orbit, about 67 million miles from the sun. Like Mercury, therefore, it stays fairly close to the sun as seen from the earth, but gets farther away than does Mercury, 47 degrees or 94 solar diameters. Figure 6 can also apply to Venus. When Venus is in position A, it rises before the sun and is called the morning star. When it is on the opposite side of the sun, it sets after the sun and is the evening star. Because of the brightly reflecting clouds which cover it, Venus is the brightest object in the sky after the sun and moon.

The three times that Venus is referred to in the Bible it is called either the morning star or the day star, and refers to the person of Christ. II Peter 1:19 says, "We have also a more sure word of prophecy; whereunto ye do well that ye take heed, as unto a light that shineth in a dark place, until the day dawn, and the day star arise in your hearts." The daylight of God's coming is at hand (Rom. 13:12). But preceding the daylight is the day star, Jesus Christ, rising in our hearts. As surely as day follows the rising of the morning star, we know that God will come to rule on earth, bringing peace and light, because Jesus has arisen in our hearts.

But the fulness of this Biblical symbol is not exhausted yet, for as the morning star rises, as if from the darkness of death into the heavens, "God hath both raised up the Lord, and will also raise us up by his power." ". . . and made us sit together in heavenly places in Christ Jesus" (I Cor. 6:14; Eph. 2:6). Thus we see that Christ was raised from the dead by the power of God, and is now in heavenly places preceding the final coming of the Lord to the earth. And we are taught that in those heavenly places we also are seated with Christ because of our faith in Him.

The planet Venus as seen through a telescope is not very interesting, for no detail can be seen on its surface. It does, however, go through phases like those of the moon. Oddly enough, Venus is brightest at the phase nearest to "new Venus," because even though the total surface is nearly obscured at that time, it is much closer to the earth and much larger in appearance. Venus is entirely covered with dense, light-colored clouds. The word *albedo* refers to the fraction of the total light received which is reflected by the planet. The albedo of Venus is .76, meaning that it reflects 76 percent of the light which falls upon it. This is the largest albedo of any planet. The moon, by contrast, has an albedo of .07.

Because the clouds on Venus are featureless, it has been difficult to determine the period of its rotation visually. In the early sixties, however, radar signals bounced back from the planet's true surface showed that its period of rotation is 243.1 days in a direction opposite to that of nearly all other planets. That is, it turns from east to west. This is called retrograde rotation. Normal rotation is in the same direction in which most of the planets rotate around the sun, counterclockwise as seen from above the north pole.

As in the case of Mercury, very little was known about Venus before it was visited by a space probe. Both American and Russian spacecraft have now visited Venus. Mariner 10, one of the most recent American craft to visit the clouded planet, did so on its journey to Mercury. Though Venus was just an added extra for Mariner 10 on its way to Mercury, it sent back much useful and surprising information about Venus. It photographed the clouds of Venus in ultraviolet light, which cannot be seen at all at the surface of the earth because it is absorbed by the atmosphere. In ultraviolet light, features are visible in the atmosphere which indicate that the clouds race around Venus at speeds up to 200 miles per hour, much faster than its slow rotation on its axis. It was also discovered that there may be as many as four different cloud layers in the atmosphere. Venus turns out to have no magnetic field, which might be expected from its slow rotation if the dynamo theory is correct. It is also 100 times closer to being an actual sphere than the earth, which is considerably flattened at the poles.

The Russian effort has been to land on Venus' surface instead of to fly by, as all American efforts have done. At least seven Russian space probes have actually landed on the surface, four of which sent back signals after landing. The conditions they found on the surface are nearly unbelievable. The atmospheric pressure at the surface is 90 times what it is on earth, which explains why some Russian probes did not even survive their descent to the surface. Surface temperatures reach 900° F., hot enough to melt lead. Venera 9 landed on Venus on October 20, 1975, and was the first probe equipped with television cameras. It was able, at long last, to send back a picture of the surface of Venus, so long shrouded in impenetrable clouds.

The result was surprising, for it showed rocks 12 to 16 inches across. They seem to be uneroded, despite the amazing wind speeds previously recorded. Strangely enough, the recorded wind speed at the surface of the planet was a leisurely two miles per hour. There still remains a great deal of mystery about the planet Venus.

Mars

Over the centuries the planet which has captured man's imagination more than any other is Mars. The famous red planet is the first of the superior planets, meaning that its orbit is outside the earth's. Mars itself is smaller than the earth, with a diameter of only 4,191 miles, slightly over half the earth's. Its distance from the sun averages 141 million miles, but every few years it comes as close as 35 million miles to the earth, and the view is especially good. Even at the best of times, however, Mars appears little larger than an average-sized crater on the moon, and little detail is visible through the largest telescopes. It is this lack of distinctness that has led to the great controversy over the Martian canals. More prominent are the light and dark areas which change their appearance with the seasons, and the polar caps, which grow in winter and retreat in summer. Occasionally even clouds are visible. White clouds are probably ice crystals high in the atmosphere. Yellow clouds appear to be dust-laden winds.

Close observations of the surface markings show that a day on Mars lasts 24 hours, 37 minutes, 23 seconds. Clouds, polar caps, seasonal changes, all join together to make us believe that Mars is a very earthlike planet. Many have taken it for granted that this resemblance also extends to the existence of life. Yet it remained for space-age observations, from close up, to clear up some of the mysteries—and to add others.

The history of man's beliefs about Mars makes interesting reading. Famous astronomers have been carried away into absurd notions without any real evidence, even to the extent of describing the beings which are supposed to inhabit the planet. Indeed, most of these speculations have to do with life. For thousands of years it has been man's desire to prove that he is not alone in the universe by finding some civilization elsewhere in space. With the advent of telescopes, and especially now with space probes actually able to visit other planets, man's hopes have grown until he is sure that it is only a matter of time until we do find such civilizations. And ever since the beginning, Mars has been the prime candidate for such a discovery. This has primarily been because it is one of the nearest and most easily observed planets, as well as because of its earthlikeness.

In the last century astronomers casually assumed that there was life on Mars. But the modern age of bioenthusiasm began in 1869, when Father Secchi observed some streak-like markings on Mars's surface and called them *canali.* In 1877 Schiaparelli took up the idea and claimed to observe a great number of them, while others began noticing them in the 1880's. The Italian word was translated as canals in English. This implied something man made, perhaps to transport water, and strengthened the early belief in intelligent life. While some, such as Abbe Moreaux, tried to explain the canals as cracks in the Martian surface, they were drowned out by those who insisted upon seeing evidences for life. The foremost proponent of the intelligent life theory was Percival Lowell, an influential American astronomer. Lowell's vivid imagination filled books and papers with descriptions of Mars and its inhabitants. He claimed that Mars was a dying world and that the canals were made to bring water from the melting polar caps to the farms which needed irrigation. Controversy raged in the 1900's, with Lowell producing a number of papers defending his own view, and with opponents bitterly attacking his position. Theories as well as observations began to indicate that the atmosphere must be thinner and colder than on earth, and a search for water and oxygen did not prove encouraging. Further, better observations with more powerful telescopes began to show that the canals might not be straight lines after all, but an unrelated grouping of spots which only looked like lines through poor telescopes.

Modern observations are too numerous to describe in detail. Temperatures were established as being quite cold most of the time, and water and oxygen were still not found. By the 1940's an inhabitable Mars was becoming difficult to believe in. Still, so influential had been the ideas of Lowell, that even in the 1950's life was considered to be the best explanation for the seasonal color changes in some areas of Mars. It remained for space probes which could actually visit Mars to dispel the strange notions built up over the centuries.

Man's first close-up look at Mars came in July, 1965, when Mariner 4 radioed back photographs taken during a fly-by mission. Although its 21 pictures covered only a small area of the planet, and each picture had less detail than an ordinary snapshot, they were enough to show that Mars was a very different place than anyone had expected. Hundreds of craters were identified in those pictures. In addition, the atmosphere turned out to be much thinner than had been foreseen and contained mostly carbon dioxide. Again in 1969 Mariners 6 and 7 flew by Mars with improved observational equipment. They confirmed the results of Mariner 4, while showing that the Martian craters were more weathered and eroded than lunar craters. They revealed areas devoid of craters as well as unfamiliar types of rugged, broken terrain. They also found that the south pole was cold enough to be dry ice.

The Mars Mariner program was crowned by the flight of Mariner 9, which actually went into a permanent orbit around the red planet. From orbit, which it reached November 14, 1971, it was able to take pictures of the entire surface of Mars. In all it returned over 7,000 photographs. When it arrived, the entire surface of Mars was obscured by the largest dust storm ever seen on the planet. All that could be discerned were four stationary dark areas. When the dust cleared, it was discovered that these had been the tops of four enormous volcanoes protruding through the upper layers of the storm. In sum, Mariner 9 was able to return enough data to give us the most complete picture of any planet other than the earth. As usual in such cases, it raised as many new questions as it answered.

Was Mariner 9 able to resolve the controversy over the canals? Probably. For example, the region known as Syrtis Major, which was the first dark marking on Mars ever recorded, has turned out to be not a single patch but a series of dark streaks. Each streak had its beginning at a small crater. The indication is that these streaks are layers of dust or sand deposited by strong winds, a theory that has been strengthened by wind tunnel experiments on earth. Further confirmation is given by high-resolution photographs, which show fields of sand dunes in some of the craters. This indicates that wind and sand are primarily responsible for many of the Martian features. However, no canals or objects which could be positively identified with previously observed canals were actually photographed by Mariner 9. It is possible that the sand storm changed many of the features of the planet. But it is more likely that the canals did not exist at all, but were in reality blotchy surface features which only looked like canals from a distance.

Large mountains had not been expected on Mars either. Actually, there aren't many, but the four mentioned earlier are truly impressive. The largest, Olympus Mons, towers 88,000 feet above the average surface level, as compared to 29,000 feet above sea level for Mount Everest. The base of Olympus Mons is as large as the state of Missouri. These Martian volcanoes resemble shield volcanoes on earth. An example is Mauna Loa in Hawaii, whose base is 75 miles wide on the sea floor. There are a few other volcanoes scattered about the surface of Mars, and nearly all are large by earthly standards.

Probably the most unexpected discovery of all was the winding channels which look undeniably like dry river beds. These bear no relationship to the canals, for they are far too small to be observed from earth, and the positions do not correspond to the canals. These, instead of being straight lines like the canals, are long meandering valleys with branches and tributaries. They show evidence of having been cut by sediment-carrying waters. At first scientists were unwilling to consider this possibility, for almost no water appears to exist on Mars at present. However, after every possible alternative had been eliminated, they returned to the possibility of water. The trouble is that even if all the water in the atmosphere were to fall as rain, it would make a layer only one-thousandth of an inch deep. Further, it is so cold that water would be frozen everywhere except under the noonday sun at the equator, and since the atmospheric pressure is so low, the water would completely boil away within hours.

A possible explanation is that conditions on Mars were different in the past than they are now, and that the atmospheric pressure was high enough to keep water from boiling away. This raises two questions: what caused the change in climate, and where is the water now? Solutions to the change in climate fall into two categories, those having to do with Mars alone, and those involving changes in the sun. In the first case, it has been proposed that if Mars's orbit were different in the past, it might have been closer to the sun and subsequently warmer, allowing water locked up in ice to melt and form a heavy atmosphere. Or perhaps some other mechanism heated Mars from within. It has also been suggested that the sun may have been warmer in the past. This is significant in that it would have affected the earth also. Evidence indicates that the earth once had a warm climate from pole to pole. However, the theory of stellar evolution says that the sun should have been cooler in the past. Whether or not any of these guesses is correct is unknown. We can be certain, though, that whichever is chosen in the end, evolutionary scientists will automatically fit it into a framework of millions or billions of years.

However, there is no reason to automatically assume such great ages. The ages are assumed first and the evidence is made to fit. Relative ages of Martian features are often gauged by means of cratering. It is assumed that the rate of crater formation has been relatively constant in the past. Regions that are more heavily cratered are thus older than those which are less heavily cratered, older craters being obscured by more recent surface activity. However, this same pattern of cratering could also be the result of much more rapid cratering in the recent past. The uncratered areas would still be due to recent activity such as volcanism, or, to irregular distribution of craters in the first place. It is only as a result of the assumptions of great age and a constant cratering rate over billions of years that crater dating yields ages of millions and billions of years.

There are two places where water could conceivably be now: either frozen beneath the soil or in the polar ice caps. There are two lines of evidence which support the first possibility. The chaotic terrain mentioned earlier resembles certain regions near the Arctic on earth. These regions, called thermokarst, result when water frozen in the ground is suddenly melted by volcanic or seasonal heat. Liquid water flows out, causing the ground to collapse into the spaces left by the water. Frequently the dry Martian "river beds" seem to have their origins in such regions. There seems to be another process at work as well, called ground ice sapping. Here, already existing channels are widened when ice in the exposed channel walls evaporates and leaves a void. As before, the soil collapses into the vacancies, widening the channel and exposing new soil, so that the process can continue. Such fractured and slumped terrain as would be caused by ice sapping is observed at the edges and sources of the channels.

The polar caps are the most visible features on the surface of Mars. For years it has been a matter of debate as to whether they consist of water or dry ice. The fact that they were observed to grow in the winter and shrink in the summer proved them to be ice of some sort. The rate at which the ice caps melted was consistent with their being primarily carbon dioxide. Photographs taken by Mariner 9 showed the ice caps to be layered. It was thought that the more permanent layered terrain may be water ice, with carbon dioxide advancing and retreating with the seasons and forming a layer over the water ice.

Mars indicates that the principles of uniformitarianism do not necessarily apply there. In *The New Mars,* Hartmann and Odell state, "Modern terrestrial geology is based upon the principle of uniformitarianism . . . the Martian studies suggest a somewhat different viewpoint: as we push farther back into ancient planetary histories, we must be prepared to meet with conditions substantially different from the present conditions. This idea, if confirmed, could alter our philosophic approach to terrestrial geology."[1] This is not the only case in which uniformitarianism is called into question within the realm of astronomy.

As we progress outward from the sun, Mars is the first planet other than the earth to possess satellites of its own. Mars's two satellites, Deimos and Phobos, are so small that they were not discovered until 1877, long after other satellites, even of Neptune and Uranus, were discovered. Many authors in past years, therefore, have pointed to a remarkable description of these two satellites given by Jonathan Swift in his book, *Gulliver's Travels,* in the year 1720, over one hundred fifty years before their actual discovery. In this fictional work he describes one moon as being three diameters of Mars away from the center of Mars and having a period of revolution of ten hours. The second is said to be five diameters away and to have a period of 21.5 hours. The truth is that the nearer moon is closer to two diameters away and has a period of 7 hours, 39 minutes, while the second is four diameters away and has a period of 30 hours, 18 minutes. Did Swift have some inside information? Certain creationists have used this as evidence for catastrophism in the solar system, saying that Mars must once have been closer to the earth, so that someone could have seen its moons. Swift then heard of these observations and included them in his work.

But there is reason to doubt that Swift ever imagined that such conclusions would be drawn from his work. Where did Swift get his information if he really obtained it from some ancient sources? No one else in history seems to know of records bearing such news. There were, however, others who predicted that Mars would have two moons. One was the famous Johannes Kepler, who predicted two moons for Mars in 1610. He arrived at this number because the earth has one moon, and Jupiter, at that time, was known to have four. What better number for the planet between the earth and Jupiter than two moons? The monk Anton Maria Schyrl claimed to have actually seen two moons orbiting Mars in 1643, but with the equipment available at that time it would have been impossible. He might have seen

---

1. W. K. Hartmann and R. Odell, *The New Mars,* NASA SP-337, p. 107.

two dim stars near Mars, and mistaken Mars's motion for the motion of its "moons." In either case, Swift undoubtedly used the number two because it had been used before.

While Swift's numbers are close, they are definitely not correct. In fact, the numbers given by Swift yield a mass for Mars which is six times too large.[2] Any arguments that the satellites' orbits may have changed since then are thus invalidated. Swift's figures were probably just a lucky guess.

The first photographs of Phobos, 17 miles long, and Deimos, 10 miles long, returned by Mariner 9 revealed heavily cratered bodies of irregular shape. Oddly, Phobos is covered with a dust layer a fraction of an inch thick. Since any meteor impact that could cause the observed craters would surely knock the dust off, and since Phobos does not have a strong enough gravitation field to hold the dust which would be knocked off, it presents quite a problem. Another problem, this time for the creationist point of view, is that Deimos and Phobos are in synchronous orbits, meaning that they keep the same face toward Mars at all times, just as the moon does toward the earth. Dynamic studies show that if any meteor impact had occurred within the last 100 million years, it would have knocked them out of this happy situation, that is, they would not have had time to stabilize back into synchronous orbits by now. From a creationist point of view, does this mean there is evidence that they are very old satellites? Or have they never really been impacted by meteors? Were they instead created in the scarred, dusty state we find them in now? Until a better interpretation emerges, this remains one of the evidences for an old solar system.

Surely one of the most dramatic moments in the history of the American space program took place at 4:53 A.M., PDT, July 20, 1976. At that moment the Viking I lander touched down on the surface of Mars on the lowland plains of the western Chryse basin. Almost immediately the onboard cameras and experiments began functioning, photographing the Martian landscape, sniffing the air, and, later, feeling for Marsquakes, analyzing the soil, and much more. Even on the way to the ground Viking I was returning evidence for creation. It determined that the Martian atmosphere consists of about one or two percent of the inert gas argon. However, if Mars has proportions of potassium-40 (which decays radioactively into argon)

---

2. Patton, *A Symposium on Creation,* p. 300.

similar to those of the earth, there should be 25 times as much argon as observed,[3] that is, of course, if Mars is 4.5 billion years old.

The first photographs revealed a dry, barren landscape consisting of sand and rugged rocks all the way to the horizon. At first sight, at least, Mars was a very dead-looking planet. This did not discourage the biologists, however, who did not really expect to see some Martian beast stalking across the landscape. They had devised much subtler ways of detecting life in case the beasts did not put in an appearance. Some of the most sophisticated space experiments ever devised were aboard Viking I, waiting for soil samples which would tell scientists whether or not any microorganisms existed on Mars. More about this in chapter 13.

The Viking probe actually consisted of two parts—the lander, which went to the surface of Mars, and the orbiter, which stayed in orbit and was able to survey large portions of the planet. Viking I was later joined by Viking II, making a total of four devices examining Mars. Together they have returned the most complete picture we have of any planet other than the earth. To tell what they have found would fill volumes, but I shall try to present some of the more interesting results here.

The polar caps, which have long been somewhat of a mystery, were finally determined to consist of ordinary water ice. Many scientists had expected them to be frozen carbon dioxide (dry ice), and some still think that it may exist beneath the ice caps. Unlike the earth's polar ice, however, the Martian ice caps seem to be only a few meters to, at most, a few hundred meters thick. One striking feature about them is that the ice caps appear to be layered. There is layer after layer of ice and dust, ice and dust. Each layer apparently represents a period of ice melting followed by a period of deposition of dust. Also near the north pole is the largest sand dune field known in the solar system.

One of the more awesome feats of the Viking II orbiter was its close-up photographs of Mars's moon Phobos. Taken from only 880 kilometers (550 miles) away, one photograph showed features as small as 40 meters across. It showed central peaks in the larger craters and chains of smaller craters. But the real surprise was a number of parallel striations, or grooves, existing over half of the visible surface. It is not known what could have caused such markings. Tidal stresses have been suggested, as have impacts from a cloud of debris which

3. *Science News,* July 24, 1976, p. 53.

Phobos may have passed through. For the time being, however, they remain a mystery.

On the surface the landers were using a device called a mass spectrometer to measure the abundances of elements in the atmosphere. One reason for this is that scientists believe the atmospheres of earthlike planets consist of gases released by the planet itself over millions of years. (Volcanoes on earth, when erupting, emit large amounts of gases, including water vapor.) They hope to be able to piece together Mars's history by analyzing the kinds and amounts of gases in its atmosphere.

Whatever the Vikings find, there is no doubt that the data will be placed into an evolutionary framework. This framework even dictates the type of experiment sent on such probes, especially the life experiments. But there is also no doubt that, since Mars was created by the living God, any experiments must ultimately reveal His hand in that creation; it is simply a matter of asking the right questions.

Bode's Law

The next planet as we move outward from the sun is Jupiter, but we have another stop to make before we get there. There is a strange gap between Mars and Jupiter (perhaps an odd word to use, because it is mostly empty space anyway). To see what we mean by this we shall look at a simple relationship called Bode's law. This mathematical relationship describes the distances at which the planets lie from the sun fairly well. It was discovered first by Titius and then rediscovered independently by Bode in 1772. It goes as follows: we take the distance from the earth to the sun as being one unit (one astronomical unit). Then we form the series of numbers, 0, 3, 6, 12, 24, and so on, doubling each time. To each of these we add four and divide by ten. This gives the series .4, .7, 1.0, 1.6, 2.8, 5.2, 10.0, 19.6, 38.8, and 77.2. These numbers give the distances from the sun to the planets in astronomical units. Table 1 shows a comparison between the predictions of Bode's law and actual observations. It can be seen that at 2.8 astronomical units the law predicts a planet between Mars and Jupiter. But there is no planet there.

This puzzled the astronomers of the day. Then, in 1801, a Sicilian astronomer named Piazzi discovered an uncharted "star." It turned out to be a body in our own solar system, orbiting the sun at a distance of 2.8 astronomical units. It was named Ceres. It was thought that Ceres, though small, was the planet which Bode's law predicted.

BODE'S LAW

Planet	*Bode's Law Distance (AU)*	*Actual Distance (AU)*
Mercury	0.4	0.387
Venus	0.7	0.723
Earth	1.0	1.000
Mars	1.6	1.524
asteroids	2.8	2.767 (Ceres)
Jupiter	5.2	5.203
Saturn	10.0	9.539
Uranus	19.6	19.191
Neptune	38.8	30.071
Pluto	77.2	39.518

Table 1

Thus it turned out to be a complete surprise when another object was discovered at the same distance from the sun in 1802. This was named Pallas. Now hundreds of objects at about the same distance are known. They are called asteroids, or minor planets, and are much smaller than the other objects which we call planets. Ceres, the first, is the largest at only 488 miles in diameter. The combined mass of all of them adds up to only about one-twentieth the mass of the moon.

Nevertheless, because of Bode's law and the idea that a planet should lie between Mars and Jupiter, some have assumed that there once really was a planet at that location, which broke up to form the asteroids. This theory has been gaining prominence again recently. Either it must have been a very small planet, or most of the material must have been lost. Recently some scientists reported that there may have been from 300 to 3,000 times more mass than is now represented in the asteroids. If this is true, they may be the result of the break-up of a very large planet.[4]

Asteroids

In the case of asteroids, scientists may have something more solid to examine than a view through a telescope. It is possible that some

4. *Science News,* November 8, 1975, p. 297.

of the meteorites that fall on the earth had their origin among the asteroids, and may actually be fragments of asteroids. Opinion varies on this point, but it does seem sure that meteorites are fragments of larger parent bodies which must have been broken up by collisions. Minerals found in meteorites are consistent with high pressures and temperatures that would be found in the interior of much larger bodies than the meteorites themselves. Veins of magnesium sulphate in some specimens may even indicate that this mineral was deposited by water on the parent body. There are three basic types of meteorites—stones, stony irons, and irons. This is consistent with the interpretation that the irons represent material which was once part of the heavy iron core of a planetlike body, while the stones were the surface rocks, and the stony irons came from the transition between. The evidence may point to the fact that meteorites came from large bodies or a single body which broke up. This is more evidence of catastrophism in the solar system and another nail in the coffin of the all-prevailing principle of uniformitarianism. And if uniformitarianism is shown not to be a valid principle in the universe, how can it be valid for the earth? Once more the possibility of sudden and large-scale changes is confirmed.

It is also possible that a knowledge of the asteroids will illuminate a passage of Scripture. We read in Revelation 8:8, "And the second angel sounded, and as it were a great mountain burning with fire was cast into the sea." While it may be fruitless to speculate on how God will bring this to pass (for He could use any supernatural means He chooses), I cannot help but be reminded of asteroids when I read this, for this is precisely what asteroids are—mountains hurtling through space.

Not all asteroids move in the same orbit between Mars and Jupiter, but there are different families of asteroids, the asteroids in each family moving together in similar orbits. One family of asteroids called the Apollo group has an orbit which crosses the orbit of the earth. This immediately presents the possibility of a collision. Only ten members of the Apollo group are known at present and all have a diameter of about 1 kilometer (5/8 of a mile). It is possible that there are as many as fifty members of that size in the group, for asteroids are usually discovered only by chance and many undoubtedly remain unseen. Given enough time (hundreds of millions of years), all of them will eventually collide with the earth. The expected time between collisions is ten million to 100 million years, so the probability of such an occurrence should cause no alarm. As an example, however, an asteroid named Icarus passed only four million miles from the earth on June 14, 1968, eliciting predictions of disaster from alarmists the world over. Actually, it passed just where astronomers said it would.

What if one of these asteroids were to strike the earth? A mass of stone nearly one mile across would look much like a large mountain. And just like shooting stars which glow white because of air friction when they pass through the atmosphere, the asteroid would heat up and appear to be burning. Because nearly three quarters of the earth is covered with water, it is most likely that such an object would fall into the sea.

In the past the earth has been struck by a number of objects smaller than the Apollo asteroids. The famous Arizona meteorite crater is 4,200 feet across and 600 feet deep, but is estimated to have been caused by a meteorite of only two million tons, or about 300 feet across. The meteorite (or comet) which fell in Siberia in 1908 devastated over 1,000 square miles. The shock was felt as far away as Europe, while trees up to twenty miles from the site were blown over. Yet this body was estimated to be only 200 feet across. Imagine how much greater damage would be done by an asteroid nearly a mile across! Its effects are nearly incalculable, and would certainly be worldwide. While I do not know that the burning mountain of Revelation is an asteroid, it is interesting to think that the Lord may have put the Apollo group in that particular orbit in the very beginning of creation, knowing that it would meet the earth at the appointed time.

There is a more applicable observation to be drawn from the Apollo group of asteroids. The time between collisions of such asteroids with the earth as given above is more correctly called the half-life. This means that in one period of time, or one half-life, half the asteroids will collide with the earth. In another such period half the remaining asteroids will collide with us, and so on. This can be run backwards as well. One half-life ago there were twice as many asteroids in the Apollo group as there are now. Another half-life ago there were twice as many again. Projected back to the beginning of the solar system, if it did indeed begin 4.5 billion years ago, the total mass of the Apollo asteroids must have been 100 times the mass of the sun! In other words, the solar system cannot be as old as the astronomers say, or there must have been an outrageous number of asteroids at the beginning. This is clear evidence for a young solar system.

Jupiter

Jupiter is the first in the group of non-terrestrial planets, or the Jovian planets. It is the largest of the planets, having more mass than all the others put together. Its diameter is 87,000 miles, or more than ten times the earth's, and its mass is 317 times larger. Nonetheless, it spins on its axis faster than any other planet, making one rotation in ten hours. At the equator the speed of the spin is 25,000 miles per hour. It has more satellites than any other planet, the highest escape velocity, and the deadliest radiation belts. Surely Jupiter is an impressive planet and well worth the study.

Jupiter averages 484 million miles from the sun, which it circles once every twelve years. Seen through a telescope, or even powerful binoculars, Jupiter is visible as a flattened disk. Its rapid rotation causes an even more severe flattening at the poles than the earth's does. Usually Jupiter's four largest moons are conspicuous as starlike points, and their movement from night to night is easily seen. With a slightly more powerful telescope, light and dark bands are seen crossing the planet, and it is possible to see the solar system's most famous blemish, the great red spot. The red spot is 30,000 miles long and 7,000 miles wide, though the size varies. It has been visible for well over 100 years, though it may really be a temporary feature. Astronomers now think it is a giant storm which has been raging in Jupiter's atmosphere for centuries.

Jupiter is unusual in other ways. It has been found to be a powerful source of radio signals. Some of these come in pulses at the rate of six or more per minute, and the total amount of energy in the radio region is larger than the radio output of the sun in its quieter moments. It is thought that this may be the result of fantastically violent electrical storms somewhere on the planet. Stranger than this is the fact that Jupiter is giving off two and a half times more energy than it receives from the sun! There must be some source for all this energy, and three possibilities are usually presented. (1) This is energy that it had from the beginning and is giving off as it cools, just as a hot burner gives off heat until it has cooled down; (2) it is the result of radioactive decay; and (3) it comes from gravitational contraction. Energy from radioactive sources is usually eliminated, since there appears not to be enough of them. Energy from gravitational contraction is the favorite candidate. (For an explanation of gravitational contraction, see chapter 6.) It has been calculated that if

Jupiter were to shrink by one millimeter (1/25 of an inch) per year, there would be enough energy released to account for Jupiter's excess radiation.[5] However, some models of Jupiter indicate that it is made of liquid hydrogen throughout, and liquids are not compressible. This would imply that Jupiter is not radiating heat because of contraction. This leaves only the first possibility, that the heat it is now radiating is the last remnant of a much greater store of heat which it had at its beginning. However, calculations show that if this were the only source of heat, Jupiter should have cooled off long ago, assuming, of course, that it is billions of years old. The fact that it has not cooled yet implies that it is not the billions of years of age that are assigned to it. For astronomers, however, the contraction hypothesis will continue to be the favorite, since it eliminates this problem. The contraction hypothesis is extremely dependent upon the model of Jupiter's interior which is used, and the final word has not yet been heard on the subject.

From earth it can be determined that the atmosphere of Jupiter consists mostly of hydrogen, helium, methane, and ammonia, not a very inviting place. The temperature is 223° Fahrenheit below zero. When Pioneers 10 and 11 visited Jupiter, they showed that the atmosphere of Jupiter is in violent turmoil. Where one cloud band sheers against another the difference in speeds may be as much as 360 miles per hour. Yet even here in an environment of violent electrical storms, cold temperatures, and poisonous gases, and without even a solid surface to the planet, some imaginative scientists have suggested that life may exist.

Jupiter has at least fourteen moons, more than any other planet. Two of them, Ganymede and Callisto, are even larger than the planet Mercury. But the strangest moon is Io, the second nearest to the surface of Jupiter. Io somehow influences the radio emissions of Jupiter, for when Jupiter, Io, and the earth are properly aligned, the radio strength increases. Another interesting effect is that after Io emerges from the shadow of Jupiter it is somewhat brighter than when it entered. The effect disappears after about fifteen minutes. This is an indication that Io has an atmosphere and that something in the atmosphere snows out during its passage through the cold shadow. The snow, which is thought to be frozen methane, increases the albedo of Io.

Pioneer 11 also indicated a thin atmosphere on Io. Now Io, even

5. H. H. Aumann, *Astrophysical Journal* 157 (1969), 169.

smaller than the moon, is not able to hold its atmosphere very long; its gravity is not strong enough. This may be evidence of a young age for Io, since it still retains an atmosphere. This is not proof of its youth, however. A torus, or doughnut-shaped ring, of gas has been observed in the orbit of Io, and it is possible that the atmosphere which Io is continually losing may be constantly replaced by the gas which it picks up from this ring. Io has also been found to be far more dense than had been expected or than can be accounted for by planetary formation theories.

Wrapped around the giant planet is its tremendous magnetic field and the deadly radiation trapped within it. Pioneer 10 showed that even 4.5 million miles from Jupiter its magnetic influence is felt. It is here that the satellite first encountered the magnetopause, the place where the solar wind and Jupiter's magnetic field meet. Trapped in Jupiter's magnetic field are charged particles just as in the earth's famous Van Allen radiation belts, except that there are more particles, and more energetic ones, in Jupiter's belts. It was at first feared, when the strength of the radiation was realized, that the probes would be destroyed by it, but they performed well at all times. It is not likely that man will ever explore Jupiter this closely in person, for this level of radiation is lethal. Even on earth we feel the influence of Jupiter's field, for every thirteen months, when Jupiter and the earth are "connected" via the sun's magnetic field lines, there is an increase in cosmic ray intensity. Energetic particles have travelled from Jupiter all the way to earth.

Saturn

Saturn's claim to fame is its beautiful ring system. The rings can be seen today with even a modest telescope, but when Galileo first observed Saturn through his early telescope, he thought the blotches he saw were two satellites of Saturn. Now we know of ten real satellites and three rings. The ring system is 170,000 miles in diameter, compared to the planet's diameter of 74,000 miles. The rings are not solid but are many small objects all in orbit together. The simplest demonstration of this fact is that stars can be seen directly through the rings. They are extremely thin on an astronomical scale and disappear entirely when seen edge on. Radar studies indicate that they may be composed of rocks or ice fragments only inches across. The whole ring system may not be more than a few feet thick.

FIGURE 7—Yerkes Observatory Photograph.

Of Saturn's ten satellites, the most interesting is the largest, Titan. Titan is one fourth as large as Mars and could be large enough to possess an atmosphere of its own. In 1944 methane was detected there, and later hydrogen was also found. Further, it appears to be warmer than it should be at its great distance from the sun. This may be due to a greenhouse effect caused by the moon's atmosphere, just as the atmosphere on Venus keeps the surface warmer than the sun alone could. However, there is not enough hydrogen in the atmosphere of Titan to produce this effect. Instead, the suggestion has been made that the greenhouse effect could be caused by the noble gas, neon. Neon, however, has never actually been observed. If it should turn out that Titan is cooling off from a higher initial temperature as Jupiter appears to be doing, it could be further evidence of a young solar system. But still more important is the fact that in four billion years the atmosphere of Titan could have boiled away many times over. Since it still has an atmosphere, it is obviously not four billion years old. Uniformitarians must find some way to explain how Titan could still have an atmosphere. Two major mechanisms have been suggested. The first is that as in the case of Io there is a ring of gas around the planet Saturn which constantly replenishes the gas lost by Titan. The second is that the gas is replaced by particles trapped in Saturn's magnetic field. There is no evidence for the ring of gas existing, however. And for the second possibility to be true Saturn would have to have a magnetic field as strong as Jupiter's, which is extremely doubtful. The best explanation is that Titan is young.

Saturn itself is very similar to Jupiter. It is yellow in color, and, like Jupiter, it has cloud bands, though they are less easy to see. It is nearly as large as Jupiter but has only one third the mass and so has a very low density. In fact, if one could find an ocean big enough, Saturn would float on water. Its day is only slightly longer than Jupiter's at 10 hours, 38 minutes. Because of the high speed of rotation, it too is flattened at the poles, more so, in fact, than any other planet. The only gases detectable are methane, ammonia, and hydrogen, but helium is undoubtedly present also. Its temperature is a chilly –230° F. And, again as in the case of Jupiter, Saturn seems to be giving off more radiation than it is receiving from the sun.

Uranus

Uranus was the first planet to be discovered in modern times. It was first seen accidentally by Sir William Herschel in 1781, when he was searching the sky through a homemade telescope. It is nearly 1.8 billion miles from the sun, and is so distant that few details can be seen on its greenish surface, even by the largest telescopes. It is one of the Jovian planets and, like Jupiter, is probably mostly atmosphere. It is smaller than Jupiter, however, only 30,000 miles in diameter. Its day is 10 hours, 49 minutes, and it takes 84 years to go around the sun once. At such great distances from the sun things get very cold—a decidedly uninviting –300° F.

The characteristic that makes Uranus unique, especially for creationists, is the tilt of its axis. Compared to the earth's tilt of 23½ degrees, Uranus tilts 98 degrees. It is tilted more than halfway over! Describing it as tilted makes it sound as if its correct position were up and down and that something forcibly made it tilt. This, of course, is what scientists assume. But there is no reason to believe that the tilt it now possesses is any different than its original tilt. Because of this tilt, we have a unique view of Uranus. At times the north or south pole can be seen face on, while at other times we have a side view as we do of the other planets. Uranus must have very peculiar seasons.

Uranus recently caused quite a stir in the scientific community, for it was accidentally discovered that Uranus shares a characteristic with the planet Saturn—rings. On March 10, 1977, Uranus occulted, or passed in front of, a bright star. These events are rare and can give a lot of information about the occulting planet, so the event was carefully observed. Unexpectedly, the star winked out a number of times before Uranus even reached it. After the occultation was over, the winking occurred again. Clearly there was something unexpected orbiting Uranus, and because of the timing of the winks, it appeared to be a set of rings. Unlike the rings of Saturn, however, Uranus' rings seem to consist of large chunks of rock, almost moon size. There may be thousands of rocks in the smaller, tens-of-kilometers, sizes in the five rings.

The rings have an inner radius of 44,000 kilometers and an outer radius of 51,000 kilometers. Another difference from Saturn's rings is that Uranus' rings do not appear perfectly circular. They are slightly elliptical, and it is difficult to see how they could maintain this shape in the presence of the perturbing effects of the other satellites' gravity.

Neptune

The discovery of the next planet, Neptune, was a triumph for the gravitational theory of Newton. After years of observations of Uranus, astronomers saw that its orbit was not the same as would be expected from the gravitational influences of the sun and the known planets. There must be some massive body beyond Uranus whose gravity caused Uranus to deviate from the calculated orbit. Two mathematicians, Adams and Leverrier, independently predicted the position of this new planet. In 1846 Neptune was discovered only one degree away from the predicted position.

Neptune lies over 2.5 billion miles from the sun. Its diameter is 28,000 miles, slightly less than Uranus', and it takes 165 years to orbit the sun. Being about the same size as Uranus but twice as far from us, Neptune's surface is more difficult to see in any detail. It too is greenish in color, and its surface temperature is –350° Fahrenheit.

Neptune has two satellites. Triton, the larger, is a little larger than earth's moon. The smaller of the two is Nereid, which has a highly eccentric (flattened) orbit, varying from one to six million miles from the planet. It is also peculiar in that it is a retrograde orbit. The Neptune-Triton relationship is unique in that it seems that most of Neptune's heat comes not from the sun but from the tides raised upon it by Triton. In the process Triton is losing orbital energy and is spiraling inward toward Neptune. It is predicted that Triton will collide with Neptune in 10 to 100 million years. This is only one percent or so of the accepted age of the solar system. Could we be so fortunate as to observe Triton's last moments of existence? While this is possible, it seems more likely that Triton has always been in the position it occupies now with respect to its planet. Its destruction is far in the future compared with the real age of the solar system.

The most distant and therefore the least known planet is Pluto. Even after the discovery of Nepture there still seemed to be unexplainable perturbations in the orbits of both Uranus and Neptune. Calculations by Percival Lowell indicated a still more distant planet. This was discovered in 1930 by Clyde Tombaugh, years after Lowell's death. As it turned out, however, Lowell's calculations were based upon bad data, and the discovery of Pluto in approximately the predicted position was pure chance.

Pluto

Pluto deviates most from Bode's law and lies 3.7 billion miles from the sun. One year on Pluto takes 248 earth years. Its orbit is the least circular of any planet, and it occasionally comes closer to the sun than does Neptune. These factors have led some astronomers to speculate that Pluto may not be a real planet after all but merely an escaped satellite of Neptune. Somehow, they say, its escape caused Triton to become a retrograde satellite. Here we have another example of catastrophism in the solar system: a moon totally escaped from its parent planet, causing the complete reversal of another moon! On the other hand, it does not seem likely that this event really happened. Though the orbits of Neptune and Pluto cross in the sense that there are times when Pluto is closer to the sun than is Neptune, they do not really intersect. The entire orbit of Pluto is inclined at 17 degrees to the ecliptic, far more than any other planet, and Neptune and Pluto are never in the same place at the same time.

Comets

The last major constituent of the solar system is the comets. Throughout history comets have variably been interpreted as omens of disaster or heralds of the birth of some great man. In reality, comets are just small bodies in orbit around the sun. Unlike planets, comets are usually in highly elliptical, or flattened, orbits, carrying some as close to the sun as a few million miles, and others farther away than Pluto. It is only when they are near the sun, usually closer than the earth, that they become visible and their spectacular tails form. Nearly every generation sees a bright comet with a tail millions of miles long. The tail is formed when the heat of the sun causes some of the more volatile components of the comet to vaporize and leave the body of the comet. They are blown away by the force of the solar wind and stream for millions of miles, illuminated by the sun.

While the visible portion of the comet itself can be up to 100,000 miles or more in diameter, this is mostly just the dust and gas evaporated from the comet by the sun's heat. The solid part of the comet, presumably all that can be seen when it is a great distance from the sun, is called the nucleus. It is believed to be only a few miles to a few hundred miles in diameter. It is not certain what the nucleus is made of, but it is thought to be a mixture of rock and ice in loose association. It has been estimated that comets lose about 1/200 of their mass each time they pass near the sun. This means that a comet like Halley's, which comes back often, would be nearly exhausted after only 10,000 years or so. Comets with short periods should not exist at all if the solar system is billions of years old. This has long been recognized as a problem by astronomers. And rather than admit that this is truly evidence for a young solar system, they have invented a mechanism to replace the comets as soon as they are burned out. They have made use of the fact that comets fall naturally into two categories—long-period comets and short-period comets. The short-period comets may have periods of a few tens to a few hundreds of years. It is the comets from this group that can be seen over and over again. Halley's comet belongs to this group and has a period of 76 years. The long-period comets are seen only once and have periods in the thousands of years.

The long-period comets seldom if ever get close to the sun, and so they do not suffer the destructive effects of the sun's heat. The long-period comets, therefore, could theoretically last for billions of years. If somehow this "reservoir" of long-period comets could be tapped to replace the short-period comets as they burned out, the problem would be solved. It has therefore been assumed that there are billions and billions of long-period comets orbiting the sun at about 150,000 astronomical units, or two light years, conveniently too distant to be observed. Every once in a while, a passing star is supposed to perturb the orbit of one of these distant comets, so that it is sent in towards the sun. The immense gravitational pull of Jupiter is then supposed to further perturb the comet's orbit, changing it into a short-period comet. There would thus be a constant replenishment of the population of short-period comets.

There are two major problems with this theory. First, there is no evidence whatever that such a comet cloud exists. It cannot be observed at the distance assumed, and there is not any physical evidence to suggest that it does exist or that it should exist, except, of course, to save the large-age solar system. Normally in the sciences such *ad hoc* assumptions are rejected out of hand. It is not proper to invent some mechanism or principle just to make a theory work. It is still done, however, in such cases as this.

The second problem is that calculations indicate that Jupiter is incapable of the celestial gyrations it is supposed to perform. It is possible that, over a long period of time and after many encounters, Jupiter could convert a long-period comet into a short-period comet.

But the *rate* at which it could do this falls far short of the required rate. There are so many short-period comets that they cannot be accounted for by this mechanism.[6] Thus the observed short-period comets have always been so, and their continued existence indicates that the age of the solar system is in the thousands and not billions of years.

We now move to a discussion about the smallest particles in the solar system, the interplanetary dust. There seems to be a cloud of dust in orbit around the sun, flattened into a disk in the plane of the ecliptic. Sunlight reflected off this dust can be seen with the naked eye shortly before sunrise or after sunset, and is called the zodiacal light. The nature of the light reflected by these particles indicates their size to be about .00004 inch in diameter. Particles this small can be influenced by the pressure of sun light. The Poynting-Robertson effect tends to slow these particles down so that they gradually spiral in towards the sun. This process tends to clean out the solar system of such dust. In fact, within 10,000 years all such dust should be completely gone. It may be inferred from this that either the solar system is less than 10,000 years old, or that there is some source constantly replenishing the diminishing dust supply. We have already seen that when comets near the sun some of their material is lost into space. This is the material that makes up the visible tail. But while the tail may be millions of miles in length, the amount of matter it contains is very small. It is estimated that the amount of matter in 2,000 cubic miles of Halley's comet's tail is less than the amount of matter in one cubic inch of air at the earth's surface. Yet, for want of a better source, astronomers assume that most of the dust causing the zodiacal light comes from comets. In fact, though, the dust would have to be replaced at the rate of eight tons per second to make up for the dust falling into the sun.[7] It is doubtful that comets contribute material at this rate.

And again, if cometary dust were the source of the zodiacal light, it would be expected that after a comet passes close to the earth, or alternately, the earth passes through a comet's tail, the zodiacal light should increase in brightness, since there would be a temporary increase in the amount of reflecting dust. Some observers have

6. H. Alfven and G. Arrhenius, *Evolution of the Solar System* (Washington, D.C.: NASA, 1976), p. 234.

7. W. K. Hartmann, *Moons and Planets* (Belmont: Wadsworth Publishing Co., 1973), p. 170.

claimed to see variations in the intensity of the zodiacal light, but Sparrow and Ney have been measuring its brightness with the satellite OSO-5 since 1969 and have noticed no change in brightness.[8] This implies that the contribution of the comets to the interplanetary dust is minimal. So, while comets may make a small contribution, perhaps lengthening the dissipation time of the dust beyond the expected 10,000 years, the very existence of zodiacal light is evidence for a young solar system.

We have examined a great variety of planets and other bodies in our study of the solar system, and have found in nearly every case that they provide evidence of a young solar system. Dr. Nicholas Short, in his book *Planetary Geology,* expresses a viewpoint with which I wholeheartedly agree. "In retrospect, as we contemplate the panorama of planets in our solar system, we can marvel at the almost providential fact that each planet seems to provide another set of essential clues for unraveling the mystery of creation."[9] I believe that each planet, each comet, each asteroid, each grain of dust in the solar system has its own contribution to make in showing the truthfulness of God's word and proclaiming His glory. This principle extends to every object in the universe, and to the nature of the universe itself. There is no object without a purpose, and man has only begun to discern what some of the purposes are.

---

8. Sparrow and Ney, *Science* 181 (1973), 438.
9. N. M. Short, *Planetary Geology* (Englewood Cliffs: Prentice Hall, Inc., 1975), p. 334.

5 THE MOON

He appointed the moon for seasons (Ps. 104:19).

After the sun, the moon is the most important astronomical object, both historically and scientifically. Historically the moon has always been used as a calendar, especially among the Jews. Scientifically it is the nearest astronomical body, the first to be studied in detail, and the first to feel the weight of a man.

FUNCTIONS OF THE MOON

The Bible's first reference to the moon is in the first chapter of Genesis. "And God said, Let there be lights in the firmament of the heaven to divide the day from the night; and let them be for signs, and for seasons, and for days, and years: and let them be for lights in the firmament of the heaven to give light upon the earth: and it was so. And God made two great lights; the greater light to rule the day, and the lesser light to rule the night: he made the stars also. And God set them in the firmament of the heaven to give light upon the earth, and to rule over the day and over the night, and to divide the light from the darkness: and God saw that it was good" (Gen. 1:14-18). The moon's principal purpose is to rule the night, and to give light. And while it is possible for the moon to appear during the day, it is obvious that its domain is the night. There are two reasons

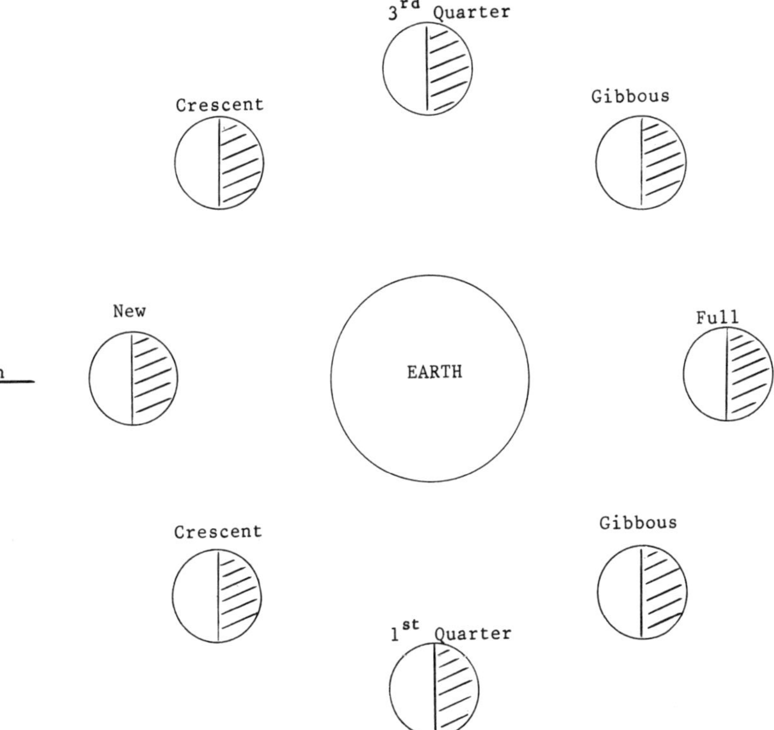

FIGURE 8.—The moon's phases throughout the month.

for this. First, the sun shines so much brighter than the moon, which shines only by reflecting the sun's light, that the moon's light is insignificant during the daylight hours. In fact, the light of the sun is 400,000 times brighter than the moon. Second, when the moon appears in the day-lit sky, it is always less than full. Figure 8 shows that when the moon is in the light half of the sky the illuminated side is primarily away from the earth. But when the moon is in the dark half of the sky, opposite the sun, it is in its fullest phases. This shows why the true domain of the moon as seen in the Bible is the night. In fact, while the moon is dim in comparison with the sun, it is so bright when full that astronomers can do very little at their telescopes. They prefer to wait until new moon, or the dark of the moon, to observe other objects in the sky.

The moon's second most important function is to mark seasons, days and years. The synodic period of the moon, which is the time it takes to go through a complete cycle of phases, is 29.53 days, hence our unit of time, the month. A calendar month, on the other hand, averages 30.42 days, or 30.5 days in leap years. They both round off to thirty days, but any calendar based upon twelve lunar months will be inaccurate by eleven days per year. The Jewish calendar was based upon lunar months, and therefore, at least in post-exilic times, to keep the prescribed feasts in the correct seasons of the year, an intercalary month was added four years out of every eleven. This was simply tacked on to the end of the year, following the month of Adar (February-March) and was called the second Adar. In the fourth century A.D. the Jews switched to a mathematical method of determining months.

The importance of the moon to the Jews may be seen in the books of Moses. Every new moon was a special day, with sacrifices being offered and trumpets blown (Num. 10:10; 28:11). The seventh new moon of the year was especially sacred, no work being done on it. This may have been because in that month, Tishri, came the Day of Atonement on the tenth day and the Feast of Tabernacles beginning on the 15th. The new moons were determined by observation, not calculation. At the end of the month, watchmen were stationed on the heights around Jerusalem to watch for the new moon. When someone saw the new moon, he would go to the president of the Sanhedrin, who would question him closely. When the president was satisfied, he would formally announce the coming of the new month with the words, "It is consecrated." Two festivals were held at the full moon instead of the new—the Feast of Tabernacles and the Passover.

The function of the moon as an indicator of months or days may be its most obvious one, but we are also told that it is for seasons. This also derives from the new moon celebrations, since it was by the observance of the full moons that the days of the month were determined. In turn, the seasonal feasts and festivals fell upon certain days of certain months. Seasons, for a people so tied to the land, referred to different periods of the planting and harvesting cycle. Pentecost, the day which celebrated the gathering of the harvest, fell 50 days after the Passover. The Passover, in turn, began on the 14th day of the month of Nisan, this day being determined by the appearance of the new moon on the first day of that month.

The most intriguing of the new moon's functions is that of giving signs. Signs in the moon are always mentioned in conjunction with signs in the sun, and I shall deal with these more fully in the next chapter. For now I shall just mention two of the signs said to appear in the moon. Joel 2:31 says, "The sun shall be turned into darkness, and the moon into blood, before the great and terrible day of the Lord come." In Matthew 24:29 Jesus said to His disciples, "Immediately after the tribulation of those days shall the sun be darkened, and the moon shall not give her light." These appear to refer to the same event. Signs in the moon as given in the Bible are always something far out of the ordinary, either in appearance or in behavior. We find no other kind of sign given for the moon. Its signs are reserved for the last days.

The first possibility that comes to mind is that these are eclipses. In fact, during an eclipse of the sun it does seem to cease to give its light. Animals have been observed to prepare for night in the middle of the day when a total eclipse of the sun occurs. During an eclipse of the moon, when the moon is entirely immersed in the earth's shadow, it takes on a coppery red color. In every case, however, the two signs are described as taking place simultaneously. This is impossible if we are to explain them on the basis of eclipses, since the moon is on opposite sides of the earth during the two types of eclipse. Further, eclipses of this sort have been going on for thousands of years and have not ushered in the Day of the Lord as yet.

Still, it is interesting to see how solar eclipses can come about. The remarkable aspect of the solar eclipse is not simply that the moon comes between the earth and the sun, blocking some of the sun's light, but that as seen from the earth the sun and moon appear to be almost exactly the same size. Even though the sun is 400 times larger than the moon, it is also 400 times farther away, giving both the same apparent diameter. This is why during an eclipse the moon's dark image shields the disk of the sun perfectly, allowing the relatively dim corona to be seen. Usually the solar corona is invisible in the much greater glare of the photosphere of the sun. The coincidence of size also means that a total eclipse may be seen from only a small area of the earth at one time. The path of the eclipse as the shadow crosses the face of the earth is only a few miles wide. Since the signs of the coming Day of the Lord will be visible to all, an eclipse is not adequate to explain them. Still, it is a remarkable "coincidence" that the sun and moon should have the same apparent diameters. The Lord certainly must have done this for some purpose not apparent to us.

THE APOLLO PROGRAM

The story of the moon has become the story of man on the moon. In the few years since the first moon rocks were returned by the astronauts, more has been learned about the moon than during all preceding history. Of course more is involved than just rocks. Many experiments were performed by the astronauts on the moon, and many other automatic devices left there by them relayed data to scientists for years about moonquakes, temperatures, and so on. I do not want to give the impression that all the evidence is in, however. There is still a great deal that is open to interpretation, and not all the experts are agreed on even some of the most fundamental aspects of lunar history or structure.

The major scientific goals of the Apollo program were to understand the structure and history of the moon as well as to look for signs of life. All are of interest for the Christian, for they bear upon the creation and age of the moon. Since all the evidence gathered will automatically be put into an evolutionary framework, it is no wonder that a picture of an extremely ancient body emerges. Looking at the data from a different point of view reveals that there is room for a youthful moon interpretation. There is no doubt, though, as in the case of the planets, that there is some evidence for a large age. This is because it is necessary to interpret the evidence in order to draw any conclusions. So far, all interpretation has been in the hands of the uniformitarian scientists.

Even with a quick glance at the moon through a pair of binoculars it is apparent that it can be roughly divided into two areas or types of terrain, the maria or "seas," and the rougher regions, which have come to be called the lunar highlands. The maria, of course, are not real seas, but vast smooth areas which appear to have been formed by huge lava flows. The maria have relatively few craters within their boundaries, while the highlands are saturated with craters. This implies that the maria were formed after most of the craters and that they covered most of the craters already existing in the mare areas. The maria are relatively dark in color (it is they which form the familiar features of the man in the moon), and the highlands are lighter.

As one of the main objectives of the Apollo program was to determine the history of the moon, nearly every resource has been brought to bear on a study of these minerals and element abundances in the returned rocks in order to find how they fit into the history of the moon. History here means assigning dates to certain events as well as identifying those events. There are two basic ways in which ages can be applied—relative and absolute. Already in the preceding paragraph I have described an instance of relative age assignments. The statement that mare formations must have followed most of the crater formation is an example of relative ages, because one can give the sequence of events but no more. Absolute ages are ages given in actual years—they go one step further than relative ages. Both types of ages are assigned to lunar events, and they always fall in the millions or billions of years.

There are many ways in which absolute ages are determined, but the primary one is always radioactive dating, a method discussed in chapter 3. There are a number of combinations of elements which are used for this purpose: uranium to lead, potassium to argon, rubidium to strontium, and others. When more than one method is used on a single rock, the ages are liable to be discordant or disagreeing. One particular rock was dated by three methods and gave three dates—3.68, 4.14, and 4.40 billion years.[1] One might argue that while these ages do differ by almost 20 percent, they agree in so far as they all indicate billions of years, and not anywhere near the few thousand creationists would hope to find. Let me answer first that this shows basic unreliability in the radioactive dating methods,

1. N. M. Short, *Planetary Geology*, p. 236.

and, second, as we have seen in chapter 3, when one assumes creation he is not under any obligation to assume all the "daughter" elements present in a rock are necessarily the result of radioactive decay. Scientists must make assumptions about how much of the daughter elements was there originally and how much is the result of radioactive processes. These assumptions are based upon theories of the formation of the solar system and of the rocks themselves. These may not be true if creation is true. In the end, results are really an end product of the assumptions one begins with, and radiometric dating is not conclusive evidence either for creation or uniformitarianism.

As another example, Apollo 12 rocks give ages nearly 25 percent higher when determined by the uranium-lead method than when determined by other methods. Since this does not look good, scientists simply bring the ages into accord by assuming that somehow two-thirds of the original lead that was in the rocks simply disappeared. This supposedly causes the uranium-lead age to agree with the rubidium-strontium and the potassium-argon ages. These, however, have already been "corrected" to bring them into agreement.[2] Some rocks appear to be billions of years older than the moon is supposed to be. In other cases regolith (soil) samples appear to be older than the rocks from which they came. While great ages appear to be indicated by radiometric methods, the discrepancies and uncertainties are great enough so as not to seriously threaten a belief in creation.

MOON TEMPERATURE AND VOLCANISM

The major features of interest on the moon are the craters. In the past there was a controversy as to the origin of the craters, some saying that they were the result of volcanism, while others maintained that they were formed by meteor impacts. In order for the former to be true, the moon must have had at one time, at least, a hot interior with magma near the surface. This is of interest to the creationist, for the moon does not now appear to be hot, although the evidence is inconclusive. Lunar geologists agree that the crust, or solid surface, is at least 60 miles thick and probably more.[3] If this is true, then volcanism cannot now be occurring on the moon. Has it in the past? Here we again encounter the time element, for if the moon were once entirely melted, it could not have cooled to the

2. Ibid., p. 239.
3. Ibid., p. 190.

present temperatures in only a few thousand years. Thus, if true volcanism has occurred on the moon, it implies that the moon has once been molten near the surface. Since the moon appears to be cool now, a large amount of time must have passed since it was hot. Let us examine some of the pertinent evidence.

One of the simplest observations that indicates a cold, solid moon is that it keeps the same face toward the earth at all times. This is due to a bulge in the moon which the earth's gravity attracts more strongly than the rest of the moon. This effect keeps the bulge closest to the earth. This theory was borne out by lunar explorations. It was shown that the center of gravity on the moon is two kilometers closer to the earth than is the geometrical center of the moon. In order to support this non-uniformity against the moon's own gravitational forces, which tend to cause the moon to be spherically symmetrical, the crust must have great strength and hence must be fairly thick. There cannot be molten rock too close to the surface.

When early satellites were placed in orbit around the moon, their orbits varied in an unexpected manner. This was found to be due to the mascons, unexpected concentrations of mass beneath the maria. For some reason the rock under the maria is denser than rock elsewhere on the moon. These density variations cause the gravitational forces to vary from place to place and hence cause the satellites' orbits to vary from the expected shape. Among the theories to explain the origin of these unexpected mass concentrations (hence mascons) is that dense iron meteorites struck the moon and lie buried beneath the maria. Whatever the origin of the mascons, they tell us something about the structure of the moon, for in order for the crust to be able to support these massive objects instead of allowing them to sink to the center of the moon, the crust must have great strength. It may be solid to a depth of hundreds of kilometers.

More direct methods of determining the structure of the moon can be used on its surface. The moon's magnetic field is small, but measurable. If magnetic fields of planets are caused by the dynamo mechanism discussed earlier, then the moon does not have such a dynamo, implying that there is no liquid center to do the circulating. The magnetic field associated with the solar wind seems to be able to pass through the moon relatively unimpeded. This fact, along with certain assumptions about what materials make up the lunar interior, imply that the moon is solid throughout.

Contradictory evidence comes from seismometers left on the moon to detect moonquakes. Moonquakes are relatively rare and weak compared to earthquakes. In one year the earth releases about 50 billion times as much energy as the moon does. Major moonquakes rate only 1 or 2 on the Richter scale. If the moon had a molten interior as does the earth, it would be expected to have more and stronger quakes than it does. Instead, the moonquakes seem to have periodicities related to its orbital motions about the earth and sun. For instance, when the moon is at its perigee (its closest point to the earth), the number of moonquakes increases, seemingly due to the greater tidal forces produced on the moon. The moon is creaking. Other moonquakes seem to be the result of meteor impacts on its surface.

Moonquakes (and earthquakes) consist of different types of motions. The two major types are called pressure waves (P waves) and shear waves (S waves). Seismometers can detect both types. Also, since there are now a number of seismometers on the moon, it is possible to tell the speed at which the waves travel by measuring the differences in time between the arrivals of the waves at various seismometers. All this tells a great deal about the structure of the moon. First, it reveals that the surface of the moon to a depth of 20 kilometers is composed of large rocks and rubble. It is unlikely that this part of the moon could ever have been molten and still have its heterogeneous nature. There is evidence that at greater depths there is a core of hot or even soft rock. This appears to contradict the earlier evidence that the moon is solid throughout.

Finally, heat flow measurements produced another unexpected result. The measurements were taken to determine the rate at which heat from the interior of the moon was escaping. One set of calculations showed that even if the moon had been entirely molten when it was formed (assuming the formation to be nearly five billion years ago), the moon would have completely cooled by now, so there should be little or no heat escaping from the moon now. Thus it came as quite a surprise when the heat flow measurements showed that two or three times as much heat was escaping as had been expected. This, then, is also evidence of a hot interior. But if the interior is hot, it has not had time to cool off and thus must be younger than the anticipated five billion years.

It is also true, however, that if the moon has ever been entirely molten, it would not have had time to cool as much as it appears to have done in only 10,000 years. Has it ever been entirely molten?

If volcanism has ever occurred on the moon, it may be evidence that the interior was once much hotter, and thus lend support to an older age for the moon. What evidence is there that volcanism did take place on the moon? Very little. Apollos 16 and 17 were expected to find evidence for volcanism, but none was forthcoming. The only evidence in favor of volcanism is in features associated with the maria. If these features are actually a result of local melting due to the impact of meteorites, there remains no evidence of lunar volcanism.

On the other hand, during the darker phases of the moon many observers have reported red glows which they have interpreted as being fresh lava from an active volcano. There have been over 1,200 such sightings recorded, reported from more than 100 locations. What this means is not clear, and little significance is usually attached to them.

As we said, there are evidences of volcanism on the maria, and the maria themselves appear to be hugh lava flows. Doesn't this contradict the contention that the crust of the moon is thick? It depends upon how the maria formed. If they are the result of the impact of a huge meteorite, the impact may have been powerful enough to penetrate all the way to the more liquid levels beneath the thick crust. The lava would have come up and spread across thousands of square miles. As the outer layer began to harden, there would still be hot lava just beneath the surface, which might cause the volcanic effects observed on the maria. This is just one of many possibilities.

Due to the somewhat contradictory nature of the evidence, it is difficult to give an unambiguous interpretation from the point of view of either the uniformitarians or the creationists. A case can be made for either a hot or cold interior and could be adapted to fit either way of thinking. As creationists we can try to see how it might fit into a young moon framework. First, even if the moon had been entirely melted at its formation billions of years ago, it should be cool by now. The apparently liquid core and the high rate of heat loss, together with the questionable observations of actual activity, contradict the great age for the moon, for it should have cooled by now. Further, most scientists agree that the moon was never entirely molten, so it should without doubt be cooler than we observe it to be.[4]

If it could be demonstrated that the entire surface of the moon had

4. Ibid., pp. 304ff.

ever been molten to any significant depth, it would be difficult to explain within a creationist viewpoint, for the surface of the moon would still be hot after less than 10,000 years. This does not appear to be the case. The few evidences of lava flow and volcanism need not be upsetting, however, for while some do suggest that the entire surface of the moon was molten at one time, others say the melting may not have been general. When we add to this the fact that the top few miles of the moon is heterogeneous enough to imply that melting never took place, the objection, that the moon must be old because it had once melted and has had time to cool, vanishes. As for the lava which does appear, scientists do not know whether it originated near the surface or deep down, or whether it was caused by internal heating or by meteorite impacts.[5]

It should be safely within the bounds of the evidence to postulate a model of the moon in which the moon has a hot if not molten core and a cool thick crust. It would not have lost much of its heat in only 10,000 years, explaining the high measured heat flow. The maria could have been formed by meteorite impacts, which either melted the rock which they struck or hit with enough energy to penetrate to the liquid regions below. As our knowledge of the moon increases, we shall probably find that we must revise our model; this is how science progresses. The thermal state of the moon as it is known now does not allow any more definite conclusions.

CRATER FORMATION

One can learn a great deal from the study of lunar craters. First, at some time in the past a large number of bodies have struck the moon (as well as Mars, Mercury, Earth, and probably Venus). At the present time there do not appear to be objects which could have caused such craters. There are the Apollo asteroids, some comets, and perhaps numerous small meteorites, but far from enough to account for all the craters observed. We are led to the conclusion that some time in the past the number of small, asteroid-sized bodies was greater than it is today. This is also the conclusion of astronomers who believe that the planets formed by the coagulation of numerous small bodies called planetesimals. To them, the lunar craters are primarily the marks which the last of these planetesimals made as they fell to form the moon. They say that we no longer see many

5. Ibid.

asteroid-sized bodies, since most of them went into the making of the planets. Thus they also believe that the impact rate (the rate of crater formation) was greater in the past than it is now. In fact, it is believed that during the period immediately after the formation of the moon the rate of crater formation was three hundred times greater than it is now. Creationists, who insist that the moon is really thousands of years old instead of billions, also must admit that all these craters must have been formed in a much shorter time, and hence that the cratering rate was even higher than that postulated by astronomers. This rapid formation of craters is difficult to account for if we assume, like astronomers, that collisions occurred by chance as planetesimal-like bodies happened to strike the moon and planets as they orbited the sun. There would have to have been so many of them that they could not possibly all be gone by now. We could simply assume that God created the moon already cratered, but I prefer to believe that effects have causes, and that God would not allow us to be so deceived as to make man think that craters were caused by meteorites when they were not.

Where, then, are all the asteroid-sized bodies now? It takes time for planets to attract all the debris floating around in space—more than ten thousand years. If the craters were formed by innumerable small meteors within the last few thousand years, there should still be a fairly large number in orbit around the sun. Only one possible explanation remains, and to introduce this I must present some remarkable observations. When the first photographs of the far side of the moon were returned from space, it was noted that the maria, which are so conspicuous on the near side, are all but absent from the far side. Mariner 9 showed that one half of Mars is considerably rougher, that is, more cratered, than the other. Finally, Mariner 10 revealed that even Mercury seems to be unsymmetrical in its crater distribution. This is a complete puzzle to astronomers. What is it about the planets that causes them to have more craters on one side than on another? Here is a case where preconceived notions have caused investigators to overlook the best explanation. Of the two possible explanations, that the asymmetry either originates within the planet itself or it is caused by an outside agency, the second is rejected by uniformitarians because the solar-system-wide effect implies that somehow, all at once, all the craters in the solar system were formed. This leaves none of the craters to have been formed by the planetesimals when they were accreting to form the planets, as uniformitarians demand. Therefore they look to the planets themselves to somehow influence where craters are formed. But how can a planet make planetesimals hit in only certain areas? If, on the other hand, they invoke some internal processes in the planet to erase craters in only certain areas, the theory founders again since for the most part the planets involved are not thought to be active enough to cause this kind of effect.

This leaves the second explanation, that some solar system catastrophe suddenly caused all the craters to be formed on all the cratered planets. If some time in the past a large cloud of asteroid-sized objects swept through the solar system and collided with the planets, it would have produced craters on just one side of each planet, assuming that the time it took the cloud to pass by was less than one period of revolution of the planet involved. This not only explains an effect already observed in the solar system, it has the added advantage that it tells us where the majority of these objects have gone, for after passing through the solar system, they just kept on going and are now very distant. We no longer need worry about how the planets could have swept all the material up in only 10,000 years, since it left the solar system.

There is further evidence for such a catastrophic event in the history of the solar system, though of course on a different time scale than ours. It appears that the ages of craters on the moon tend to cluster around certain values. That is, there was a period when a large amount of cratering took place in a short time. Nicholas Short, author of *Planetary Geology,* says, "This doctrine of cataclysm, tied to a single brief interval of large-scale impacts that tore apart the outer crust over the entire moon, has now become widely accepted by most investigators."[6]

This finding is in direct opposition to the doctrine of uniformitarianism, which maintains that all presently observed processes have always continued at their same slow rate. It is even in disagreement with the theory of planetary formation which states that the impact of planetesimals was rapid at first, and constantly decreasing as they were depleted through formation of the planets. Instead, evidence indicates that there was, according to uniformitarian dating methods, a period between 300 million and 600 million years *after* the formation of the moon when the impact rate increased dramatically for a

6. Ibid., p. 321.

short period of time.[7] A sudden but short-lived bombardment of the type indicated by the evidence is, in fact, just what I have proposed above. As always, the time scale is stretched far beyond that of creationists, but facts support a sudden catastrophic formation of craters after planets already existed, instead of the steady process of the infall of planetesimals during planetary formation.

The assignment of relative ages of craters is fairly straightforward. A study of the sizes and overlapping of craters shows that certain craters were formed before others. In some cases craters which are presumed to be older show the usual sharp edges to have eroded away or to have fallen inwards. Classifications have been devised which assign craters relative ages according to the features they possess or lack. These criteria are sufficient to establish relative ages but not absolute ages. Other methods, primarily radiometric dating, are used to establish absolute ages.

Other means also serve to establish relative ages for craters and surrounding features. For instance, craters will often possess rays of light-colored material radiating in all directions from the crater like spokes on a wheel. The freshness of these rays, when present, is one indication of relative age. If rays from two craters overlap, the ones on top obviously belong to the younger crater, and anything underneath the rays must have been there before the crater. Extensive studies of lava flows which overlap each other as well as the analysis of differing crater densities appearing on each show one deposit to be older than another. In all these cases it is impossible by simply observing the shapes and relative positions of various lunar features to assign absolute ages to them. One may try to do so by making assumptions as to the crater formation rate in the past, but these assumptions are totally unverifiable. As Nicholas Short says, "There is still no way to determine whether these events were completed rapidly in succession over a short duration (from tens to a few hundred million years) or took place uniformly over most of this lunar geologic time or have proceeded intermittently at nonuniform rates with indeterminate intervals."[8]

According to planetary formation theory, cratering rates near the beginning must have been much higher than at present. If one assumes cratering rates to increase linearly into the past, then in order to account for the large numbers of craters on the moon the in-

---

7. Ibid.
8. Ibid., p. 117.

crease must be allowed to continue for 10 to 100 billion years. This is far older than the moon is thought to be. This is based upon calculations of what the cratering rates should be now and is derived from terrestrial crater densities and measurements of the number of small bodies in the solar system. This is complicated for scientists by two factors. First, seismographs placed on the moon indicate that the present cratering is ten to a thousand times lower than expected.[9] If cratering rates are extended into the past using the *observed* rate instead of the theoretical rate, which is much higher, it would have taken ten to a thousand times longer to make all the craters. Second, the observed crater density in the lunar highlands was used to judge the total number of impacts which have occurred. However, after the surface has been entirely covered with craters, or saturated, as it is called, any further impacts will, on the average, destroy as many craters as they form. Thus, after the surface has become saturated, it is impossible to tell just how many meteors have struck the surface, and the counts actually yield only a lower limit. This means that scientists must account for even more craters than they actually count, and the time it took for them to form must be pushed back correspondingly further. Actually, scientists assume that the cratering rate has been decreasing exponentially with time and not linearly, which is in accord with the idea that originally there were many more planetesimals than at present and that the number has been declining over a long period of time. Still, it would seem that the time required for the formation of all the lunar craters, especially considering the unexpectedly low present impact rate, is longer than the age of the moon.

In answer to criticisms of the practical value of the space program, scientists often say that the study of other planets will aid in understanding our own earth. The assumption behind this answer is that all planets formed according to natural physical laws over long periods of time. Hence there would be a similarity in the way the planets formed and presumably also in their structure and histories. Other planets with less active surfaces would not have changed as much as the earth in the time since their formation, so that an examination of them would tell us what the earth was once like. Only such evolutionary assumptions could cause people to expect one planet to shed light upon another. On the other hand, if creation is true, then the

9. Ibid., p. 175.

planets were created essentially as they are now; the differences are innate and not indications of different stages in a similar evolution. We would not expect an examination of other planets to yield significant information about the history of the earth.* We might, though, learn something about the structure of the earth, since the other terrestrial planets are made out of similar materials. Consequently, one of the major goals of the lunar exploration was to determine the moon's origin. Tentative conclusions have been drawn—mostly negative. They concern which of the three major theories of lunar formation is most likely, or as it turns out, least likely.

MOON FORMATION THEORIES

The three basic moon formation theories are fission from the earth, accretion while in orbit around the earth, and independent accretion with a later capture of the moon by the earth. Accretion means the growth of planets or moons by the continuous addition of smaller bodies, the planetesimals. Fission refers to the splitting off of a large portion of the mass of the earth, which then went into orbit around the earth to become the moon. This would be the result of an initially high rate of spin for the earth, high enough so that some of the surface was thrown off by centrifugal force. This sounds strange, since if the earth were spinning fast enough to throw off some of its material, that material should not have been able to accrete on the earth to begin with. It has not yet been shown to be a feasible theory. At first, when the moonrocks were returned, it seemed that they supported the fission theory, since some patterns of element abundances were common to both the earth and the moon. Further, from a simple measurement of the mass and size of the moon it can be determined that the density of the moon is not great enough for it to have a dense core as does the earth. If the moon had once been part of the surface of the earth, it would have been primarily the light surface material and not any of the heavier core materials. More recent studies, however, tend to emphasize the difference in the element abundances and not the similarities. These are significant enough to indicate different origins for the moon and earth.

If the moon and earth had both formed from the same cloud of

* Though we do not believe that much light will be shed upon the history of the earth as a result of the space program, as Christians we still have reason to rejoice in the results of the space program, for it has enabled us to see more of God's creation and has provided further confirmation of His word which would not have been available without it.

dust or the same group of planetesimals, as in the accretion theories, they would be expected to have the same chemical compositions. We have just seen that they do not. Besides the chemical differences in the surface rocks, the moon does not have an iron core. It is strongly depleted in some elements, compared to the earth. Chemical analysis tends to indicate that the earth and moon did not form from the same bunch of stuff. Further, in this theory the moon accreted from matter originally in orbit around the earth. It is even postulated that the earth had rings of its own at one time. If so, what has happened to them? Scientists may affirm that the matter outside the earth's Roche limit formed into the moon, but what about the material inside Roche's limit? The material that makes up Saturn's rings is inside its Roche limit and hence cannot coalesce into a solid body. The same should be true of any material inside the earth's Roche limit. And if planets formed this way, why are Saturn and Uranus the only ones with rings?

All the available evidence serves to eliminate these two models. The third possibility is that the moon formed somewhere else in the solar system and was captured later by the earth. This, however, is also fraught with problems. No planets except Pluto cross the orbit of another planet. Presumably the moon also would have been in its own nearly circular orbit around the sun. How could it ever have come close enough to the earth to be captured? And even if it did, the chances are that it would not simply fall into a nice orbit around the earth—celestial mechanics are more complicated than that. It would most likely have an excess of energy, causing its orbit to be hyperbolic, that is, it would not be captured by the earth but would swing by and keep on going. And, if it should be captured, why should it fall into such a nearly perfect orbit about the earth, nearly in the ecliptic plane?

Though the differences in chemical composition between the earth and the moon cause astronomers to believe that the moon did indeed originate elsewhere in the solar system, they do not seem to be able to agree on where it must have formed in order to have the observed properties. Some astronomers maintain that it must have formed farther from the sun than did the earth,[10] while others say that it formed even closer to the sun than did Mercury.[11] It seems that

10. Ibid., p. 298.

11. J. Cornell, ed., *Man and Cosmos* (New York: W. W. Norton and Co., 1975), p. 35.

every prominent theory for the formation of the moon has fatal problems. But while the moon's nature is impossible to account for on natural grounds, creationism has no problems. God made it where it is and the way it is.

We have seen in this chapter that the moon is a much more unusual and inexplicable object than was once thought. Is it hot or cold? How did it form in the first place? Why is one side different than the other? The moon is so full of contradictory evidence and other perplexities that it is hard to explain its features, no matter what presuppositions one starts out with. Evidence exists for both creation and evolutionary theories. We are a long, long way from understanding even our nearest neighbor in space. As we are able to examine other planets more and more closely, we might expect difficulties to proliferate there as well, making evolutionary theories seem less and less reasonable. But for now the moon has quite enough problems for everyone. Because of this, William Hartmann in *Moons and Planets* says, ". . . the moon seems a highly unlikely object. Theoreticians have been led by frustration on more than one occasion to suggest facetiously that it does not exist."[12]

---

12. Hartmann, *Moons and Planets,* p. 127.

6 THE SUN

Praise ye him, sun and moon: praise him, all ye stars of light (Ps. 148:3).

Not enough can be said about the sun. It is the center of the solar system, the controller of planetary motions, the source of warmth and light, the life sustainer. No wonder it was worshiped by many ancient civilizations, and that even in the Bible it is used metaphorically for God.

FOR DAYS, SEASONS, YEARS

Because of the sun's importance to earth and its prominence in the heavens, it is the first heavenly object mentioned in the Bible. Its creation is described in Genesis 1:16, where it is the greater light, in contrast to the lesser light, the moon. The major purpose of the sun is "to rule the day . . . and to divide the light from the darkness" (Gen. 1:18). In addition to this are its lesser roles as a sign and as an indicator of seasons and days and years. Its role as a divider of light from darkness is apparent every day. We saw in chapter 3 how the seasons come about due to the tilt of the earth's axis; how in the summer the northern hemisphere points toward the sun, so the sun's rays are more direct. From our point of view, during the course of a year the sun's position changes, being higher overhead in the summer and lower in the winter. Along with this change, the point of the sun's rising and setting shifts northward in summer and southward in winter. This seasonal change is spoken of by God in the book of Job. "Have you ever in your life commanded the morning, and caused the dawn to know its place . . .?" (Job 38:12). In all these ways the sun is an indicator of seasons.

Of days and years not much need be said. The light of the sun brings day and its absence brings night. For hundreds of years now it has been known that this is due to the earth's spin and not the revolution of the sun about the earth. The passing of a seasonal cycle tells us when a year has passed. Were it not for the tilt of the earth's axis we could still discern the passing of a year by the stars which are visible, but it would be difficult to tell by observing the sun. The tilt of the earth is a simple fact, but it has great effects on the inhabitants of the earth, and it enables the sun to fulfill the role it is given in the Bible.

A SIGN GIVER

As with the moon, the most intriguing aspect of the sun's function is that of a sign giver. The word *sign* usually brings to mind a vision of some spectacular display in the sun and moon—something entirely foreign to normal experience. This is what is implied by such passages as Joel 2:10, 31; Acts 2:19, 20; Revelation 6:12; Isaiah 13: 9, 10; and Ezekiel 32:7, which reads, "And when I shall put thee out, I will cover the heaven, and make the stars thereof dark; I will cover the sun with a cloud, and the moon shall not give her light." I cannot agree with those expositors who endeavor to write these signs off as eclipses. First, while eclipses have always been regarded as signs by the superstitious, they are too common, and in fact entirely too predictable to serve as signs. If eclipses were the signs of the Bible, we could easily predict future signs, and our Christianity would begin to look dangerously like astrology. The basic nature of signs and miracles is the divine act of intervention in a supernatural and unpredictable manner.

Second, in each of the references given except for the last, the events in the sun are explicitly associated with the coming great and terrible Day of the Lord. They all refer to the same event, the one of which Jesus spoke in Matthew 24:29: "Immediately after the tribulation of those days the sun shall be darkened, and the moon shall not give her light, and the stars shall fall from heaven, and the powers of the heavens shall be shaken." Eclipses have been occurring regularly throughout all history and have not heralded the return of Christ. Yet the signs point only to that event; they cannot be eclipses.

The final reason for rejecting eclipses is that they cannot explain all the described events. Nearly every instance describes the sun and the moon as being dark at the same time. We saw in chapter 5 that this cannot happen. Further, it is typical of the Biblical descriptions to include other events as well. In this respect Isaiah 13:10 is representative. "For the stars of heaven and the constellations thereof shall not give their light: the sun shall be darkened in his going forth, and the moon shall not cause her light to shine." The signs are seen to be nearly universal in extent, blocking out the light of the distant stars as well as that of the sun and moon. There is nothing that can happen during an eclipse that can account for these events, or for the falling stars foretold by Jesus.

And again, there is no reason to suppose that any known events in history have coincided with any past eclipses. Some "scholars" with little confidence in Scriptural authority would say that these predicted signs were merely eclipses which happened to occur at the same time as important events in Israel's history. They later were incorporated as a sort of nature myth into Israel's history. But besides missing the point of these signs, these people disregard the divine inspiration of the Scriptures, saying that the events were not predicted at all, but rather the "predictions" were written after the events in question. These wanderers from the truth need not be heeded.

The Sign to Joshua

It is useless to speculate as to what might cause these unusual events in the end time. They are of supernatural origin and cannot be explained by simple, known processes. There are, however, examples of signs in the sun found elsewhere in the Bible. They illustrate how the Lord works in the heavens and give a clearer idea of what He meant when He said the sun is for signs. The first of these major signs is found in the book of Joshua, the well-known battle when Joshua commanded the sun and moon to stand still. "Then spake Joshua to the Lord in the day when the Lord delivered up the Amorites before the children of Israel, and he said in the sight of Israel, Sun, stand thou still upon Gibeon; and thou, Moon, in the Valley of Ajalon. And the sun stood still, and the moon stayed, until the people had avenged themselves upon their enemies. . . . So the sun stood still in the midst of heaven, and hasted not to go down about a whole day. And there was no day like that before it or after it, that the Lord hearkened unto the voice of a man: for the Lord fought for Israel" (Josh. 10:12-14).

This remarkable event was a sign in many ways. Its main purpose, of course, was to give Israel an added advantage over the Amorites and insure Israel's victory. It was utilitarian, as are most of the recorded signs and miracles. It was also a sign of God's power and authority both to the Israelites and to the Amorites—to the Israelites because, as the Bible tells us repeatedly, the Israelites seek signs, and they were prone to follow the idolatrous practices of the Canaanites. It was a sign to the Amorites of the authenticity of Israel's God and the ineffectiveness of their own. It was also a confirmation of the power which God had invested in Joshua as the leader of Israel. In fact, it is the Lord hearkening to the voice of a man that impressed the writer of Joshua.

In modern times the existence of this and other Biblical miracles has been discounted by both scientists and scholars. This is because of a weakening of faith in the Scriptures as authoritative, and in the power, if not the existence, of God Himself. These scientists stress the fact that tampering with the laws of motion of the universe simply cannot occur. But believers know the God of the Scriptures, who not only could stop the earth if He chose, but could create the whole universe with a single word. If He could do the latter, He could easily do the former.

Even liberal Bible scholars, the few who admit that the book of Joshua is based upon fact at all, interpret this in other ways. For instance, they say that Joshua was simply calling for a lessening of the heat of the sun, and that a storm began, whose hailstones killed the Amorites. A careful reading and a little thought, however, reveal that this must have been a literal stopping of the sun and moon. The cool of the storm would have been as helpful to the Amorites as to the Israelites. But prolonged light would enable the Israelites to pursue the enemies who might otherwise have escaped in darkness.

This record also contains, almost as an aside, a point which not only confirms that this was a real event, but also that the writer realized that days were not caused by the sun orbiting the earth, but by the spin of the earth. Joshua issues a command for the sun to stand still in order to prolong the daylight. At the same time, he commands the moon to stand still. Now if Joshua believed the sun went around the earth, it would have been sufficient to command the sun to stand still in order to prolong the daylight. But since, in reality, the sun and moon continued in their normal motions and it was the earth that stopped, the moon must necessarily have appeared to stand still as well. The inclusion of this seemingly insignificant detail affirms the truth of the account.

The Sign to Hezekiah

The fact that God has, at times, interfered with the normal course of planetary motions is also evident from another example. When King Hezekiah was ill and told that he would die, he prayed that he might recover. The Lord sent Isaiah to him with the message that his prayer would be answered and that he would recover. He was told that he would live an additional 15 years. In an action that seems strange to us, Hezekiah asked for a sign that this message was true. Through Isaiah God offered Hezekiah a choice between two signs—that the shadow on a certain staircase would go either forward 10 steps or backward 10 steps. It has been conjectured that the shadow on this staircase was used somehow as a sundial, and that as the day passed, the shadow of a certain building would progress along the steps. Hezekiah reasoned that it would be easy for the shadow to go forward 10 steps; it did this every day. Hence he requested that the shadow go back 10 steps. "And Isaiah the prophet cried to the Lord, and He brought the shadow on the stairway back ten steps by which it had gone down the stairway of Ahaz" (II Kings 20:11, NASB). The sign required not only that the sun stop, but that it go backwards! This has variously been explained as a defect in the sundial (as the King James Version calls it) or as some freak atmospheric phenomenon. Again, this is a result of the fact that people do not believe in God's power to do as He wills. Objections that disastrous side effects would result from such a stoppage of the earth are of no import; if God can stop the earth, He can also stop the side effects.

As before, there is confirmation of the truth of this event from a seemingly insignificant detail elsewhere in Scripture. When the rulers of Babylon sent envoys to King Hezekiah to congratulate him on his recovery, they were also instructed to ask what this wonder was that had happened in the land (II Chron. 32:31). Apparently this remarkable reversal of the motion of the sun had been observed as far away as Babylon. It could thus not have been anything wrong with the sundial or any atmospheric disturbance, which must by nature have been relatively localized. The earth really did reverse its spin, causing the shadow to regress on the stairs.

A third example of a sign in the sun is the darkness at the time of Jesus' crucifixion. After Jesus had been nailed to the cross, "from the sixth hour there was darkness over all the land unto the ninth hour" (Matt. 27:45), that is, from noon until 3 P.M. It has been pointed out many times to those who insist that this was a simple eclipse that the Passover, when Jesus was crucified, occurs only at the full moon. Solar eclipses occur only at new moon, two weeks away. Further, the longest that any total eclipse of the sun can last is seven minutes. Whether or not the moon also was darkened at this time we cannot say, since it was below the horizon. But the fact remains that this was a supernatural darkness caused by the intervention of God in natural affairs. It was a sign which God wrought in the sun, illustrating one of the purposes for which the sun was created. It may well be that, if the Lord returns soon, some people now living will see the most spectacular signs yet in the sun, moon, and stars, and then the return of the Lord Jesus Christ.

THE SUN'S ENERGY

The ordinary sun as we observe it every day is hardly less remarkable than some of the signs we have read about. Describing it as big and hot is an understatement. It is 864,000 miles in diameter, over 100 times the diameter of the earth, and could hold 1.3 million earths within it. The mass, though, is only 300,000 times the earth's, making it considerably less dense on the average. This is because the sun is gaseous, not solid. It shines because it is hot, 6,000 degrees Kelvin (10,800° F.) on the surface. At this temperature each square yard of the surface generates 70,000 horsepower, and its surface area is 7×10^{18} (7 billion billion) square yards! At this unbelievable rate of energy generation it is no wonder that even at earth, 93 million miles away, we feel its warmth, sometimes painfully. Yet the fraction of the sun's energy that actually arrives on the earth is only one two-billionth. The rest, except for a little that strikes the other planets, is radiated profligately away into space.

The part of the sun that can actually be seen is called the photosphere. While this appears to be the surface, there is much more to the sun than this, as those who have been fortunate enough to see a total solar eclipse can testify. Lying above the photosphere and about 5,000 miles thick is the chromosphere, made up of gases which

FIGURE 9.—The sun's corona during a total eclipse. Lick Observatory Photograph.

are nearly transparent. Only just before and after the totality of the eclipse, when the moon is covering the much brighter photosphere, can the chromosphere be seen. Much better known is the solar corona, which is easily visible during a total eclipse as a bright but variable-sized ring of light. It looks like a halo around the sun and may be more than one million miles thick. As one moves (if one could!) upward through the chromosphere and into the solar corona, the gases become thinner but hotter. At places in the corona the temperature is 2 million degrees Kelvin. If the surface of the sun were this hot, we would instantly be burned to a cinder. But the gases in the corona are so thin that they give off little radiation.

What maintains these temperatures, and what is the source of this fantastic energy? This question was not a problem until the last century, for no one realized how great the output of the sun is. Then Sir John Herschel, a famous astronomer of the nineteenth century, performed an experiment enabling him to measure the amount of heat arriving at the earth from the sun. His results gave such a large amount of energy that scientists of the day were hard pressed to explain how the sun could maintain it. The natural first thought, that some kind of fuel was burning, had to be ruled out. It is easily calculated that if the sun were made of coal and had always burned at the observed rate, it would last only 5,000 years. This is not long enough even for creationists, who believe that creation took place about 10,000 years ago.

The first reasonable explanation was that of Herman Von Helmholtz, who in 1871 suggested that the sun's energy comes from the contraction of the sun. This is the same process that was suggested as the energy source for Jupiter and the other giant planets. This concept can be made clear from a simple example. If an object is carried to a great height above the surface of the earth and then dropped, it gains speed as it falls. By the time it finally hits the earth it has acquired a great deal of energy. When it hits the ground, assuming it does not bounce, this energy is transformed into heat. When the object is high above the earth, it is said to possess gravitational potential energy—gravitational because it is the earth's gravity which accelerates it downward, and potential because the energy, in a tangible form, so to speak, was only potentially there. It did not become a tangible form, motion or heat, until later. Now, instead of a falling object, consider the whole surface of the sun contracting inward. This would obviously contribute a great deal of energy to the sun and would appear as heat. Of course, even if this were the source of the sun's energy, the surface of the sun would not be falling inward as fast as a free-falling object. It would contract gradually, adding energy to the sun at the same rate at which it is radiating it away. If this really were the source of the sun's energy, the sun would be shrinking at the rate of 400 feet per year, a change too small to detect.

This theory, while thought for a while to be the final answer, was ultimately rejected, because even if the sun had contracted from a larger size to its present size, it could have been giving off heat for only 20 million years. Biologists, in the meantime, were formulating the theory of evolution and decided that more time was needed than the contraction theory allowed. Geologists also said that 20 million years was not enough time for some of their rocks. Many other theories were advanced, some more reasonable and some less. For instance, it was proposed that meteorites were continually striking the sun, heating it up by their impacts. However, the total mass of the meteorites required to heat the sun for millions or billions of years is greater than the mass of the sun itself. What, then, is the source of the sun's great energy? To see what astronomers think, let us return first to the surface of the sun itself.

Moving downward from the photosphere, we find the temperature rising. The pressure of the gas increases, because each lower layer is supporting the weight of all the layers above itself. In order for the sun to be able to support these progressively heavier layers, the temperature of the gas must increase accordingly. This is called the condition of hydrostatic equilibrium. The simple fact that the sun is able to exist without collapsing under its own weight indicates that certain pressure and temperature conditions must prevail in the interior, assuming that the known physical laws are valid there. When we reach the center of the sun, the temperature has climbed to about 15 million degrees Kelvin (27 million° F.). It is here, theoretically, that certain nuclear reactions are able to take place.

The Hydrogen Atom

Before these can be understood, however, we must change our perspective from one of the larger objects we know of to one of the smallest, the hydrogen atom. The sun itself is made primarily of hydrogen, the lightest element, along with 20 to 40 percent helium by weight. All other types of atoms put together comprise only about one percent of the sun's mass. These abundances may be determined spectroscopically as we described in chapter 2. These abundances are determined for the surface of the sun only, but it is reasonable to presume that hydrogen is the dominant element in the center as well.

Now, what are these reactions? It was noted by Hans Bethe in the 1930's that it might be possible to combine hydrogen nuclei and make a helium nucleus out of them. How can this be if helium nuclei have two protons and two neutrons while hydrogen nuclei have only protons? The transformation can be visualized simply as shown in figure 10. If two hydrogen nuclei, or protons, combine, an odd thing happens—one of them gives up its charge and becomes a neutron. This is an example of what is called the weak interaction in nuclear physics, and it is fairly improbable. However, there are so many free protons in the center of the sun that it may actually happen fairly often. The positive charge of one proton cannot simply disappear; it is gotten rid of when the former proton emits a new particle called a positron. The positron is identical to an electron except that it is oppositely charged. It is the antiparticle of the electron. The positron, which has small mass compared to the protons involved, leaves the scene and is not involved in other nuclear reactions. There is now a new nucleus consisting of a neutron and a proton. Recall that an atom's type is determined only by the number of protons in the nucleus. Hence the new nucleus is still hydrogen, but of a heavier variety called deuterium. If this deuterium nucleus collides with another proton and they stick, they will form a nucleus with two protons and a neutron which is helium. This is one neutron short of a normal helium nucleus. The next step occurs when this light helium nucleus collides with another like itself, resulting in a normal helium nucleus with two protons and two neutrons, and with two protons left over. These are free to participate in more reactions like the first in this chain.

The remarkable thing is that this new nucleus, along with the two positrons which were emitted in the process, weighs less than the four original particles from which the helium nucleus was made. This, it is believed, is the source of the sun's energy. According to Einstein's famous formula, $E=mc^2$, the missing mass has appeared in a new form—energy! This transformation does not take place under normal circumstances, for these reactions are not very probable. But two conditions in the sun cause it to be more probable there: the density and the temperature. The density is so great at the center of the sun

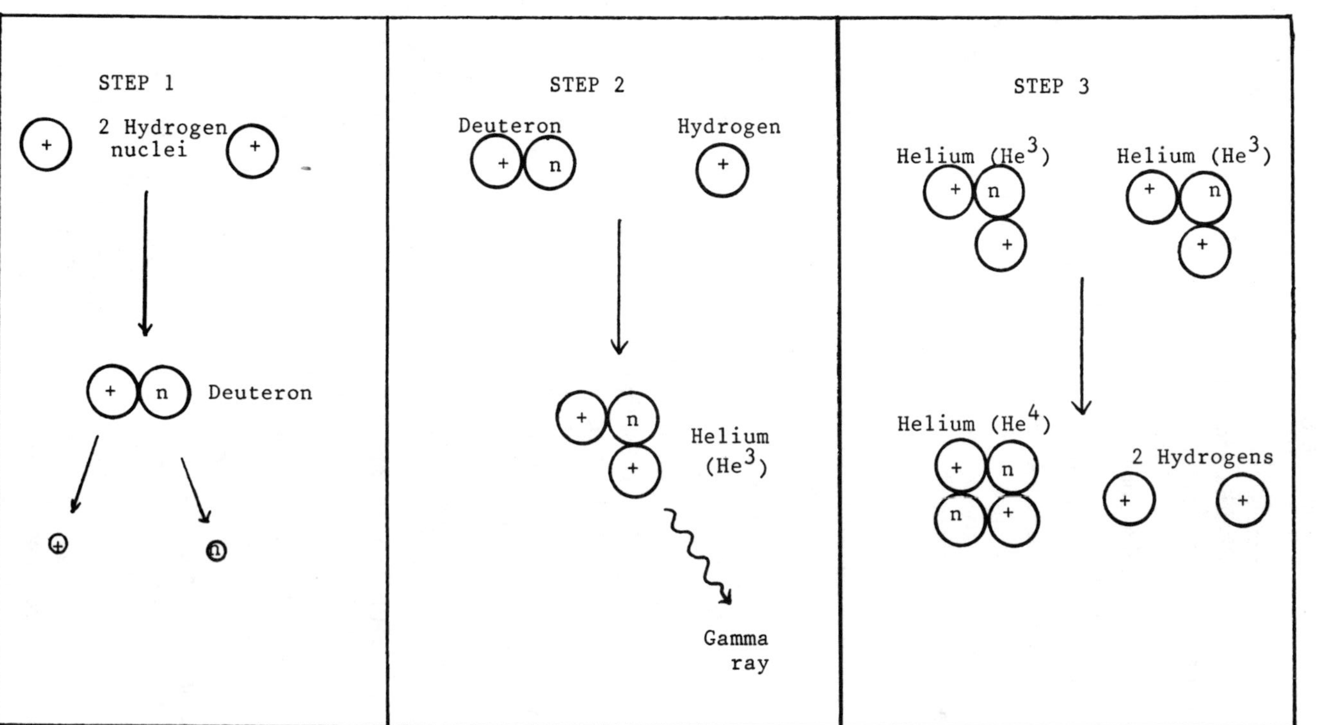

FIGURE 10.—The proton-proton chain as it is thought to be taking place in the sun.

that collisions are constantly occurring there, and the more collisions there are, the more there will be which result in the nuclear transformations. The temperature is important because at high temperatures the particles are moving faster, and hence they hit harder, making it more likely that they will "stick." Of course, the energy released by a single reaction is not very much. At the rate the sun is giving off its energy, it must be changing its mass into energy at the rate of five million tons per second! There is no need to worry about running out of energy, however, for if the sun started out as pure hydrogen, it could burn at its present rate for ten billion years. It is this extremely long potential lifetime which causes astronomers to believe that nuclear reactions are the energy source for the sun. They need a mechanism allowing the solar system to be billions of years old.

Scientists at last were able to come up with an energy-producing process to satisfy their needs. What does this mean to the Christian? Probably if everyone were creationist, we would have been perfectly happy to stick with Helmholtz's contraction theory; twenty million years is more than enough. However, nuclear fusion is a perfectly legitimate energy source. Just because it has the potential to go on for billions of years does not mean that it already has been doing so. If the sun does derive its energy from fusion, the sun is not necessarily as old as the scientists say. Nuclear fusion could just as easily have started 10,000 years ago as five billion. Further, calculations appear to indicate that when hydrogen is made hot enough and dense enough, as it is in the center of the sun, nuclear fusion will take place.* So there seems to be no reason to reject fusion as the solar energy source. Therefore it is an interesting development that a way has been tested which should be able to detect this process if it is occurring.

Is There Nuclear Fusion in the Sun?

To understand this experiment we must go back to the details of the fusion process. The chain of events described earlier is just one of a number of paths that hydrogen nuclei can take as they convert to helium. Usually one process will be the predominant one, while the others occur at a slower rate. The rates of the various paths are determined by the conditions within the star, namely temperature, pressure, and the amounts of other elements present. The process be-

---

* We should stress here that calculations of this sort are subject to much uncertainty and should serve to illustrate possibilities instead of facts.

lieved to be dominant in the sun is called the proton-proton chain, since it starts with two protons. Even the proton-proton chain has three different branches, some of which involve elements other than hydrogen and helium. The rates at which these three different branches proceed depends upon the abundances of the elements present. It is time to remember the positrons which carried away the positive charges when the protons became neutrons. Nature has certain conservation laws which state basically that if you start out with so many of a certain kind of particle, you have to have that many when the process is over. This law applies to a certain class of particles called leptons. Included in this class are electrons. Positrons, as antiparticles, belong to the class of antileptons. One cannot simply create an antilepton; there must be a lepton created at the same time to cancel out the antilepton, keeping the total number of leptons at zero as it was before the reaction. What is the lepton which appears at the same time to cancel out the positron? It cannot be an electron, since an electron has a negative charge. There is a conservation law for charge too; there must be the same total charge after the reaction as before. To satisfy all the conservation laws, the lepton must be one which has no charge. This lepton is called a neutrino. This is not a fantasy which grows more and more complex in an effort to keep the bookkeeping straight—all these particles have actually been observed. All the particles involved have now been accounted for. Each time a helium nucleus is made from hydrogen, there must be two positrons and two neutrinoes produced as well. This is true no matter which branch of the proton-proton cycle is followed. The neutrinoes from different branches of the cycle, however, have different energies. One particular branch has exceptionally energetic neutrinoes. It is only the neutrinos from this branch that are detectable with the detectors now in use. The rate at which this branch proceeds depends upon the amount of helium present—the more helium there is the faster the branch proceeds and the more energetic neutrinoes are produced.

Now neutrinoes are peculiar little objects, for they have the ability to pass through matter almost as if it were not there. Thus, while all the other particles produced in the nuclear reactions are trapped inside the sun, the neutrinoes are free to escape from the sun and into space. If these could somehow be detected on earth, we would be able to "see" for the first time what is taking place at the center of the sun. How could we hope to detect on earth such evasive particles which have no trouble passing through hundreds of thousands of miles of sun? Couldn't they pass through any of our detectors just as easily and not be seen at all? Yes, for the most part. However, if the energetic branch of the proton-proton cycle is occurring as fast as is believed, then there should be an incredible number of neutrinoes passing through the earth every second. The vast majority do simply pass through the detector, but an extremely small percentage will strike an atom within a detector and be stopped.

One scientist, Raymond Davis of the Brookhaven National Laboratory, has constructed an apparatus which he hoped would enable him to detect the few neutrinoes which could be stopped. He filled a huge tank with 100,000 gallons of the cleaning fluid dichloroethylene and placed it one mile deep at the bottom of the Homestake Gold Mine in South Dakota. The reason for placing it at the bottom of a mine is to shield the experiment from the effects of cosmic rays, which would overwhelm the effect of any neutrinoes. The reason for the choice of the cleaning fluid is that it contains mostly chlorine atoms. When a chlorine atom is struck by a neutrino, it may be changed into a radioactive argon atom. These radioactive atoms are detected by their radioactivity. Thus, if there is a flux of neutrinoes from the sun which result from the energetic branch of the proton-proton cycle, Davis should find radioactive argon atoms in his tank.

And the results? After years of looking, almost no neutrinoes have been found. Does this mean that nuclear reactions are not taking place in the sun? That may be the case, but not necessarily. Dozens of theories have been advanced in an effort to explain this predicament. Most require rather strange conditions or processes and none have been entirely successful. The reason is that all have been proposed in an effort to maintain the viability of the high age for the sun. Recall that the energetic branch had to have helium present before it could take place. Astronomers expect that, since the sun has been burning hydrogen into helium for billions of years, there would be sufficient helium present for the energetic branch to occur. However, that branch apparently does not occur. Now Davis is sure that his experiment is correct and looks to astronomers to make some corrections to their theory about the sun's interior. Astronomers, on the other hand, are sure that they have done their calculations correctly and cannot understand why the neutrinoes have not been detected. The obvious answer is simply that there is not enough helium for this branch. The reason that there is not enough helium is that the sun has not been converting hydrogen into helium for as long as scientists believe, but for only a few thousand years. The lack of neutrinoes in Davis' experiment is strong evidence that the sun is not billions of years old, and if the sun is not, then the earth is not.

This has not caused astronomers to switch to creationism in droves, perhaps understandably. The entire scientific community has accepted the great age of the universe; indeed, it has built all its science upon that supposition. They will not give it up without a fight. In fact, they will never give it up, even if it means compromising their reason or even their professional integrity, for to admit creation is to admit the existence of the God of the Bible. This is exactly what the world system will not do. Consequently, many strange theories have emerged to account for the lack of neutrinoes. One even says that the sun is temporarily shut off and no nuclear reactions are occurring. This obviously cannot continue very long before we feel a chill.

There is absolutely no way that one can tell the age of a star simply by looking at it. For all stars this is all we can do, look at them. The sun is the only exception in that we can look for neutrinoes. Those neutrinoes, the only way we have to prove the existence of nuclear reactions in the sun, are not found. When this is added to the evidence we have for the youth of other solar system objects, is there any reason to doubt the truth of the word of God? How can one account for the blindness of scientists toward these truths? ". . . the god of this world hath blinded the minds of them which believe not, lest the light of the glorious gospel of Christ, who is the image of God, should shine unto them" (II Cor. 4:4).

CHANGES IN SOLAR BEHAVIOR

Since scientists believe that the present is the key to the past and thus that the sun has been shining steadily and benevolently for billions of years at almost the same rate, it is interesting to note that recently astronomers have come to the conclusion that the sun is not so steady after all. It was pointed out by Gustav Sporer of Germany and E. W. Maunder (a Christian astronomer) of England in the late nineteenth century that the sun has undergone changes within recorded history. They based this upon the fact that almost no observations of sunspots had been made between the years 1645 and 1715. This is unusual, because in more modern times the sun has been observed to follow a regular cycle with a duration of 11.2 years, during which the number of sunspots increases to a maximum and decreases to a minimum. Because of scientists' deep-seated notions that nothing ever changes, Maunder was ignored.

But recently further evidence has come to light. Aurorae (northern lights) which often accompany high sunspot activity were not recorded during this period. Newly discovered oriental sunspot observations also showed no evidence of spots during those lean years. Even the amount of radioactive carbon 14 (the famous radioisotope, used in dating) found in tree rings shows that solar activity was extremely low during that period. Studies of climate indicate that when the sun passes through such a low period, the temperature of the earth's atmosphere decreases. This corresponds to the "little ice age" previously recognized to have happened during that time.

What does all this mean? John Eddy, the astronomer who has brought the subject to light once more, said, "We've shattered the principle of uniformitarianism for the sun. . . . We've finally broken a block that has held us back—uniformitarianism. It was an assumption we took as fact."[1] What more need be said? We now have an example where not only uniformitarianism is shown to be untrue, but actually a hindrance. The assumption was taken as fact without good reason and proved to stand in the way of the truth. This is what creationists have been maintaining all along.

Actually, astronomers do not say the sun has been constant in brightness since its beginning. If the sun really did result from a condensation of a cloud of dust and gas as modern theories declare, there must have been a time when it was considerably dimmer than now. Part of the theory of stellar evolution says that the sun has gradually been increasing in brightness since its beginning. This has profound significance for uniformitarian theories. If, when the earth was young, the sun was really as much cooler as the theory states, the oceans would have frozen. Life obviously could not have evolved in frozen oceans. Further, since the albedo of the earth would have been greater due to the ice, the earth could never have absorbed enough heat to melt the oceans. They would still be frozen today.[2]

But do not expect great and permanent reverberations throughout the scientific community as a result of the evidences presented here. Scientists will not suddenly scrap all their theories, which are built upon uniformitarian presuppositions. Undoubtedly the effect will

---

1. *Science News* 109 (1976), 157.
2. E. H. Avrett, ed., *Frontiers of Astrophysics* (Cambridge: Harvard University Press, 1976), p. 45.

be felt only among solar studies, and even here a new form of uniformitarianism will be adopted. The fuss over the abandonment of uniformitarianism will quickly and quietly disappear. The significance here is not that creationism is somehow proved, but that for one brief shining moment scientists saw clearly enough to realize that their basic assumptions were at fault, and that much shattering of hitherto unquestioned beliefs must occur before a complete understanding of our universe can be possible.

7 THE FORMATION OF THE SOLAR SYSTEM

Through faith we understand that the worlds were framed by the word of God, so that things which are seen were not made of things which do appear (Heb. 11:3).

Since the beginning of recorded history man has wondered and speculated about his origins. The earliest civilizations whose literature still exists are filled with stories explaining the beginning of the world and the human race. Mythology is filled with tales of fights among the gods, with the loser's carcass becoming the earth or the sky. More recently, in the last two centuries, the speculations have begun to take on a more scientific and respectable air. Instead of coming from the body of a dead giant, the earth is supposed to have formed by itself from a cloud of dust and gas in orbit around a not-quite star. The Biblical story, the true one, has been relegated to the ranks of the mythologies of the world. In reality, though, the modern myths are simply a more sophisticated attempt at the same explanation of our origin that the mythmakers of the past were trying to formulate. The ancients had giants and gods, so they invoked these as the formers of the cosmos. Modern man has science, so he attempts with the science he has to explain his origin. In a very real way the myths of the ancients were as naturalistic an attempt at explanation as are the scientific theories of today. They have something else in common—they are both wrong.

Unfortunately, because science is the god of this day, and because scientists are believed by the public to possess all knowledge and all reason, theories tend to be accepted as fact, just as the myths were once believed in implicitly by the people of that day. Many Christians as well have fallen into this trap, believing that what scientists say must be true, even if it contradicts the word of God. Are Christians foolish to believe in the creation of the universe as told in the Bible, especially in the face of so much scientific knowledge? Is the creation story really just mythology? In this chapter we shall examine the modern theories of the solar system formation in a new light—that of Scripture. We shall see that there is little reason to believe that the sun and planets took millions of years to form and that they have been around for billions of years. In short, we shall look at the evidence against the accepted theories. We do not apologize for not countering this with the evidence in favor of these theories. All this is presented elsewhere and gets adequate treatment in every textbook ever printed on the subject. The problem is that every astronomer already assumes that the evolutionary theories are true before even examining the evidence. That evolutionary theories and long time periods are required is a result of modern man's rejection of God and dependence upon natural processes. We, as Christians, are delivered from such restricted views and freed to believe in a God who has the power to create.

THE BIBLICAL PICTURE

The Bible provides a clear and succinct description of the formation of the solar system. "For in six days the Lord made heaven and earth, the sea, and all that in them is . . ." (Ex. 20:11). "He hath made the earth by his power, he hath established the world by his wisdom, and hath stretched out the heaven by his understanding" (Jer. 51:15). While other verses and chapters elaborate on these thoughts, these verses, and the one with which this chapter is headed, give the major points to be noted about creation. The first is the most relevant, for what we are about to examine is evidence relating to the age of the solar system (as well as to insurmountable problems faced by modern theories). If it can be demonstrated that the solar system is only a few thousand years old, it shows the truth of the word of God and the futility of man's efforts without God's help, thereby glorifying His name. The verse from Exodus, along with the creation account in Genesis, makes it abundantly clear that the creation took place in six literal days and that this event was in the recent past.

Second, creation was by the power of God. He had the authority and wisdom to do it. This has been called creation by fiat, a positive and authoritative command. This also implies suddenness in the creation event. A command is given all at once. God said, "Let there be . . . ," and there was. No long periods of time are implied or needed.

Finally, what exists now was made from nothing. This is called creation *ex nihilo*. It is the essence of the meaning of the word *create*, and only God can do this. Some theories of the origin of the universe postulate a continuous creation of matter in the universe even now; matter appears all by itself. This is necessary to make the theory work, but its inventors are at a loss to explain how this process can occur all by itself. In fact, this is the real failure of every theory of origins, whether it be of things on earth or of the universe itself. Ultimately, you can imagine a time when the things which now exist had to come into being. Scientists recognize this fact, and while some feel forced to admit that here at last is a place where God must really enter into the picture, most simply write off the question as "unscientific." Origins are either unknowable, or matter is postulated to have existed into the infinite past, no matter how hard this may be to accept scientifically or aesthetically.

Alternative Views

It is understandable that those who believe in a recent creation should be regarded with skepticism by the scientific community. But it is harder to understand why some Christians also look upon creation in this way. They, too, readily place their trust in man-made theories. Therefore, for purposes of completeness, I will mention some of the many interpretations given to the first two chapters of Genesis. These fall roughly into two groups. The first leans more toward a uniformitarian view and allows room for huge amounts of time and, according to some, evolutionary processes. This group includes the gap theory and the spiritual interpretations. The gap theory states that between verses 1 and 2 of Genesis chapter 1 there is a gap of indefinite duration, presumably a few billion years, to be consistent with modern dating methods. Often the gap theory includes the acceptance of the theory of evolution, but states that all that this might entail was destroyed before verse 2. Afterward came the literal six-day creation. This enables the gap theorists to accept nearly any theory of origins, and they can easily accommodate changes as scientists invent them. The spiritual interpretations call the Biblical creation account a reverent but misguided myth, thereby disposing of the entire problem with a wave of the hand. The second group is basically a single method of interpretation, the literal one, and the one adopted in this book.

There have been a number of books published in recent years which try to reconcile the creation of Genesis with scientific cosmogonies (theories of the origin of the universe). All such attempts have failed. For example, one author equates the "without form and void" of Genesis 1:2 with a nebula, a cloud of dust and gas in space. He says that the solar system condensed from such a nebula as modern theories state. There are many objections to such attempts at reconciliation. First, the Bible does not lend itself to such interpretations, either in Genesis or elsewhere. The description in Scripture, even with such an interpretation in the back of one's mind, simply does not sound like the description of a nebula. This description is followed immediately by the statement that there were waters upon the earth, but there is no mention of an intervening period during which the earth could have condensed from a cloud. The Bible also says that the heavens and the earth were formed in six days. But no matter how one defines a day (unless one refuses to define it), condensation from an interstellar gas cloud does not seem to fit.

The second objection is simple—the first chapter of Genesis and modern theories say completely different things; they cannot be reconciled. The most pertinent example in a study of astronomy is the creation of the sun, moon, and stars. The Bible says that these were formed on the fourth day of creation. Astronomers insist that many stars, and especially the sun, were formed before the earth. Stretching the days of Genesis into billions of years does not remove this difficulty but makes it worse. No one would venture to say that the sun formed billions of years after the earth. The same problem applies to those who accept the gap theory, for the sun certainly was not formed after the first creation was created, evolved, destroyed, and a new creation had begun. It is beyond the scope of this book to enter into a detailed comparison between creation and the theory of evolution, but the reader can see for himself that the order given for the appearance of animals on earth in Genesis chapter 1 differs from that given by the theory of evolution. In short, the creation of Genesis and modern cosmogonical theories seem irreconcilable. Acceptance of one means rejection of the other.

The third objection is that there is no reason for Christians to adopt someone else's problems as their own. Scientists have as yet been unable to understand how a solar system could form from a cloud of gas and dust, despite what the reader may have heard to the contrary. There are too many hurdles to cross, physical laws to be reckoned with, and improbable occurrences to invoke before any semblance of our solar system emerges from a cloud. Since scientists have been unable to explain it, why should some Christians be so eager to reject the simple and reasonable Biblical explanation in favor of a complex and incomplete "scientific" theory? As Paul wrote to the Galatians, "I marvel that ye are so soon removed from him that called you into the grace of Christ unto another gospel: which is not another; but there be some that trouble you, and would pervert the gospel of Christ" (Gal. 1:6, 7). This is certainly not to say that a Christian should be reluctant to accept advances in science, but neither should he be eager to embrace any scientific theory into his theology at the expense of his faith in the inerrant word of God. This is especially true when scientists themselves face insoluble problems with their own theories.

One aspect of the scientific method (as well as of the Scriptural interpretation) is that the simplest is likely to be the best. In Scripture there is a beautifully simple explanation of our origin. Far from being naive, it fits more easily into a framework of what we know of man and God than any other system of thought there is. It is consistent with what God tells us of His sovereignty and power, as well as His love. It provides a reason for the existence of heavenly as well as earthly bodies. It presents the fall of man and the reason for sin in the world, and the need for a Saviour. Opposed to this is a monumentally complex and yet inadequate theory being developed to explain naturally the origin of the earth and the universe. Paper after paper and book after book appear, filled with clever reasoning and shot-in-the-dark guesses. Yet they are still unable to account for even the sun's existence, much less the earth and all that is upon it. And even if they succeed in time in presenting a reasonably complete physical theory, they still cannot explain the origin of the original material, or the reason for man's sinful nature. The simplest and best explanation is given in God's word, as it always is.

MODERN THEORIES

Modern theories of solar system formation have been developing for more than two centuries but have not really changed much from the original versions proposed by Kant and Laplace. They start with a proto-sun surrounded by a solar nebula. Proto-sun is a word referring to the early sun in a supposedly incomplete state. The solar nebula is the cloud of dust and gas surrounding the proto-sun and from which the planets formed. This nebula is flattened into a disk shape because of its rotation. Within the nebula condensations occur which in time grow into planets. Usually no explanation is given as to the origin of this nebula. Assumptions that the sun acquired it while passing through interstellar clouds do not give satisfactory results. It is usually assumed that it was made from material left over from the formation of the sun.

Astronomers point to certain types of celestial objects called cocoon nebulae and infrared stars in support of this. These are objects which emit infrared (heat) radiation and appear to be a few hundred degrees above absolute zero. Astronomers think these are really young stars surrounded by their own solar nebulae. This is interpreted as evidence that solar nebulae are the natural result of star formation and that many will eventually form planets of their own. This, however, is not necessarily true. First, according to the theory of stellar evolution, old stars should appear about the same but require a very different interpretation of the evidence. Second, the existence of warm clouds does not prove planetary or star formation. Far too much interpretation goes into some observations. In short, one cannot simply find a warm object in the sky and say it proves the present theories of planet formation.

Nearly all theories, or as they are also called, models, follow the general outline given above, but details differ considerably. Usually each astronomer will have his own model, differing in some details from all others. There is much room for variation among models, since there is so little basis in observational fact to build models on. One astronomer who formulates his model on the basis of meteorite studies will arrive at one conclusion, while another who uses only mathematical analysis will reach another. None of them, however, prove entirely satisfactory. They cannot account for all the facts.

The most relevant facts which any model must explain are:

1) All planetary orbits fall more or less in the same plane, the ecliptic.
2) The sun's spin axis is tilted seven degrees with respect to this plane.
3) Planetary orbits are nearly circular.

4) The directions in which the planets revolve around the sun are the same, and in the same direction as the rotation of the sun.
5) With two exceptions the planets also rotate in this direction.
6) The distances of the planets from the sun fall into a simple relationship (Bode's law).
7) The satellites of the planets resemble smaller versions of the solar system, with some moons orbiting the same direction as the planets and some in the opposite direction (retrograde).
8) The planets contain 98 percent of the angular momentum of the solar system.
9) The sun has a small magnetic field.
10) Comets have randomly oriented orbits of high eccentricity.
11) Different planets have different chemical compositions.
12) With a few exceptions the planets have similar periods of rotation.
13) Planets fall into two basic groups, Jovian and terrestrial.

At the starting point of most theories is the young sun, which has not yet started its nuclear burning but is hot solely through contraction. It is surrounded by an extensive cloud of hot gas. This is left over from the formation of the sun itself and is also hot because of contraction. It is hottest and densest near the sun, cooling and thinning as it reaches out past Pluto's orbit. It is somewhat flattened due to rotation, being thickest near the sun. As it cools, certain elements begin to condense out in the form of microscopic grains, just as a snowflake condenses out of the air. The elements with the highest vaporization temperature condense first, as the temperature falls low enough, about 1680° Kelvin. As the nebula cools further, elements with progressively lower melting points condense out as grains, using the previously existing grains as condensation nuclei. Eventually much of the mass of the nebula is in the form of grains. Due to their mutual gravitational attraction, the disk flattens more, so that the grains form an extremely thin disk about the sun. The uncondensed gases, mostly hydrogen and helium, do not concentrate so much in this plane.

When the grains flatten into the disk, they are closer together, increasing the chance of collisions among them. They begin to collide and stick together to form somewhat larger particles, assuming they do stick when they collide. These larger particles are the planetesimals, as are all the progressively larger bodies formed by their coagulation. Eventually they become large enough so that some, which happen to have grown larger than the rest, have a strong gravitational field. These attract all other particles in their vicinity. Thus they "sweep" their domain of influence free of smaller particles and leave only a few very large bodies, the planets. A similar process is imagined to be going on around each of the planets, forming the satellite systems. Alternately, the satellites may be thought to be some of the planetesimals which, instead of going to form the planets, were captured into orbit about the planets. Asteroids are usually thought to be some of the planetesimals which were never captured by a planet. This process of smaller particles sticking together to form larger and larger particles is called accretion.

PROBLEMS WITH THE ACCRETION MODEL

There are a number of major problems with this model. One of the biggest is the process of accretion. First, what assurance is there that when these first grains collide they will really stick together? It is usually assumed that they do. In fact, though, it has been calculated that with all these grains moving independently about the sun their relative velocities would be on the order of the speed of a .22 caliber bullet. The grains would not stick together but would pulverize each other. Amazingly, a typical response to this type of problem comes from a scientist who says, since we know that the planets really do exist, the grains must have stuck together in spite of what the calculations show.[1] Besides being simply unsatisfying, this response is highly unscientific. It is a circular argument, in that it presupposes that the solar system did indeed form as astronomers say. The existence of the solar system is then used as proof that their theory must have worked.

Actual experiments with colliding grains have been made. Though iron grains did tend to stick on the average when caused to collide at various speeds, silicate grains, of which most rocks are composed, always tended to erode instead of accrete. This is true even at low speeds.[2] Thus ordinary silicate materials, which make up most of the surface of the earth and other terrestrial planets, could not have formed. Most small solid bodies such as asteroids as well as our own

1. Hartmann, *Moons and Planets,* p. 116.
2. J. F. Kerridge and James F. Vedder, "An Experimental Approach to Circumsolar Accretion," *On the Origin of the Solar System* (Paris: Centre National de la Recherche Scientifique, 1974), p. 282.

moon are composed substantially or even primarily of silicates, and could thus not have formed by accretion. Here is an actual case of a theory being disproved by experiment, and yet the theory persists.

In answer to this there are those who say that the dust particles would move at different speeds from the gas within which they moved, thus producing a sort of "air resistance" to the particles, and slowing them down. There are two reasons why this cannot be true. First, the particles would have to be slowed down so much that the probability of collisions occurring at all is much reduced, and it would take too long for the planets to grow. Second, if the particles were slowed down by the gas, they would no longer have the speed they needed to stay in orbit, and they would gradually spiral inward to be burned up by the sun.

The second major problem with accretion is that there are certain gaps in size which do not seem passable. For instance, it seems theorists can demonstrate how the fine grains can accrete to the size of golf balls, and they can explain how large rocks can accrete to form planets, but there seems to be no process by which the golf-ball-sized planetesimals can accumulate to form the large rocks.[3] Another estimate has it that before an object is large enough to attract to itself a significant number of planetesimals in order to grow, it already has be the size of the moon![4] Advocates of this theory have to start out with a full-grown moon in order to have a moon formed. This begins to sound like creationism.

Another strong objection to the accretion model is that the tidal effect of the sun on the protoplanets would prevent them from forming. This is because of the principle of the Roche limit. When two objects are in orbit about each other, they exert tidal forces on each other. The best known example, of course, is the ocean tides caused by the gravity of the moon. But a less obvious effect in the earth-moon system is the earth tides. Not only does the moon's gravity cause ocean tides, but earth tides as well. There is an actual rise and fall in the surface of the earth. While water tides rise and fall by many feet each day, earth tides rise only about 15 inches. The effect is less because the earth is rigid. In the same way, the earth causes tides on the moon, which are proportionately larger than

3. W. McCrea, "Difficulties Encountered by Various Theories," in ibid., p. 368.

4. J. C. Whitcomb, *The Early Earth* (Grand Rapids: Baker Book House, 1972), p. 50.

earth tides because the earth's gravitational field is stronger. The rigidity of the moon resists this effect, but if the moon were closer the tides would be stronger, until if the moon were close enough the tidal forces would tear it apart. The distance inside of which the forces are strong enough to do this is called the Roche limit. If the moon were less rigid—for instance, made of liquid—it would not have to come so close to be torn apart. Thus the Roche limit depends upon the density and rigidity of the objects involved.

The same principle applies to the sun and planets. The sun is the central object causing tides on the protoplanets. For protoplanets of low density, which is the case for clouds of gas and small grains, the Roche limit of the sun is about a billion kilometers from the sun, which would be outside the orbit of Jupiter.[5] This means that the dust and gases could never have condensed to form planets; they would have been torn apart by the sun's tidal forces first. The reason the planets now exist within this Roche limit is that they are more rigid than the clouds from which they are supposed to have formed, and for rigid bodies the sun's Roche limit is smaller. Some astronomers believe that the rings of Saturn were formed as a result of a satellite straying within Saturn's Roche limit and being torn apart. While this may or may not be true, one thing is certain—the particles which make up the rings of Saturn will never coalesce into a new satellite. They cannot because they are within Saturn's Roche limit.

There has been a great deal of analysis done of the time scale involved in the accretion of planets from the solar nebula as well as the time over which the nebula could have lasted. Estimates of formation times for the planets vary considerably, ranging from 10 million to hundreds of millions of years.[6] The formation times are greater for planets farther from the sun. For some of the outer planets the estimated formation times exceed the postulated age of the universe! On the other hand, there are constant influences tending to disrupt the solar nebula. First, for those theories which rely upon roller bearing eddies (like those seen in a flowing stream), which concentrate matter in one place, it turns out that these convenient formations can last only a few hundred years at most. In fact, the dissipation time of the entire solar nebula is bad news for all models because it would simply disappear in only one hundred years at the distance of the

---

5. W. McCrea, "Origin of the Solar System: Review of Concepts and Theories," *On the Origin of the Solar System*, p. 2.
6. Hartmann, *Moons and Planets*, pp. 71, 110, 116.

earth, and in 10,000 years at the distance of Jupiter. The formation of planets from the solar nebula in all cases is seen to require a great deal more time than the lifetime of the nebula. Planets did not and could not have evolved. The only way they can exist is for them to have been created.

The Ecliptic Planetary Orbits

Now that we have seen some of the major difficulties of modern models of planetary formation, let us see how well they account for the 13 points which must be explained by a good theory. Many are explained in a qualitative way by assuming that the planets formed from a flattened solar nebula. For instance, the first requirement of all planets to have orbits in the same plane follows naturally. However, most models still do not provide detailed predictions which may be checked against observations. Instead, they are satisfied to say, as we just did, that the qualitative agreement follows naturally.

When astronomers decide to start at an early point in the development of the solar system, before the nebula became flattened, they get unexpected results. They begin with a spherical cloud of gas, which has to be spinning since the planets which formed from it are. Instead of collapsing into a sun and a flattened solar nebula, it collapsed into a spinning ring with nothing in the center. This, they say, is more likely to form a double star than a solar system.[7] It implies that the planets did not form from material left over from the formation of the sun.

An alternate hypothesis is that the already existing sun passed through an interstellar cloud and picked up some of its material. However, because of point two above, that the tilt of the sun's axis is only seven degrees with respect to the ecliptic, it does not seem likely that the sun acquired its solar nebula by chance. Further, it is not likely that the sun could have acquired enough material to form all the planets this way. There seems to be no way in which the solar nebula could have formed.

The Tilt of the Sun

Returning again to point two, we ask why is there an inclination at all. If the solar nebula formed from the same material as the sun, they should spin in the same plane. This means either that something

7. R. B. Larson, "Collapse Calculations and Their Implications for the Formation of the Solar System," *On the Origin of the Solar System,* p. 142.

tilted the sun, a rather unlikely occurrence, or that something tilted all the planets by the same amount, a still less likely possibility. Yet this tilt is close enough to zero to indicate that the nebula was not captured by chance, for one would not expect the tilt to be as little as seven degrees. It would seem that the Lord chose a tilt of seven degrees, a fact which makes a solar nebula unlikely by any theory.

Planetary Rotations and Circular Orbits

Facts three and four, that the planets' orbits are circular, and that the planets all revolve around the sun in the same direction as the rotation of the sun, are answered qualitatively by the flattened solar nebula model. Point five, however, is most important, for while seven planets rotate in the same direction, two do not. Theory demands that all planets rotate in the same direction. Venus has a period of 243 days and rotates in a retrograde manner, just the opposite of what theory requires. This is impossible without some formidable outside influences. To save the theory, these influences are invoked.

Accordingly, the retrograde spin of Venus is said to be due to the gravitational influence of the earth. The effect is called a resonance and theoretically results from the earth's gravitational pull upon irregularities in Venus' shape each time their orbits bring them close together, in a similar manner to the earth's causing the moon to keep the same side towards us at all times. Unfortunately for evolutionists, the relationship does not give exactly the right period of rotation for Venus. Venus is one of the most nearly perfect spherical planets in the solar system and has virtually no bumps for earth's gravity to pull on.

A similar problem is the period of rotation of Venus, which is by far the slowest in the solar system. Most planets as well as their satellites and the asteroids whose periods have been measured all have rotational periods of a few hours. According to theory, Venus should also. But calculations have shown that the earth's influence upon Venus is not great enough to slow it as much as must have occurred.[8] The retrograde motion and slow rotational period of Venus are evidence against the evolutionary theories of planetary formation.

Far more impressive in this connection is the planet Uranus. As we saw in an earlier chapter, Uranus' axis is tilted 98 degrees with

8. S. F. Singer, *Science* 170 (1970), 1196.

respect to the ecliptic, so that it is "turned" more than halfway over. Its motion, therefore, is termed retrograde, but this term is inadequate to describe the uniqueness of Uranus' position. This tilt is entirely incompatible with any evolutionary theory of solar system formation. In order to remedy this, Uranus too must be imagined to have undergone some calamitous experience in the past. It has been calculated that if Uranus had been struck by an object with five percent of its mass the tilt might be accounted for. This is equivalent to 36 percent of the earth's mass. No objects, whether they be asteroids or moons in the solar system, have this much mass except for the planets themselves. Where would such an object come from? Theory says it must have been a planetesimal. But if such large planetesimals were around after the planets were nearly complete (so as to tilt an already existing axis), where is the evidence for them? The largest craters on the earth or moon show no impacts of objects anywhere near this size. And if one of the largest planets could have its axis tilted by 98 degrees, think what would be done to a smaller planet by such an impact. The axes of the rest of the planets are reasonably perpendicular to the ecliptic, but one would expect them to be considerably more askew than Uranus if such large objects were hurtling about. It is much more logical to assume that Uranus was created as it is.

But even more important is the effect that such a collision would have upon the Uranus system. First, the impact of such a large object should radically change Uranus' orbit about the sun. Instead of this we find that its orbit is more nearly circular than all but three other planets, and its orbit falls more nearly in the ecliptic plane than any other planet but earth. Its orbit is nearly perfect and shows no effect at all of having been struck by such a disrupting object as a 5×10^{21}-ton planetesimal. Finally, and most important of all, is Uranus' satellite system. All of Uranus' satellites orbit in the plane of Uranus' equator, not the ecliptic. In fact, they fall more perfectly in their planet's equatorial plane than any other satellites in the solar system. Now if the satellites had been formed according to the nebular hypothesis, they would fall in the ecliptic plane, the plane of the nebular disk. No large body striking Uranus could conceivably have altered the orbits of all five satellites so they orbit in nearly perfect circles in the plane of Uranus' equator. Instead, no matter where the satellites were before the impact, a large body striking Uranus would have completely disrupted all the satellites' orbits, causing them to be randomized in orientation and perhaps causing them to escape from Uranus altogether. In conclusion, all properties of the planet Uranus demonstrate that its history has been relatively quiet and that the tilt of its axis has always been as it is now. It stands near the edge of the solar system as a signpost, saying, "I am proof that the solar system did not evolve."

Bode's law is remarkable in that it is not only followed by the planets in their orbits around the sun, but it is also followed approximately by the orbits of satellites around their planets. This is difficult to explain. It does not just drop naturally out of solar system models. Some models are formulated with the intent of producing Bode's law, which they then do. The agreement is then presented as proof of the theory![9] This circular argument, needless to say, does not constitute proof. Methods which attempt to produce Bode's law for planets do not succeed in doing so for the satellites. Evolutionary theories have not as yet been able to account for these remarkable regularities.

Point seven is that planets and their satellites resemble small versions of the solar system, with some moons revolving in prograde orbits and some in retrograde. The satellites in the retrograde orbits are the interesting ones. While it is not expected that the nebular hypothesis could lead to satellites in retrograde orbits, this is not proof against the nebular hypothesis, despite what many creationist authors have written. They have not taken all the evidence into account, and astronomers' explanation that these represent captured satellites may not be without support. If one counts Uranus' five satellites, there are 11 retrograde satellites out of a total of 34 in the solar system. However, it is not really legitimate to count Uranus' five as retrograde, since they orbit in the same direction as Uranus' rotation. This leaves six retrograde moons which astronomers say are captured asteroids. These six are JVIII, JIX, JXI, JXII, SIX (Phoebe), and Neptune's Triton. The letters in the satellites' names are the first letter of the planet's name, while the Roman numerals represent the order of the discovery of the satellite. If it were true that these are really captured asteroids, they should, as a class, have certain characteristics, most notably in their orbits. While most satellites should fall in the same plane as the rest of the solar system, captured satellites could have any orbit in the plane. The angular difference between the ecliptic

9. H. Reeves, "Seven Questions Related to the Origin of the Solar System and the Answers Given in Various Models," *On the Origin of the Solar System*, p. 28.

and the plane of the satellites' orbit is called the inclination. Further, the satellites' orbit should have an equal probability of being prograde or retrograde. Last they would not be expected to fall into perfectly circular orbits but to have a large eccentricity or flattening of the orbit. An eccentricity of zero means the orbit is circular; an eccentricity of close to one means it is highly flattened. These characteristics should give a good indication of whether or not a satellite was captured.

Orbital Characteristics of Satellites

What is found when we examine the orbital characteristics of the satellites? There are about 11 (counting JXIII but not JXIV, whose characteristics are not yet known) which display either large eccentricities or high inclinations or both. These are the ones which have the highest probability of having been captured. They are: SVIII, JX, JVI, SIX, JXII, JVII, JXI, JIX, JVIII, JXIII, and NII. Of these, six are prograde and five retrograde, about half and half as expected for captured satellites.

The gravitational effect of the planet upon its satellites tends to cause them to move into the same plane as the equator of the planet. But this is an extremely slow process, and there is not time for it in the creationist framework. Therefore, the fact that some satellites are not in the orbital planes of their planets may imply a young age. It might also simply imply a relatively recent capture.

Mars's two satellites Phobos and Deimos are the only ones in the solar system to be photographed close up. They are irregularly shaped and quite small. This seems to be characteristic of asteroids, hence astronomers believe Mars's satellites to be captured asteroids.

The above discussion does not prove that retrograde satellites are captured asteroids, but it demonstrates that this is consistent with the evidence. Hence it is not legitimate to say that retrograde satellites disprove the nebular hypothesis. I am certainly not saying that captured satellites are evidence for the nebular hypothesis; the satellites could as easily have been captured in the last 5,000 years as in five billion. In fact, there is some evidence indicating that 5,000 is more nearly correct. If such captures have been going on for five billion years, the approximate size distribution of asteroids indicates that Jupiter should have a great many more satellites than it does. In fact, as one looks for smaller and smaller satellites, there should be more and more of them. At least 14 Jovian satellites the size of JXIV should be observable. Instead, only one is seen.[10] Jupiter has not been capturing satellites for as long as scientists think. There is always the possibility, of course, that more small moons will be discovered.

The example of the retrograde satellites shows how careful one must be in interpreting evidence before presenting it as proof of creation. Many well-meaning authors have made mistaken statements about creation based upon an incomplete understanding of the situation. It also points out the fact that there is a need for more qualified people to devote their learning to creationism. Fortunately, recent years have seen a great increase in interest in Biblical creationism and the application of science to the Bible. The future should bring some startling developments, and it will be interesting to observe how these are received by the scientific community.

The Angular Momentum of the Solar System

Point eight has to do with the angular momentum of the solar system. It can be described roughly as the amount of spin something has. The faster something spins, the more angular momentum it has. For two similarly shaped objects spinning at the same rate, the more massive of the two will have the greater angular momentum. A more difficult point to appreciate is that a more extended object spinning at the same rate as a smaller object will have the greater angular momentum. A well-known example may serve to clarify this. When a skater spins with his arms extended, he possesses a certain amount of angular momentum. When he pulls his arms inward, his spin rate increases to keep the angular momentum constant. This also illustrates the importance of the law called the conservation of angular momentum. That is, angular momentum within a system tends to remain constant unless some outside force disturbs it.

Applying this to the solar system, it becomes apparent that if the sun had contracted from a spinning ball of gas, it would have had to spin faster as it contracted, to conserve its angular momentum. By the time it had shrunk to its present size, it would have been spinning very rapidly. However, in reality 98 percent of the solar system's angular momentum is in the planets and their satellites. This is a result of their revolution around the sun, and to a lesser extent a result of their rotation, and of the revolution of the satellites. If the

10. *Science News* 107 (1975), 367.

nebular hypothesis were true, most of the angular momentum should reside in the sun instead of its satellites.

This has been a major point of creationists ever since the problem was realized, and astronomers have admitted it to be a fundamental problem. In fact, when astronomers develop a solar system model, they simply assume that something has already happened to slow the sun down, and start from there. However, in recent years some partially satisfactory answers have been forthcoming. Ways have been devised to transport this angular momentum to other parts of the solar system, usually beyond the orbit of Pluto, where scientists will never be able to make the necessary observations.

One mechanism whereby angular momentum is thought to be

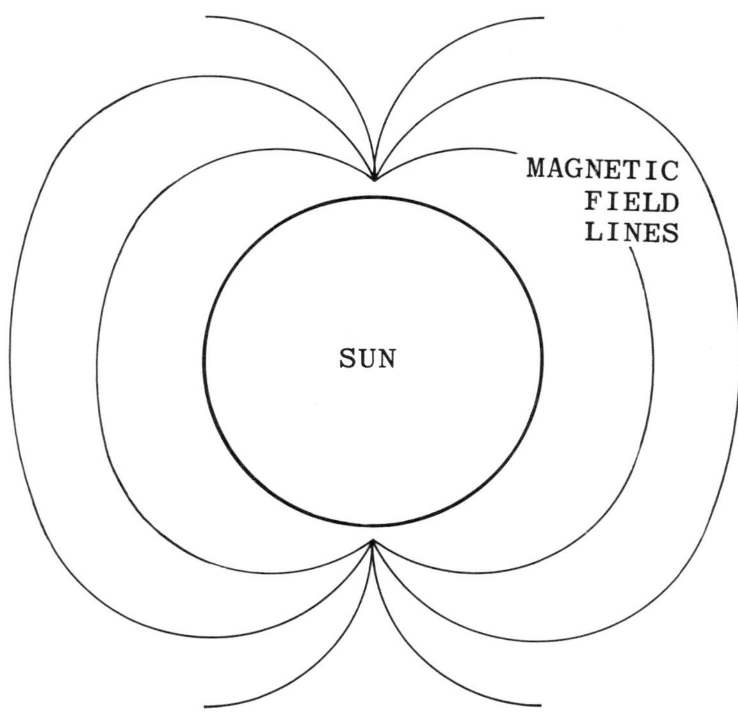

FIGURE 11.—The sun's magnetic field.

transferred utilizes the sun's magnetic field. Figure 11 shows magnetic field lines around the sun in the same way that such lines are drawn around an ordinary bar magnet for purposes of illustration. The sun, astronomers postulate, had a higher magnetic field in the beginning. As the sun spun quickly on its axis, it attempted to carry the field lines with it. Astronomers maintain that the solar nebula at this time contained a large number of ions, atoms which had lost electrons and were thus positively charged. Charged particles have the ability to "lock in" a magnetic field. Thus when the sun tried to carry its field along, it dragged the solar nebula with it. The solar nebula resisted this movement and slowed down the sun. This, however, has been shown to be unstable. It will not work.[11]

Another proposed mechanism is the solar wind. The solar wind is a "wind" of charged particles constantly leaving the surface of the sun at hundreds or thousands of miles per second. In a complex interaction between these moving charged particles and the sun's magnetic field, the wind carried off the sun's angular momentum into space. Scientists believe that the solar wind was considerably stronger in its youth. The higher rate would be required to reduce the solar angular momentum to its present value. Based upon uniformitarian principles, however, studies indicate that the solar wind has been constant for at least two billion years, and evidence for an intense early wind is entirely absent.[12]

There are many variations and uncertainties in these explanations, and whether or not they will prove satisfactory is unknown. The significant point is that they enable scientists to sweep the angular momentum problem under a rug and to start their models with a slowly spinning sun. Someone else has supposedly already answered the angular momentum problem. The sun's lack of angular momentum may still be a valid objection to nebular models, but it need no longer be admitted.

The Sun's Magnetic Field

Closely related to the angular momentum problem is the problem of the intensity of the sun's magnetic field. For the magnetic field slowdown theories to work, the sun must have had a higher magnetic field at first than it does now. There is another reason to expect the

11. Alfven and Arrhenius, *Evolution of the Solar System,* p. 259.
12. F. Begeman, "On the Early Irradiation of Matter in the Solar System," *On the Origin of the Solar System,* p. 250.

sun to have had a high magnetic field. There is a small magnetic field that pervades the whole galaxy. If the sun had contracted from a solar nebula, the nebula would have had this field within itself also. Now, as the ionized cloud contracted, it would condense this locked-in field, increasing its intensity. By the time the sun reached its present size, the field would have been intensified to one billion times what it is today. There seems to be no explanation as to why the sun should have lost this intense magnetic field. This is another problem model makers usually assume to be already solved before they begin, simply because they do not know what else to do.

Cometary Orbits

While the assumption of a flattened solar nebula qualitatively accounts for the orbits of the planets lying in the ecliptic, it does not account for the orbits of the comets. Cometary orbits, instead of lying in the plane of the solar system, are randomly oriented and come at the sun from all angles. Some, like Halley's comet, are in retrograde orbits. Because of this, and because the gravitational field of Jupiter has been observed to influence the orbits of certain comets, astronomers have assumed that Jupiter is responsible for changing long-period comets into short-period comets. In other words, it has changed the orbits of comets whose revolution periods were thousands of years into comets whose periods are in the tens or hundreds of years. These supposedly come from the Oort cloud which was described earlier. But there are two comets, Schwassmann-Wachmann and Oterma, which have circular orbits and do not intersect the orbits of any planets. They appear to have always been in the orbits they occupy now, and not to have been introduced from the depths of space. The randomized orbits imply that comets did not form according to the nebular hypothesis, and the fact that they have not disintegrated shows their youth.

In addition to this there are some asteroids whose orbits are difficult to explain using the nebular hypothesis. Pallas, the second largest asteroid, is particularly difficult because of its size. Since asteroids are considered to be some of the original planetesimals, they are thought to be some of the oldest solar system objects to have accreted from the original solar nebula. Astronomers are not surprised if some asteroids have noncircular orbits. They explain the fact that planets, which supposedly formed from planetesimals, have circular orbits by saying that the smaller planetesimals stuck together and averaged each other out. Pallas, if it is one of these larger planetesimals, should have formed from enough smaller ones that their random qualities would have cancelled each other out, and Pallas' orbit should be circular and in the ecliptic.

Instead, Pallas has an eccentricity of .24, twice the average for asteroids, and an inclination to the ecliptic of 35 degrees, which is four times the average value for asteroids.[13] The only way such a large asteroid could have been perturbed into such an orbit, assuming it had originally been in a circular orbit, is through the influence of one of the giant planets. Computer calculations, however, indicated that encounters with Jupiter or Saturn were not enough to bring about the type of orbit Pallas has. And Pallas is just one of a number of asteroids with similarly inexplicable characteristics. Another family of asteroids which also has high inclination is called the Trojan group. All are examples of the fact that the nebular hypothesis is inadequate to explain the solar system.

The Chemical Composition of Planets

It is obvious that the planets all have differing chemical composition, that is, different types and amounts of elements and compounds. As point eleven says, the nebular hypothesis must explain these differences. The most notable difference is that the terrestrial planets are composed of solids and rocklike materials, but Jovian planets are mostly hydrogen and gaseous compounds. Astronomers realize the importance of this fact, and an integral part of every model is an attempt at explanation. Astronomers believe that in the early solar nebula the chemical composition was fairly uniform; it was about the same as observed elsewhere in the universe and, most important, in the sun itself. Thus the standard of comparison is usually taken as the solar abundance, or cosmic abundance, as it is also called. Their task becomes to explain how differences among the planets came about from initially homogeneous cosmic abundances.

There are two basic approaches to producing different chemical compositions among the planets. The first is to assume that within the solar nebula different regions acquired larger proportions of particular elements before planetary formation took place. When planets did form, they simply formed from different elements, depending

---

13. F. L. Whipple, *et al.*, "The Strange Case of Pallas," *On the Origin of the Solar System*, p. 312.

upon where they formed in the solar system. The second approach is to assume that all planets started out with similar compositions and that chemical differentiation appeared later.

Within the first model there must be a reason for differing chemical compositions in different parts of the nebula. Because different elements have different temperatures at which they condense, some would form earlier than others as the temperature of the nebula decreased. It would seem that nearer the sun, where the temperatures are higher, only those elements which condense at a higher temperature would solidify. Farther away, where temperatures are lower, other elements would be able to condense out. Thus there would emerge a differentiation in element abundances. The sun would be surrounded by "rings" or zones, sometimes called jet streams, of differing chemical composition. It is assumed that once such rings are formed they will condense into planets. But there is no reason to think they really would. The rings of Saturn cannot coalesce into a larger body because they are within the Roche limit of Saturn. In the same way these rings around the sun, at least out to the orbit of Jupiter, are within the sun's Roche limit. Astronomers appeal to the Roche limit of the sun to tear away excess atmosphere of the already formed planets to make observations agree with theory, but they forget that this same law applied earlier would have prevented the formation of the planets in the first place.

There are other reasons for not believing that material in these rings would form planets. When comets approach the sun, they begin to lose some of their material because it is evaporated from their surfaces by the heat of the sun. This material becomes strung out over the entire orbit of the comet to form a sort of ring around the sun, only elliptically shaped. Meteor showers are evidences of this, for times of intense shooting star activity occur as the earth passes through the orbit of the comet. All this lost material, instead of being condensed into a single body, is dispersed and strung out along millions of miles of the comet's orbit. A second example is the families of asteroids. Examples are the Trojans and the Apollos. It is unlikely that asteroids in a family are in similar orbits by coincidence. The most likely explanation is that they came from a single large asteroid which through collision broke up into a number of smaller asteroids, each of which had approximately the same orbit as the original. There are a number of such families, called Hiryama families. In the same way as cometary particles, these asteroid fragments have now become strung out along the orbit of the original asteroid. Again, the smaller bodies do not coalesce, they spread out. In fact, this is always the tendency. It is a manifestation of a law of physics, called the second law of thermodynamics. When a large enough number of particles is involved, their behavior is governed by statistical laws which state that particles left to themselves will take the state of greatest disorder, or least organization. These fragments will never condense into a single body; planets could not have formed this way either.

The second explanation for the differences in chemical composition postulates that all protoplanets had approximately the same composition. They possessed a cosmic abundance and were a great deal larger than at present, being more like Jupiter in size. Now, in the sun about 90 percent of the atoms are hydrogen, eight percent helium, and the rest belong to all the other elements. The terrestrial planets are made mostly of those other elements, so if they started out with cosmic abundances, they must have lost nearly all the matter they started out with. Somehow all that hydrogen and helium had to be blown away, leaving only the other elements in the final earth. The hydrogen and helium in the Jovian planets would not have been blown away, thus leaving the large gaseous planets as they exist now. If it is assumed that somehow it was the sun which did the blowing, the planets lying nearer the sun would have been blown harder than those far away. Thus many of the lighter elements were blown from Mercury, less from Venus, still less from Earth, and so on. On the average, the planets near the sun would possess relatively more very heavy elements, with the average amount of lighter elements per planet increasing outwards from the sun. In general this describes the situation correctly. However, the relationship is not exact. Also, one might expect Mars to be larger than Earth, since it should have lost less of its mass. And how could the asteroid belt have formed?

How could the sun have blown all this mass away? There is an unusual type of star called the T Tauri star. Astronomers consider these to be very young on an astronomical scale, only a few million years old. This star type appears to be losing mass at a high rate by spewing matter into space in an intense solar wind. Astronomers seized upon this as a mechanism to blow away the excess gases of the terrestrial protoplanets. Without any real understanding as to why the T Tauri stars were losing mass, they have now assumed that the sun was at one time a T Tauri star with a solar wind one to ten million times stronger than it is now. There is, however, no evidence that this ever took place.[14] And this model also faces the same problem as the other—the Roche limit.

The T Tauri stars create more problems for astronomers than they solve. T Tauri stars are considerably enriched in the element lithium. In fact, they have more lithium than the material around the stars from which they supposedly formed.[15] Where could this excess lithium have come from? One possibility is that it was formed within the star itself by nuclear reactions. The problem with this is that nuclear reactions destroy lithium, not create it. The only alternative explanation is that lithium formed by a special kind of nuclear reaction, called spallation reactions, on the surface of the stars. It may have been formed in solar flares, where temperatures and high energy particle conditions might be right for forming lithium from some other element. Calculations have shown this to be impossible, though, because there is not enough energy available in the whole star.[16] The same problem exists for the elements beryllium and boron. The best explanation is that these stars were created with the elements they possess now.

There is an internal contradiction in the functions attributed to the "T Tauri" phase of the sun. In earth rocks and meteorites there is also a relatively high abundance of lithium. This is somehow supposed to have been created in the early sun and deposited in the planets during the high solar wind phase. But how can this high solar wind blow away a large portion of the matter in the solar system on the one hand, and at the same time deposit it into rocks on the planets?

Another example of a hard to explain element is deuterium, a heavy form of hydrogen. Recall that normal hydrogen has one proton in the nucleus and one electron. But deuterium has an additional neutron in the nucleus, making it twice as heavy as normal hydrogen. In the sun, and indeed in all the universe, deuterium abundance seems relatively small. On earth, however, the ratio of deuterium to hydrogen is at least three times higher than in interstellar gas and about 40 times what it is in the sun.[17] We shall hear more about deuterium later.

Another example is the abundances of the gases helium, neon,

14. H. Reeves, "Seven Questions," p. 52.
15. Hartmann, *Moons and Planets,* p. 97.
16. Ryter *et al., Astronomy and Astrophysics* 8 (1970), 389.
17. H. Reeves, "Seven Questions," p. 52.

argon, krypton, xenon, and radon. The abundances of neon and xenon vary widely when measured in the sun, in the earth's atmosphere, and in meteorites. Xenon in particular is tens or hundreds of times more abundant on the earth and in meteorites than on the sun. Any theories which try to account for this succeed only in producing odd abundances of krypton and argon which are not observed.[18] Presently there is no satisfactory answer except to assume that the abundances were created as they exist now and are not a result of evolutionary processes.

The moon also possesses different chemical abundances than the earth. Extremely complex physical processes have been invoked to explain why such differences should exist. Inconsistency and contradictions among these theories indicate that little weight need be attached to them.

A problem similar to differing element abundances is differing isotopic ratios. As in the example of deuterium, other elements may also possess more or less neutrons than is normal without being a different kind of atom. Atoms which have the same number of protons but different numbers of neutrons are called isotopes of that type of element. An isotopic ratio is the ratio of the abundance of one isotope of a given element to the abundance of another isotope of the same element. For example, $O^{17}/O^{18}=.2$ means that the ratio of the number of oxygen atoms weighing 17 to the number weighing 18 is two tenths. (The superscript really is the combined number of protons and neutrons in the nucleus.) Since oxygen normally has eight protons and eight neutrons, giving a weight of 16, O^{17} must have nine neutrons, and O^{18} ten.

There are some ways in which isotopic ratios can be changed by physical processes, but this is far less likely to happen than a change in the *kinds* of elements involved. Different isotopes of a given element behave the same chemically, and therefore most chemical reactions will not affect isotopic ratios. Thus, if all the planets and the sun formed out of a cloud with given isotopic ratios, the measured isotopic ratios should be the same everywhere in the solar system.

We have already discussed one type of isotopic ratio—deuterium and hydrogen. Another example is the element neon. The isotopic ratio of Ne^{20}/Ne^{22} is low in meteorites as compared to the earth.

---

18. J. Geiss, "Noble Gas Isotopes and Deuterium in the Solar System," *On the Origin of the Solar System,* p. 217.

There are dozens of other examples. Any process which discriminates between different isotopes is called fractionation, and some isotopic ratios have been explained by fractionation processes. For the most part, however, there is no satisfactory explanation for the variation in isotopic ratios from one place in the solar system to another.

So difficult has the problem of isotopic abundances become that in recent years a third explanation of the formation of the solar system has emerged. It has been postulated that a supernova—a star which undergoes a titanic explosion—occurred near the cloud from which the solar system was supposed to have formed. The shock wave from this event struck the cloud and caused it to condense into the sun and planets. At the same time a fresh supply of elements from the supernova, heavier than hydrogen and helium, was deposited in the cloud. These elements, however, were not thoroughly mixed in, with some parts of the solar system receiving more and some less. This, scientists hoped, would explain how different planets came to have differing chemical and isotopic compositions.

Alas, the situation proved to be not quite so simple. A great deal of study has been done very recently on a meteorite called the Allende meteorite, which fell in Mexico in 1969. Two small inclusions of about one-centimeter size have revealed a number of isotopic anomalies, that is, abundances of isotopes which do not fit with what had been expected. Some isotopes which had been expected to be present in high amounts were actually relatively rare, and some which were not expected were present in relatively high amounts. Some of these combinations were explainable on the basis of the proposed supernova, but others could not have been formed by that event. They would require entirely different conditions. The entire scenario, as astronomers have come to refer to events they do not understand very well, has become more and more complicated. Instead of simply having to invoke an extra supernova to account for the isotopic anomalies, the anomalies have become so abundant that new processes would be needed to explain them. And this result is from the study of only one part of one meteorite. Other parts of the same meteorite tell different stories entirely.[19] Clearly if astronomers plan to explain all the isotopic anomalies in the solar system as resulting from injections of material from supernovae during its formation, that event would have to have been quite a fireworks display! It is apparent that even the most

19. *Science* 202 (1978), 203.

recent dead end down which astronomers have chosen to travel will become more and more complex until, like its cousins in biological evolution and geology, it will collapse under its own weight.

If the solar system formed according to natural laws which apply at all times and all places in the universe, there should be numerous examples of other solar systems being formed at the present time. When scientists search for systems actually forming, however, there is a surprising result. There seems to be a gap between very tenuous objects and fairly dense objects. That is, there exist many thin clouds (nebulae), but these appear to be far too thin to ever collapse into stars. Next are found stars which are formed already. There is virtually nothing in between. Just as fossils intermediate between two species are entirely missing from the fossil record, even though one is supposed to have evolved from the other, so also there is little evidence by way of intermediate objects to suggest that stars really do form from condensed gas clouds. This suggests that there is no link between the two, but that stars and nebulae are entirely different and unrelated objects.

When astronomers point to an object in the sky and say they see a star forming, what they really mean is that they see a region of space where the conditions appear to be similar to those which astronomers expect to see when a star forms. A star is theorized to take millions of years to form, and in one human generation no change at all in a "contracting star" could be detected. In the very few cases where actual changes have been observed in the brightness of a star, far too little is known about the causes to state that this is a new star which has just begun.

A major criticism of all solar system formation models is given by L. Mestel. He states that in order for any bodies to wind up orbiting the sun they must form in pairs. Both members of the pair would be in the same orbit. In reality there are no paired planets at all. Why is there only one planet per orbit?

A Speculative Dead End

Theories of planetary and solar system formation can become extremely complex, especially when trying to surmount some of the difficulties described in this chapter. It is not necessary or possible to review all the variations that occur in the literature. Each may succeed in explaining one or two difficulties out of hundreds, invariably bringing up new ones as well. It is significant that on nearly every page in every article one finds the phrase, "if we assume," or "we shall suppose." There is no certainty in this pursuit, and to cast away one's faith in the word of God, only to embrace a confused and incomplete scientific explanation, is foolish.

Among the conclusions reached at the 1972 international colloquium on solar system formation is the following, "This symposium showed that we know next to nothing about the formation process of the solar nebula and its early evolution."[20] In speaking about condensation of gas and accretion of particles into larger bodies, Reeves said, "We enter here into one of the most obscure chapters of our book."[21] Of the supposed growth of planets from small bodies into larger ones: "They have not given a plausible account of any process by which golf balls might be caused to produce an asteroid."[22]

The conclusion of the world's experts on planetary formation is that they know nothing about the evolution and early history of the solar nebula, or how gas condensed and particles began to accrete, or how small particles could have accreted into larger ones. What, then, do they know? Despite volume after volume and year after year in solar system research, scientists have not made even a significant step in explaining how the solar system could have formed by natural processes. What they have done instead is to show the impossibility of natural formation and to leave special creation by the living God as the only explanation.

---

20. B. J. Levin, "Comments on a Few Questions of Interest," in ibid., p. 370.
21. H. Reeves, "Seven Questions," p. 41.
22. W. McCrea, "Origin of the Solar System," p. 368.

8 STARS

He telleth the number of the stars; He calleth them all by their names (Ps. 147:4).

Nearly all the matter in the universe is bound up in a single type of object—stars. There is some gas, a little dust, and maybe there is even a small amount of mass bound up in solid objects like planets or asteroids. But stars are the primary inhabitants of the heavens. Stars come in all sizes and colors, and, more recently, we recognize all sorts of unusual properties. In recent years so many strange objects have been discovered in the universe that it is getting more and more difficult to give a definition of a star. It can be said with relative safety, though, that all stars have at least one property in common—they are light-givers. This is how we know they are there. Of course, in this context the word *light* means the entire electromagnetic spectrum. We are about to see that as far as their purpose as revealed in Scripture is concerned, their light-giving properties are the most important ones.

STARS AS SYMBOLS IN SCRIPTURE

The first mention of stars in the Bible is, again, in the first chapter of Genesis. "And God made two great lights; the greater light to rule the day, and the lesser light to rule the night: he made the stars also"

(Gen. 1:16). Oddly enough, stars are hardly mentioned at all; they are an afterthought. How can it be that stars, which make up the bulk of the mass of this huge universe, are treated so lightly in Scripture? Could it be that Moses did not know how big the stars are? If not, he at least knew how many there are (Gen. 15:5). A skeptic might be inclined to say that Moses simply wrote down heavenly objects in the order in which they seemed important to man. To this I would reply, "Precisely!" though for a different reason than he. The skeptic would say that Moses wrote through ignorance of the nature of stars. Christians say that he wrote out of knowledge of God's relationship to man and of the importance of stars to that relationship. The answer is simple. In God's revelation of Himself to man the stars are almost totally unimportant. The great lights are mentioned because they are there, and because of their usefulness as seasonal indicators, navigational aids, and so forth. But the stars do not give enough light to see by. They do not give us warmth. Their humble purpose is to serve as signs and as indicators of seasons and days and years, things which could be determined without the help of stars. The stars were created for man, along with everything else in the material universe, and their importance exists only in so far as they affect mankind.

This may sound like ethnocentrism on a cosmic scale. And it would indeed be just cosmic-sized pride if the statement were made without Scriptural support. But I believe the Bible teaches that stars, as well as all other things, were created for man's benefit. The Bible tells of signs appearing in the stars for matters which happen only here on earth. This is an answer to those who hope to find intelligent life on other planets. Their argument is always based upon the fact that the universe is so large that God must have made other civilizations to make the whole thing worthwhile. Or from a naturalistic point of view they say that the probability is that there must be life somewhere else. But if they realized that God made the stars for man's benefit as well as His own glory, they would not feel the need to find life anywhere else. God may not have created it.

Hereafter in the Bible, stars are usually used as symbols, either of people or as representatives of God's glory and power. Genesis 37 tells of Joseph's dream in which the sun, moon, and stars bowed down to him. These, of course, are his family. In Genesis 15 Abraham is promised seed as numerous as the stars of heaven, showing both the magnitude of God's promise and the extent of His power. When Judges 5:20 speaks of the stars in their courses fighting against

Sisera, it probably means that God, in His power, is bringing all the forces of nature to bear against His enemies.

The stars, in their brilliance, are often symbols of supernatural beings. Job 38:7 speaks of the morning stars singing together at the creation of the earth. Here they must be heavenly beings rejoicing to see the works of God. In Isaiah 14:13 we read that Satan exalted himself above the stars, perhaps meaning all the glorious beings created by God. Here he is even called Lucifer, which means bright star or morning star. He was the greatest of all God's created things before he fell.

But the Lord Jesus Himself is the ultimate example of the stars as symbols. Numbers 24:17 says, "I shall see him, but not now; I shall behold him, but not nigh: there shall come a Star out of Jacob, and a Scepter shall rise out of Israel, and shall smite the corners of Moab, and destroy all the children of Sheth." In this we have one of the first prophecies of the coming Messiah, who shall appear as the brilliant light among the descendants of Israel. This is why Isaiah said, "The people that walked in darkness have seen a great light: they that dwell in the land of the shadow of death, upon them hath the light shined" (Isa. 9:2). And how fitting it is that the Star out of Jacob should be announced to those wise enough to see it by a shining star above a manger in Bethlehem.

The Bible mentions stars as real bodies also. Looking in the book of Job, we find constellations and stars mentioned which are familiar to us today. Arcturus, Orion, and the Pleiades are spoken of in Job 9:9. The Pleiades are actually a cluster of hundreds of stars. Paul made the observation in I Corinthians that "star differeth from star in glory." This was undoubtedly based upon his observations that visible stars vary in brightness and color. Indeed, the word he uses for glory means literally brightness or radiance. He may not have had any idea, however, of how much stars really do differ in brightness. Some stars are as small as the earth and are entirely invisible beyond a few light years' distance. Others are as much as a million times brighter than the sun and can be seen individually in distant galaxies.

The Star of Bethlehem

The most intriguing star of all is the star of Bethlehem. What was it really? In the characteristically practical manner of the word of God, the Bible does not tell us much about the star of Bethlehem. It never dwells on the sensational or gives details just to satisfy our curiosity. Instead, the star is named only as it points to Jesus. It was mentioned because it was there and played a part in the coming of the wise men, not because it was the center of attention. Since nearly every heavenly object was called a star by ancient writers, a marvelous amount of speculation has been done. If it was God's pleasure to be silent, it is man's pleasure to be verbose. There is no need for a complete review of all the theories that have been propounded over the ages; none of them are correct.

As usual, all man can do when faced with the unknown, especially when it is of a spiritual nature, is to explain it as a natural phenomenon. Among the natural means used to explain the star of Bethlehem are real stars, planets, and comets. Let us read the account in Matthew to see if any of these fit the facts as given by him. "Now when Jesus was born in Bethlehem of Judea in the days of Herod the king, behold, there came wise men from the east to Jerusalem, saying, Where is he that is born king of the Jews? for we have seen his star in the east, and are come to worship him. . . . When they had heard the king, they departed; and, lo, the star, which they saw in the east, went before them, till it came and stood over where the young child was. When they saw the star, they rejoiced with exceeding great joy" (Matt. 2:1, 2, 9, 10). The meager facts are these: The wise men saw the star from the east and were directed by it to Jerusalem. The star went before them and stood over the place where Jesus was.

Could it have been a real star? A normal star would not have aroused the attention of the wise men. If it had been a star, then to attract their notice it must have either moved or noticeably changed in brightness. Now even the nearest star is so far away that its motions are far too difficult to observe without careful telescopic observations over many years. It must, then, have changed in brightness, probably increasing. Variable stars are known, but to catch the attention of the wise men it would have to have increased above the normal change for a variable star. It must have been a nova or a supernova. But still, the star moved and stopped over the manger in Bethlehem. Supernovae do not move. The only motion observable to the eye of any stars is the simple diurnal motion of the sky as the earth turns under it. If this is the motion referred to, how could the star have stopped over the manger? It is apparent that a star will not fill the bill.

A comet would be a more likely candidate. Its appearance would be enough to arouse the attention of the wise men, and comets do move. But again, comets share the motion of the sky as the earth turns. How could it stop over the manger? How could it remain visible for the months it must have required for the wise men to make their way to Jerusalem? And, in fact, how could anyone hope to tell what point of the earth the comet was over? The point above which a comet lies changes constantly as the earth turns under it.

The same objections apply to planets, and to every attempt to explain the star of Bethlehem as some astronomical event. It has been suggested that the star was really the conjunction, or the apparent meeting, of two planets. But only on exceedingly rare occasions would two planets be close enough together to appear as one star, and this would not last very long. Had this been the case, we would not expect them to have been described as a star, for their coming together as two separate objects would have been obvious to the wise men.

In the face of these objections it becomes apparent that astronomical objects are ruled out. In order for the star to have appeared to be so localized as to rest above a single building, it must have been very close to the earth and have possessed the ability to move by itself. It is far more reasonable to believe that the star of Bethlehem was a supernatural event created by God for the special purpose of announcing the birth of His Son Jesus Christ. The angels which appeared to the shepherds were sent for that purpose, and so was the star. Why must the miracles of the Bible always be explained away as natural occurrences? Is it because our belief in God's power is far too small? I think so.

Martin Harwit is a refreshing author as far as astronomy texts go. He often, for the sake of argument, presents a view opposite to the accepted view. Of course, he ultimately rejects the unorthodox view, seemingly because it requires events not obviously part of natural science. About stars he says, "We do not know how stars are formed, nor just how they die. But we think we understand the structure of the most commonly found stars and the mechanisms by which they generate the energy we see as starlight."[1] This statement is highly unusual in the literature but nonetheless true. It would be well to remember it through the rest of this chapter.

1. M. Harwit, *Astrophysical Concepts* (New York: John Wiley and Sons, 1973), p. 303.

HOW WE LEARN ABOUT STARS

All the information man has about stars—the very fact that they exist—comes through a feeble signal of light. Stars are large, but even the nearest are so distant that even through the most powerful telescope they appear only as points of light, and even the brightest stars are 30,000 times dimmer than the full moon. How is it possible to know as much about stars as we do? First, we do not always know as much as is implied in popular literature. Much, if not most, of what scientists claim to know about stars is a result of mathematical reasoning based upon laws or observations made in a laboratory, or formulated at someone's desk. Along the way many assumptions are made concerning what the interior or even the surface of a star ought to be like. No one has ever observed nuclear reactions occurring in a star, nor taken its temperature, at least in the center; and no one has ever gone to a star to measure the pressure or the density of the material. Still, the light from a star does convey a great deal of information. It tells the surface temperature, it tells what the surface of the star is made of, it indicates the presence of magnetic fields, or the spin of the star, turbulence in its atmosphere, and much more. This is all accomplished by analysis of the star's spectrum as discussed in chapter 2.

The only other way anything can be learned about a star is by the way it moves in the sky. The movement of stars in the sky is so slow that you could watch for years and detect no movement at all. But through the use of telescopes, and by comparing the positions of stars in photographs taken years apart, it is possible to measure some stars' movements from year to year. The fastest moving star is called Barnard's star, which takes about 180 years to move the same distance as the diameter of the full moon. Barnard's star is a lone star making its way through the Galaxy. It appears to move because it really is moving quickly, but this is more apparent because it is one of the nearest stars to the sun. There are other stars which appear to move because they are members of a double star, or binary star. Often two, and sometimes more, stars are in orbit about each other, just as a planet orbits the sun. But because they are nearly the same size, each is really orbiting the other. If the stars are not too close together, so that they can be seen as distinct points of light, they can be seen following elliptical paths in the sky. The last kind of motion is only an apparent motion, due to the fact that the earth changes its position with respect to the stars as it moves around the sun. This is called parallax. As figure 12 shows in an exaggerated way, a nearby star, as seen from earth when it is in different parts of its orbit, will appear in front of a different set of background stars. By measuring the amount the star appears to shift, and knowing the size of the earth's orbit, one can use trigonometry to find the distance to that star. The distance of stars out to about 300 light years is measurable in this way. This is only a fraction of the size of our galaxy, the Milky Way, let alone the rest of the universe. Other methods of distance measurement will be presented as we proceed.

Amazingly enough, the theoretical existence of parallax was realized as long ago as Aristotle. He pointed out that the *lack* of parallax proved that the earth does not go around the sun but is the center of the universe! The reason why he could not discern the parallax was that the effect is so small. Now the existence of parallax is regarded as one of the prime proofs that the earth does indeed go around the sun.

From the motions of binary stars it is sometimes possible to determine the masses of the stars involved. Mass is one of the prime ways of categorizing a star, and it is from binaries that the most precise mass determinations come. Actually, what is usually found is the relative mass, the ratio of the masses of the two stars. More information is required to find the actual masses.

CLASSIFYING STARS

Now that we have some idea as to how information about stars is gathered, what do we find? To answer this would fill many volumes, but I shall attempt a brief overview. There are several ways that stars may be classified; these include by mass, by brightness, and by temperature. As it turns out, all these properties are closely related, and since it is the spectrum which is most easily observed, it would be most convenient to classify them by their *spectral type.* It is observed that there are smooth variations in the spectra from one star to another. Some spectral lines become weaker, while others become stronger. If the spectra of all stars were arranged in a row by spectral type, there would be a smooth variation, and the line would include nearly every type of star. When this ordering is done, the stars are divided into spectral types by rather arbitrary boundaries. There are seven major spectral types, which are labeled O, B, A, F, G, K, and M. This turns out to be a good arrangement because, as one goes from O to M types, he also goes from the brightest to the

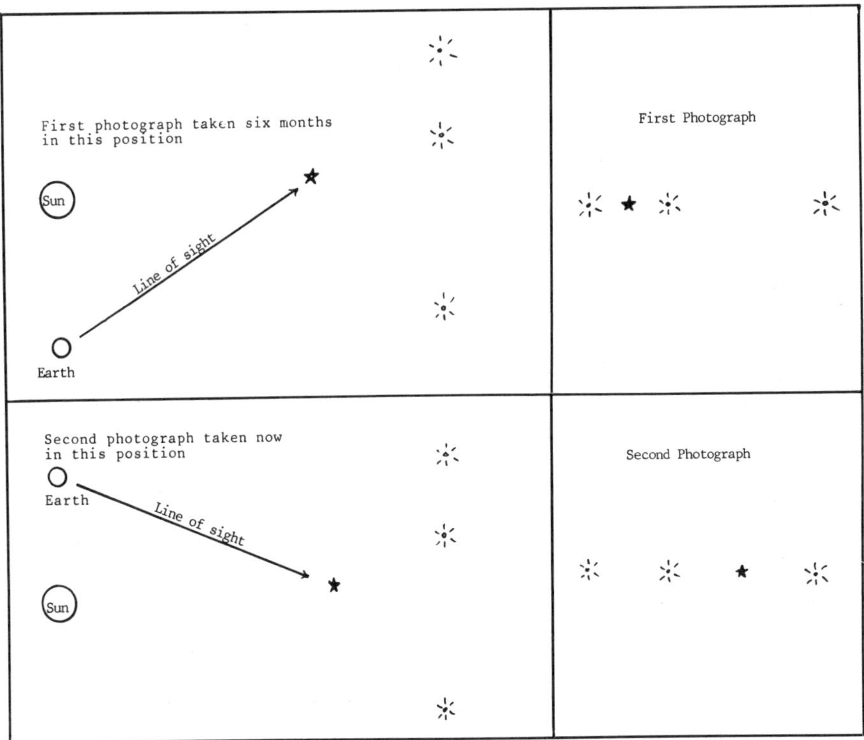

FIGURE 12.—The apparent motion of a nearby star against background stars due to the motion of the earth around the sun is called parallax.

dimmest, as well as from the hottest to the coolest stars, from largest to smallest, and from the heaviest to the lightest. Obviously there is a close relationship among all these properties.

The masses do not vary a great deal. The smallest stars are about a tenth the mass of the sun and the largest have about fifty times the sun's mass. The diameters of the stars vary even less for most normal stars. However, the differences in brightness can be enormous. The O type stars, at most fifty times as massive as the sun, are as much as half a million times brighter. M stars, at about a tenth of the sun's mass, are only a thousandth as bright as the sun. This great range is due mainly to the difference in temperature, for doubling the temperature produces a sixteenfold increase in brightness. O stars are as hot as 35,000° K. and M stars as low as 2700° K.

SPECIAL CHARACTERISTICS OF STARS

Spectral Class	*Color*	*Typical Temp. °K.*
O	blue-white	35,000
B	blue-white	21,000
A	white	10,000
F	creamy	7,200
G	yellow	6,000
K	orange	4,700
M	red	3,300

Table 2

It is also true that the bright O's and A's are fairly rare and the cooler K's and M's are the most plentiful. One would thus expect that when he looks at the sky he will see mostly K and M stars. This is not entirely true, however, because the O's and A's are so much brighter that they can be seen to a much greater distance, distances at which the later stars are entirely invisible. So the night sky appears to have a relatively larger number of O and A stars. To give an idea of the distances involved, the average distance between stars in the solar neighborhood is six or seven light years.

The stars that fall nicely into the pattern described above are the "normal" stars and constitute 90 percent of all stars. They are called main sequence stars, for reasons we shall see in a moment. There are also giant stars, supergiant stars, white dwarfs, and even more exotic types. A giant or supergiant star has about the same mass as a normal star such as the sun, but can be 400 times the diameter and 4,000 times as bright. The large size is possible because the materials in the outer portions of the star are extremely tenuous. In fact, it would be considered a good vacuum if we could obtain the same density in an earth laboratory. The tremendous brightness comes from the large surface area, not the temperature, which is usually relatively low.

The giants and supergiants are rare, and most of the ten percent of the stars which do not belong to the main sequence are white dwarfs. White dwarfs are the opposite of giants, being small, dense, and hot. In fact, they may be as small as the earth and twice the temperature of the sun. Amazingly, they have about the same mass as the sun crammed into their small size. Though they are hot, they are also dim, due to their small size, and cannot be seen at great distances.

Stars may be further classified by what are called stellar populations, according to the relative amounts of heavier elements they have. Heavy, again, means elements other than hydrogen and helium. The stars falling into the group called Population I contain large amounts of heavy elements, also called metals, compared to the Population II stars. The two populations tend to fall in different locations within our galaxy. The Population I stars, which include the sun, are located in the spiral arms and disk regions of the galaxy, while the Population II stars are more concentrated towards the center of the galaxy. Population II stars tend to be late type stars, meaning, it will be recalled, late in the sequence O, B, A, F, G, K, and M. This means they tend to be less massive and cooler than Population I stars.

Within the galaxy, stars tend to group themselves not only according to populations, but they also fall into smaller, tighter groups called clusters. There are three general cluster types: galactic clusters (also called open clusters), globular clusters, and stellar associations. Galactic clusters consist primarily of Population I stars and hence fall in the spiral arms of the galaxy. They are generally loose, irregular groups, having from a few dozen to a few hundred stars. An example is the Pleiades, whose "seven sisters" are the seven brightest members of the cluster, which really contains hundreds of stars.

Globular clusters are more spectacular in appearance, but unfortunately always require a telescope to be seen. Globulars contain thousands to hundreds of thousands of stars in a distinctly spherical distribution. They consist primarily of Population II stars and concentrate around the center of the galaxy. In fact, they appear to be in orbit around the center of the galaxy, and thus they mark out the center, which cannot be seen directly from earth due to intervening clouds of obscuring dust.

Stellar associations are striking in that they contain primarily O and B type stars belonging, of course, to Population I. There are not many stars in an association, and they have the peculiar characteristic that all the stars are flying away from each other.

STELLAR EVOLUTION

The preceding discussion should serve to familiarize the reader with the nature and distribution of stars in our galaxy, and should help him to understand the arguments which follow. These have to do with the modern theories of the formation and evolution of stars. The information given above is derived from observations and is probably all correct. Theory, which plays at least as large a part as observation, is almost the only source of information about stellar evolution. Stellar evolution is the supposed processes by which stars form, grow old, and die. Stellar evolution requires billions of years and is the supposed process by which stars have come into being. It is thus of great interest to the Christian who is concerned about how his faith is challenged by such concepts.

Astronomers usually begin by assuming that stars form out of condensed clouds of gas and dust. Often it is the very nearness of clouds to certain stars which causes astronomers to classify the stars as recently formed, thus producing a circular argument. Again, it is Martin Harwit, in his *Astrophysical Concepts,* who has the freshness of thought to say, "The association of dust clouds with recently formed stars is not absolute proof that stars formed from these clouds. Some causal relationship presumably exists, but is it impossible that stars just form out of nothing at all? and that a lot of dust gets raised in the process? Such a picture, though unsatisfying because it postulates an apparently unphysical origin, after all at least avoids the angular momentum and magnetic field difficulties. We should keep this important point in mind: Perhaps stars do form out of 'nothing'! For the moment, however, we prefer to work, as far as we are able, within the framework of ordinary physics."[2]

His statement is significant. Stars forming out of nothing, of course,

---

2. Ibid., p. 14.

is really a form of creationism. Note that he does not reject this because there is evidence against it. In fact, he seems to consider it a real possibility. He simply prefers to stay within the framework of ordinary physics as long as possible. It is necessary at least to start in this way if we ever hope to gain any physical understanding of any objects or processes. However, implicit in this is the assumption that stars originated and continue to exist by purely natural means. While we do not doubt that stars' continued existence is describable by physical laws, their origin was not by means of physical laws. Creation is something that cannot be understood within the framework of physical laws. God had to intervene to create and thus suspended, or superseded, those laws temporarily. Astronomers are doing nothing wrong in applying physical laws to aid in understanding stars. The error comes when they also try to apply those laws to origins in contradiction to the revealed word of God. They then substitute natural laws for the supernatural Creator, and worship and serve the creature rather than the Creator.

Population I and Population II Stars

While we are on the subject of star formation, it is the proper place to explain how astronomers think the difference between Population I stars and Population II stars came about. The origin of the elements, the abundances of which distinguish the two populations, is a continuing problem for astronomers. Astronomers believe one of the most likely places for element formation is through the energy-producing nuclear reactions in the interiors of stars. Thus stars which formed early in the universe must have been deficient in the metals, for these elements had not yet been created. These would be the Population II stars. During their lifetimes these stars would produce metals, but these metals would not show up on their surfaces, which should still reflect the low metal abundances of the clouds from which they were formed.

I have briefly mentioned supernovae—stars which undergo titanic explosions, causing them to lose much of their mass. Astronomers postulate that during a supernova much of the metals produced in the interior of the star would be released into space and mingle with the other material in the interstellar clouds. Subsequently new stars form from these clouds and possess a large metal abundance to begin with. These are the Population I stars. The high metal abundances are observable on their surfaces. This sequence of events is a guess to explain why there should be two different stellar populations. It is on the basis of this guess that astronomers say that Population II stars are older than Population I stars.

Again I quote Martin Harwit. "These differences in the surface composition of the very oldest stars do indicate that they were formed out of a chemically different medium. Moreover, the basic physical processes that should occur in the interior of stars—if our theories of stellar evolution are correct—are in good agreement with the observation that stars forming today contain more of the heavier chemical elements than stars formed in the earliest stages of galactic evolution. . . . Only if such views were to lead to incompatible results, would we wish to switch to a theory that required the spontaneous formation of stars out of nothing. But then we would still not be home free. We would still have to explain why stars formed from 'nothing' some ten aeons ago had low metal abundance, while stars formed in the same way, but within the past few million years, have higher metal abundances. We would have to face the somewhat uncomfortable implication that 'nothing' had changed."[3]

But *has* "nothing" changed? He makes the implicit assumption that Population II stars are older than Population I stars, and then states that their chemical differences prove that the medium from which they formed has changed. However, the basic reason that the Population II stars are thought to be older than the Population I stars is precisely that their chemical compositions are different! Thus we find astronomers caught in another circular argument. We could instead assume that all stars formed at the same time. Then all that is proved is that there are stars with differing chemical compositions; there are differences from one star to another, a fact which is obvious anyway! We can make no statements about how the interstellar medium has changed, because there is no evidence that it has.

Is there any independent way to tell the age of a star? For a single star the answer is, no. There is absolutely no way one can tell the age of a single star by looking at it. Differences in chemical composition indicate different ages only if one starts with certain assumptions. The only conceivable way one could tell the age of an individual star would be by the amount of heavy elements it has created in its lifetime of nuclear reactions, and even this is entirely dependent upon the assumptions one makes about how much of what element a star started out with, about whether it really is deriving its energy from nuclear reactions, and about how much of these

3. Ibid.

newly created elements might reach the surface and be observable. However, even if this element formation is taking place within stars, it is not observable. "The chemical makeup of the outermost portions of the stars, the ones we actually see, therefore show no evidence of the complicated changes that have occurred in the star's interior, even at this advanced stage of evolution."[4] The sole evidence about an individual star's age, therefore, is entirely negative.

There is even a point of view in which the chemical composition of stars actually contradicts the theory of stellar evolution. We have already learned that supposedly the "older" stars have a lower abundance of heavier elements than the "younger" stars, and that this is so because the medium out of which they formed has changed in the intervening years. However, Dr. Harwit says elsewhere, "The similarity in abundances for stars of as widely differing ages as a BO star, which probably formed only a few million years ago, and a red giant or the planetary nebulae, which should be among the oldest objects in the galaxy and hence seven or more aeons old, indicates that the interstellar medium may not have changed much during the time between the formation of these various stars. The lack of evidence for chemical evolution is somewhat puzzling . . . clearly the evidence is ambiguous."[5] The evidence is not ambiguous in the least. It is extremely clear that there are irreconcilable contradictions in the theory of stellar evolution. Harwit said that when these views lead to incompatible results he would accept a theory where stars form out of nothing. The incompatible results have just been presented, but the normal response is that the evidence is ambiguous or requires further investigation. Scientists, like the rest of us, are reluctant to change their minds.

The argument can be restated for clarity. First, the differences in chemical composition between the "older," metal deficient Population II stars and the "younger," metal rich Population I stars are explained in this way: the older stars formed when there were few metals in the universe, but during their lifetimes they created these elements in their interiors through nuclear reactions. Somehow at the end of their lives, perhaps through a supernova explosion, these old stars released their heavy elements into space. These metals mingled with the hydrogen gas already there, and the new mixture subsequently formed into a new population of stars which were rich in

4. Ibid., p. 121.
5. Ibid., pp. 345, 347.

metals. Hence one should be able to say that Population II stars are older than Population I stars because they have less metals. The age determination is made on the basis of differing chemical composition.

On the other hand, if we determine the ages of stars on another basis, we get contradictory results. Examining the metal abundances of a B type star, a star which because of its extremely high energy production cannot be more than a few million years old, and comparing it to a supergiant star which is supposed to be an old star at the end of its lifetime, or to a planetary nebula which, according to the theory of stellar evolution, is a very old object, show that there is no difference in chemical composition. If they really did form billions of years apart from clouds in the interstellar medium, this is proof that the medium did not change during those years. If it has not changed, then we cannot account for difference in the Population I and Population II stars by saying they formed at different times when the interstellar medium was different. Thus there is no basis for saying that Population II stars are older than Population I stars. Also it must be explained how these two populations came to have differing compositions, since the material of which they formed *did not*. An unchanging medium simply could not produce two populations of differing compositions at different times. Thus different populations must have had their differing compositions since the time they were formed, since evidence of internal reactions is not manifested on the surfaces, nor can the differing compositions be accounted for on the basis of differing materials from which they are supposed to have formed. The only possibility remaining is that the two population groups were created with different chemical compositions and did not form from the interstellar medium.

Assumed Sequence in Stellar Evolution

The reader may have noticed that despite the fact that I said one cannot tell the age of a star by looking at it, Dr. Harwit's quote said that a B star is a young star and a red giant, or a planetary nebula is very old. These assigned ages are the result of a number of assumptions which we shall deal with as we now explore the theory of stellar evolution further. To see why astronomers think certain types of stars are older than others, I shall now give an overview of the sequence of events as presented by the theory of stellar evolution. A star is thought to begin when a cloud, made primarily of hydrogen gas, begins to contract under the influence of its own gravity. Because of dynamical difficulties with the formation of a single star in this way (it is impossible), it is thought that this large cloud will break up into smaller clouds, each of which will become a star. The whole will form a cluster of stars bound together by gravity. As in the case of the sun, each star contracts and heats up as it does so. Sometime during this period the protostar must somehow rid itself of an excess of angular momentum and magnetic field. (However, earlier types of stars—O's, B's, and A's—are found to be spinning rapidly, and other types of stars have a high magnetic field.) When the center of the star is hot enough (millions of degrees), nuclear reactions begin, converting hydrogen to helium. With the onset of these nuclear reactions its lifetime as a main sequence star has begun. It will remain this way until its fuel is used up. When its supply of hydrogen eventually does run out, there is no longer any energy being produced which can maintain the high central heat and pressure and thus hold up the upper layers of the star. The star must then begin to contract once more due to its own gravity, and again the contraction causes heating until central temperatures are high enough to allow another kind of nuclear reaction, changing helium into carbon. This produces more energy, temporarily halting the contraction. But less total energy is available in converting helium to carbon than in changing hydrogen into helium, and this fuel runs out quickly. During the time of this second contraction, it is primarily the core of the star which contracts. The outer layers expand and cool producing a red giant star. When the helium burning actually begins, this envelope, as it is called, shrinks and the star resembles a main sequence star once more.

After the helium runs out, any of several things are thought to be possible. If the star is massive enough, the contraction following the exhaustion of the helium again raises the temperature of the core to a point where carbon is used as fuel. Carbon nuclei may combine with leftover helium, other carbon, or other atoms, producing a host of different kinds of elements. Or the star may become a supernova, exploding so powerfully that for a time it is one of the brightest objects in the universe. The by-product of a supernova explosion is thought sometimes to be a strange object called a neutron star, one of the many wonders of modern astronomy. A neutron star is what is left after the mighty explosion has forced the central portions of a star into an extremely tiny volume. It might have the mass of the sun with a diameter of only twenty miles. Or it might become the even more mysterious black hole, made famous by the popular media.

A black hole is an object predicted by the theory of general relativity. It is a star which, after it started to collapse, couldn't stop. It continues shrinking until it disappears into nothing at all. All the mass is still there, as can be determined by the influence of its gravity. Nothing can escape from it, not even light, and it swallows everything which comes too close. From the outside, however, it does not appear to disappear into a point, for time is affected as well as space in such an intense gravitational field, and when the contraction reaches a certain point, called the Schwartzschild radius, time appears to stop altogether. As yet none of these has been positively identified. On the other hand, the star might contract peacefully into a white dwarf which can do nothing but cool and glow until the end of time.

It has become apparent now why astronomers think certain stars are older than others. A red giant is thought to be a star which has already burned up its hydrogen and is on its way to burning helium or some other element. Hence it is older than a main sequence star of the same mass. A planetary nebula is thought to be a star on its way toward becoming a white dwarf, shedding mass as it does so. This is an even later stage than red giantism.

Is the Sequence Reliable?

The sequence explained above is the universally accepted process of stellar evolution. It sounds clear and reasonable, and because all the objects described appear to exist, it seems consistent with observations as well. However, though popular media may lead one to believe that this is indeed the case, and that stellar evolution is well understood, it is really an incomplete and disjointed theory. Astronomers are not very certain how a star should move smoothly from one state to the next, but such changes are the very basis of an evolutionary theory. The sequence is an attempt to unite a number of different objects into an evolutionary sequence. They are placed in this evolutionary sequence because they exist and scientists feel that they ought to fit together, not because the theory of stellar evolution really predicts them or requires them. The observed objects had to be fitted together into an evolutionary scheme because it is obvious that, if the universe is really 20 billion years old, some changes must have taken place in that time; certain objects cannot have existed as they are for that long a time. And so it is assumed that every object in the universe, and even the universe itself, undergoes some process of evolution on its way from its beginning to its end, and that all observed objects must fit into that sequence. The sequence described above is the one scientists decided on. As new objects are discovered in the heavens, they also find their way into the sequence of stellar evolution, not because they are predicted by stellar evolution, or even because they fit the sequence especially well, but simply because they have to be put somewhere.

This does not mean that the theory is totally wrong in all respects. Limited calculations have been done on computers and show that a star which has been burning hydrogen will expand into a red giant when the hydrogen runs out. This is as far as a continuous sequence of models has gone at present. Some calculations also have been done on the early stages of contraction. It is well to remember that all these computer models are based upon the same assumptions as go into the theory. If these assumptions are wrong, the computer models will be wrong also. If it turns out that stars are really burning hydrogen, a real possibility, then perhaps, if allowed to continue unhindered, they will follow a course similar to that predicted by the theory (that is if we assume that the fiery end of the heavens described in II Peter is a long way off). The point is that the theory as it now stands is incomplete and unreliable, and certainly not attested well enough to stand as proof that the stars have been burning for millions and billions of years.

The Hertzsprung-Russell Diagram

Stellar evolution, however, is not a random attempt to lump together all types of stars. There are limitations to the variety of characteristics a star may have. This is best illustrated by the Hertzsprung-Russell (HR) diagram. An example is shown in figure 13. On this graph each star is represented by a point. The horizontal axis is the temperature (or spectral type) increasing to the left. The vertical axis is the brightness, which increases upwards. It is obvious from looking at the diagram that stars do not fall randomly over the whole graph. There are only certain areas where stars are permitted, and this expresses some underlying physical laws which govern the nature of stars. The vast majority of stars fall approximately on a line which goes from upper left (hot and bright) to lower right (cool and dim). This should sound familiar; it is the same sequence we saw earlier when we examined spectral types, O through M. The stars that fall on the line are the normal stars we have discussed, and the line is called the main sequence.

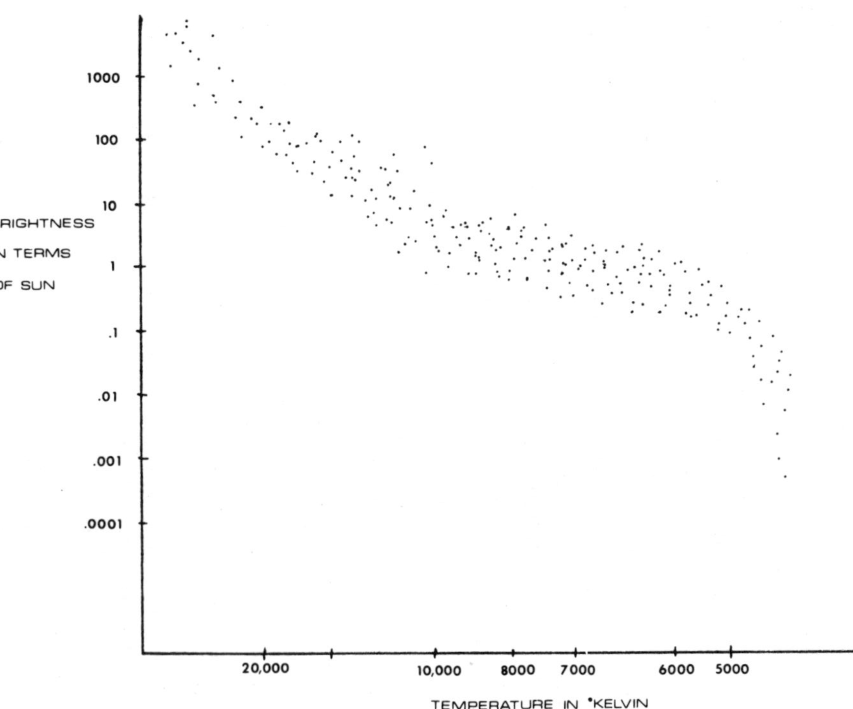

FIGURE 13.—The Hertzsprung-Russell diagram showing the main sequence.

There are few stars elsewhere on the diagram. The giants and supergiants are found in the upper right portions of the diagram. They are cool, but extremely bright due to their immense size. The white dwarfs fall in the lower left, hot but dim. Stellar evolution is an attempt to unify these objects under a single theory of the development of stars. This means that according to the theory the stars will move around on the HR diagram, first being on the main sequence, then moving to the giant regions, and finally winding up as white dwarfs in the opposite corner of the graph. Let us follow a hypothetical star along the path proposed by astronomers.

A star starting out as a contracting gas cloud will be large but extremely cool by star standards. Thus it will start out on the HR diagram far to the right and near the bottom. As the cloud contracts and heats, it will move toward the left to higher temperatures, also gaining somewhat in brightness. Newspapers will often quote an astronomer who says he has seen a star form, but as I said earlier, the theory says that it will take from 100,000 to 150 million years to form. No one has ever seen a star form. They may have seen an O type star in regions of dust and gas, or some unexplained light that changes in brightness. O type stars are called young simply because they would exhaust their complement of hydrogen in only a few million years and hence are younger than other types of stars. (Do other types of stars start out old? From the way they are discussed, one would think they did.) Some objects which vary in brightness are assumed to be young, unstable stars.

In fact, astronomers are uncertain as to how stars form. To the quote at the beginning of this chapter we can add the following: "The process by which an interstellar cloud is concentrated until it is held together gravitationally to become a protostar is not known."[6] "Summing it up, we can say that the transformation of an ordinary small globule into a star is improbable, since it requires special conditions, but it is in general not ruled out."[7] "Literally hundreds of ideas on how stars are formed have been advanced in the past decade. However we are still far from any real solution."[8] "There are so many uncertainties in this picture that at present we do not really have a

6. E. Novotny, *Introduction to Stellar Atmospheres and Interiors* (New York: Oxford University Press, 1973), p. 279.

7. S. A. Kaplan and S. B. Pikelner, *The Interstellar Medium* (Cambridge: Harvard University Press, 1970), p. 366.

8. Harwit, *Astrophysical Concepts*, p. 405.

theory of star formation."[9] "There are no known nebulae in the interstellar medium small enough and dense enough to collapse into single stars."[10] Five authors, one after another, admit that either they do not know how stars are formed, or that it is almost impossible! Stellar evolution is off to a bad start already, and we have hardly begun. Since there is no acceptable theory of star formation, and since it does not appear possible anyway, it would seem that creation provides by far the superior explanation.

Protostars

The word *protostar* refers to an object believed to be a star which has not yet reached the main sequence on the HR diagram. It would thus not yet have begun its nuclear burning stage and would not be a quiet, stable star. One type of star which is almost unanimously believed to be a protostar is the T Tauri star. There are about 1,000 of these known at present. The reasons they are thought to be young are:

1) They are found in regions of interstellar dust where stars are assumed to form.
2) They are found near O type stars, which are thought to be young.
3) They fall to the right of the main sequence in the HR diagram.
4) They are rapidly expelling material into space, at the rate of one solar mass every 30 million years.
5) They have large amounts of the element lithium, which is rapidly destroyed by nuclear processes.

These pieces of evidence taken together would give strong testimony to the youth of these stars. The first point, of course, depends upon the assumption that stars form by contraction of gas clouds, which has already been seen to be impossible. Nevertheless, the apparent fact that stars must form from something and the obvious fact that not all dust and gas in the vicinity of these stars have yet been used in star formation implies to astronomers that T Tauri stars have recently formed from this material.

The second point assumes that because they are nearby to O stars they formed at the same time and in the same manner. About this I ask, where are the G, K, and M stars, which should have formed at

9. B. M. Middlehurst and L. H. Aller, eds., *Nebulae and Interstellar Matter* (Chicago: University of Chicago Press, 1968), p. 58.
10. Hartmann, *Moons and Planets,* p. 86.

the same time and in greater numbers? It would seem that different processes must be at work in the formation of these different types of stars, in which case their assumption is not valid. The third point, their position in the HR diagram, indicates their youth only if they really are in the process of contraction from a gas cloud. If this is true, then T Tauri stars may be moving toward the main sequence. On the other hand, they may be stable and belong where they are found in the HR diagram. Can a star in this position really be stable? It is impossible to tell simply by looking at it. Astronomers assume they are not stable because they do not fall in the "permitted" region of the HR diagram. But this is purely empirical. This region is considered not permitted only because many stars are found there. However, T Tauri stars *are* found there, so this must be a permitted region after all. The fourth point, that they are losing matter very rapidly, shows that they cannot have existed as they are now for long. At the rate they are losing mass they must be either young compared to the high ages for most stars, or they were ridiculously large a long time ago. The fifth point is quite compelling, for the element lithium cannot exist for long where nuclear transformations are taking place. Hence either those transformations are not taking place or the star is very young. And if those transformations are not taking place, the star must be young anyway, since it has no energy source to keep it radiating.

In sum, points four and five, the only ones not implicitly assuming the correctness of stellar evolution, are enough to indicate that T Tauri stars are young. But this is what I have been saying all along, that stars are very young. Astronomers have proven it for us in the case of T Tauri stars. For other stars, definite ages cannot be assigned.

But what if stellar evolution should prove to be true? Are not T Tauri stars strong evidence that stars really do contract from gas clouds and approach the main sequence from the right on the HR diagram, as the theory says? Don't they form a consistent body of evidence in favor of stellar evolution? Recall how we said that new and strange objects are sometimes forced into the evolutionary sequence. This has been the case with T Tauri stars also. It may seem at first glance that they fit nicely into the theory and lend it valid support, but reading a little closer reveals that they are not predicted by the theory after all! "What physical processes or attributes could account for the distinctive features of the T Tauri stars? . . . None of these phenomena are predicted by the modern theory of young stars. Each is still a complete mystery."[11] If each property of the T Tauri stars is a complete mystery, and the accepted theory predicts none of them, it is contrary to reason to say that T Tauri stars lend support to the theory of stellar evolution. All that can be said without further evidence is that they are independent objects with no evolutionary path to other objects. It is a complete mystery how these stars can be cited as proof of the theory since (1) the theory is not able to describe how these stars might form, and (2) when young stars are actually identified the theory cannot explain any of their properties.

Next, according to the theory, the young star reaches the main sequence with the onset of hydrogen burning. The consumption of hydrogen is amazing in terms of the number of tons of matter that are burned per second. It is only in virtue of the fact that a star has such a tremendous amount of hydrogen that it could possibly burn for billions of years. During this stage there is little change in the appearance of the star. It is only after the exhaustion of hydrogen that new changes take place. The rate of hydrogen burning is described by what is called the mass-luminosity relation. It is a quantitative statement of the earlier assertion that more massive stars burn their fuel faster, not simply in proportion to their sizes, but much faster. Stated mathematically it is $L \propto m^{3.5}$. For example, a star twice as massive as the sun burns its fuel $2^{3.5}$ or about 11 times faster. But since it has only twice the fuel to begin with, it lives only 2/11 as long as the sun. Simply stated, the more massive a star is, the shorter is its lifetime. This is an empirical fact and is true no matter what the real energy source is.

Recall now, that stars arranged in order of decreasing mass are also arranged in order of decreasing temperature. Thus stars on the main sequence of the HR diagram are ordered according to decreasing mass as one goes from the upper left to the lower right. So those stars on the upper left on the main sequence are those which most quickly exhaust their fuel. As time passes, stars farther and farther down the main sequence, those with progressively longer and longer lifetimes, eventually run out of fuel. According to the theory, the stage to which they then pass is the red giant branch of the HR diagram. Calculations do tend to indicate such a swelling as a star which has been burning hydrogen finally runs out.

11. G. H. Herbig, "The Youngest Stars," in *Frontiers in Astronomy* (San Francisco: W. H. Freeman and Co., 1970), p. 145.

One assumption implicit in the above discussion is that all stars on the main sequence are the same age. Only if all the stars on the main sequence were formed at the same time would those at the upper left run out of fuel first. If stars are forming all the time and joining the main sequence, then one would expect to find stars in every permitted part of the HR diagram. There would be old red giants as well as young main sequence O and B stars. When all the stars within a certain distance of the sun are plotted on an HR diagram, it does indeed have stars in every permitted part of the diagram. This might be interpreted to imply that stars did not all form at the same time, as opposed to the creation model in which they were all created at once. Or does it? Again, it depends upon the assumptions with which one starts. If stars do indeed contract from gas clouds and then spend their lifetimes on the main sequence burning hydrogen as fuel, then the distribution of stars on the HR diagram implies that the stars were formed at differing times. An equally plausible explanation is that God created a number of different types of stars. Why should He have made them all the same? No evolutionary relationship is proved at all. Even if such an evolutionary relationship should some day be demonstrated, it is still valid to say that God created all types at once; He created an entire functioning universe. If, after they were created, stars continued on an evolutionary course, it in no way weakens the fact of creation.

Clusters

There is another way to choose stars to graph on the HR diagram. Instead of choosing stars within a certain distance of the sun, which we might expect to be a reasonably random distribution, we can choose stars which tend to fall into natural groups, the clusters. Astronomers believe that stars form in large numbers at once from a single gas cloud. Later the stars separate and move individually. This is the theory of the formation of clusters. A cluster may be such a group which has not yet broken up. One feature about a cluster, then, is that all stars within it would be of the same age. (Though this conclusion is arrived at on evolutionary grounds, creationists would have no trouble agreeing with the conclusion!) Theory thus predicts that all stars would start out on the main sequence at about the same time. As time goes on, those stars at the top of the main sequence would be the first to leave it and become giants. At later times less massive stars would also exhaust their fuel and go to the red giant

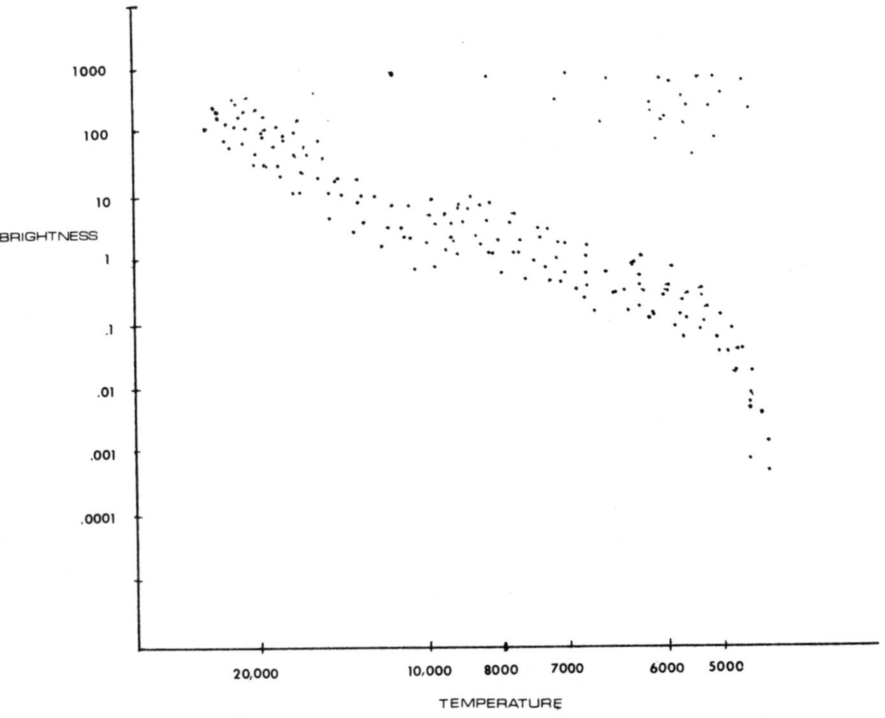

FIGURE 14.—The HR diagram for a cluster of stars showing the turnoff point.

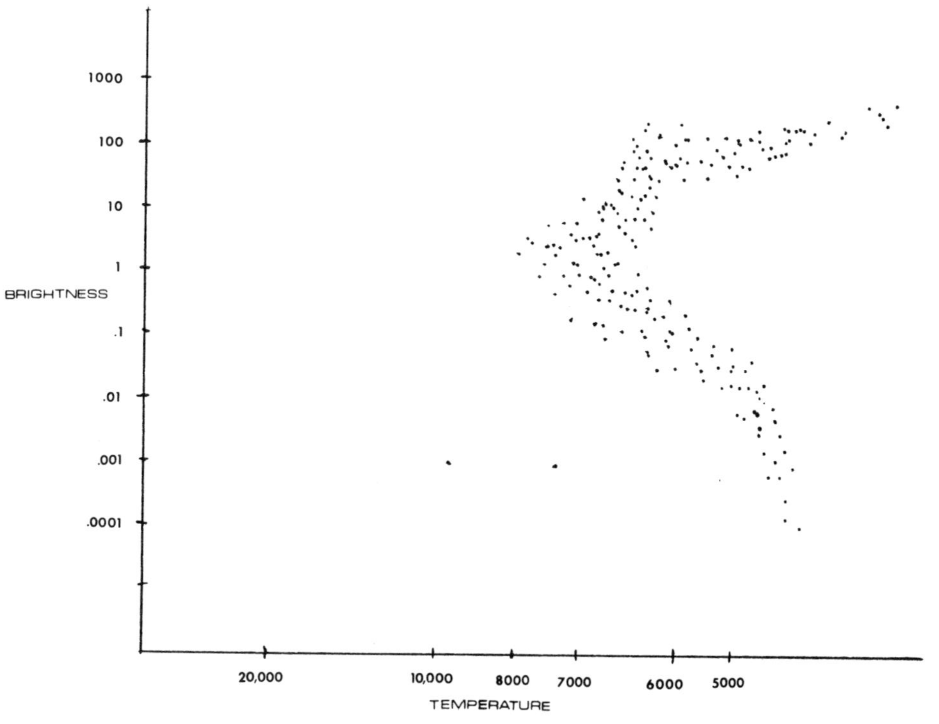

FIGURE 15.—The HR diagram for a different cluster with a lower turnoff point and a more developed giant branch.

branch. Thus, if we looked at the HR diagram for a cluster at progressively later times, we would see that the *turnoff point,* the point at which stars were just leaving the main sequence, would progress down the line. Another way to obtain the same picture without the long waiting period is to look at the HR diagrams of successively older clusters whose turnoff points have moved farther and farther down the main sequence line. Figures 14 and 15 show the HR diagram of two different clusters. The turnoff point is different in each, and there is a line of stars connecting the turnoff point with the giant region. On the basis of the difference of the turnoff points, an astronomer would say that the cluster with the lower turnoff point is the older. In fact, assuming nuclear burning, he would say how long a star could remain on the main sequence and give an actual age for the cluster based upon the mass of the stars which were just leaving the main sequence.

Because the appearance of the HR diagrams for various clusters appears to be consistent with the theory of stellar evolution, they are cited as proof of the theory. Such an interpretation is self-consistent, and if one starts with the right assumptions, it is strong evidence in favor of the theory. A creationist could, of course, reply that God made the clusters with the observed distribution of stars. But why did He choose a different set of stars to put in one cluster than in another? It would be much more satisfying to produce an explanation based upon physical principles yet without invoking uniformitarian assumptions. We might guess, for example, that stars do evolve as predicted but much more rapidly. If they are not burning hydrogen, their lifetimes would be considerably shorter than is now believed, and they might go through the stages of stellar evolution at a much greater rate. The trouble with this is that we would expect to be able to see changes taking place in stars which evolved at this rate, and we do not. Besides, if stars do derive their energy from the gravitational method, their lifetimes would still be in the millions of years. There is as yet no complete creationist theory to explain the appearance of the HR diagrams of clusters other than to assume that God made them that way.

The Basic Assumption of Stellar Evolution

We must still, however, return to the fact that the entire theory of stellar evolution is based upon the assumption of nuclear burning of hydrogen. This is the most important assumption in the theory, and yet there is still no indication that such burning is really happening. I repeat, the *only* reason that nuclear burning was proposed in the first place was to give the sun a lifetime great enough to allow for the evolution of life on earth.[12]

Attempts to find nuclear reactions in the sun have failed, and there is no indication that they are taking place in the stars. "The calculations are based on nuclear reaction rates, computed for different stages of a star's life. . . . We very much depend upon nuclear burning theories."[13] Some have cited the discovery of the element technetium in stars as evidence of nuclear reactions. The reason for this is that technetium is a radioactive element and quickly decays into another element (within a few hundred years). Hence, since this element exists, it must have been created recently by nuclear reactions in the stars. This carries into the implicit assumption that the star is old enough for all the original technetium to have vanished. One could equally well interpret this as evidence that the star is young. Some isotopes of technetium have half-lives in the millions of years, and the abundances visible now could well represent the original abundances of that element in those stars. If the stars were billions of years old, however, even this technetium should have decayed away. This explanation is especially to be favored, since even stars late in life show no evidence of the reactions that have been proceeding within. It would be strange if technetium were the only element which succeeded in reaching the surface. There are also the spallation reactions which could produce new elements on the surfaces of stars without nuclear reactions being the real source of the star's energy.

Some remarkable recent observations of the sun have shown it to be pulsating at a number of different periods ranging from a few minutes to a few hours. These pulsations were a complete surprise, and as yet no explanation has arisen. They can be useful, however. Just

---

12. A. Unsold, *The New Cosmos* (New York: Springer-Verlag, 1969), p. 274; Harwit, *Astrophysical Concepts,* p. 307; J. C. Brandt, *The Sun and Stars* (San Francisco: McGraw Hill, 1966), p. 60; Novotny, *Introduction,* p. 248; M. Schwarzschild, *Structure and Evolution of the Stars* (New York: Dover Publications, Inc., 1958), p. 73; S. Chandrasekhar, *Stellar Structure* (New York: Dover Publications, Inc., 1967), p. 455; L. Motz and A. Duveen, *Essentials of Astronomy* (Belmont: Wadsworth Publishing Co., Inc., 1968), p. 383; G. Abell, *Exploration of the Universe* (San Francisco: Holt, Rinehart, and Winston, 1964), p. 506; W. Ley, *Watchers of the Skies* (New York: Viking Press, 1966), p. 457.

13. Harwit, *Astrophysical Concepts,* pp. 18-19.

as earthquakes and the following seismic waves can be used as probes to tell us what the interior of the earth is like, the nature of the solar pulsations is dependent upon the density and nature of the interior materials. These factors, in turn, are important in determining whether or not nuclear reactions can take place in the interior. The result, according to Andrei B. Severny, is that the conditions in the solar interior are not right for nuclear reactions to take place.[14] This remarkable result seems not to have fully impacted the astronomical community as yet. However, taken together with the solar neutrino problem, this constitutes strong evidence that nuclear reactions are not taking place in the sun.

Is There Proof of Stellar Evolution?

But what if scientists are correct about the sun being temporarily turned off? Even if nuclear reactions are the source of the sun's energy, stellar evolution is not proved. Nuclear burning is as good a source of energy as any other, and the fact that it gives potential for long ages does not mean that the sun is already old. Stellar evolution has failed to provide a coherent and continuous explanation of the relationship among stellar types. "What happens next is not well known. Somehow the red giant stars shed some of their mass and eventually end up to the left of the main sequence and below it, in the form of *white dwarfs!*"[15] Stated this way it seems somewhat far-fetched to believe that a giant star with a large mass and low temperature should, in some unknown way, become a small star with low mass and a high temperature. They are as opposite as can be. With no connecting link, either observational or theoretical, it is unreasonable to expect anyone to believe that this really happens. They are obviously two entirely different, unrelated objects. Observations can never prove a theory which does not make predictions.

The question can be approached in another way. Does the existence of giant stars support stellar evolution and nuclear burning since some calculations, at least, show that such an expansion should occur? Not necessarily. Usually in the sciences a given result can be arrived at in more than one way. The calculations based upon the assumptions of nuclear energy sources may be only one way of arriving at a conclusion. It is not surprising that calculations do give the correct re-

14. A. B. Severny, *et al., Nature* 259 (1976), 87.
15. Harwit, *Astrophysical Concepts,* p. 344.

sult for this isolated case, since that is what they were designed to do. The very purpose of the theory of stellar evolution is "to explain the distribution of stars within the HR diagram, showing not only why some regions are populated and others not, but also why some regions —particularly the main sequence—are heavily populated, while stars are very sparse in others."[16] It would be remarkable if, after these years, astronomers had not succeeded in at least partially explaining the HR diagram. But just as, for example, quantum mechanics has replaced classical mechanics because of the old theory's inability to explain all the facts, so it seems the present theory of stellar evolution is also unable to explain most of the characteristics of the HR diagram. It must be improved or replaced. The limited agreement between theory and observation is inadequate to prove the theory. On the contrary, the weakness of the theory is more apparent because the agreement is so limited.

Perhaps the most important remaining question for creationists is the origin of the turnoff points in the HR diagrams of different clusters. The stars are real, physical objects and presumably follow physical laws; we would rather not take the easy way out by saying simply, "God made them that way." But if creationists take the position of rejecting stellar evolution, they should provide a feasible alternative. Astronomers have tried to provide one which has not proved entirely successful. Hopefully an alternative theory will be forthcoming.

If it should turn out that the theory of stellar evolution is true, creation is still not disproved. Stars that now exist would follow the course predicted for them if the Lord permits them to burn that long. They would have been created in the states in which they are now found, already partially through their lives, in the same way that Adam was not created a baby but a grown man. If we still feel obligated to ask why, for instance, star clusters have an appearance of age, we would answer, for the same reason that Adam had an appearance of age. Why do the clusters appear to have different ages? Why did Adam have a different apparent age than a tree, or a chipmunk?

The next stage in the history of stellar evolution is the onset of helium burning. After the star has swollen to a red giant (during which time the star's core is contracting and heating), helium atoms can combine to form carbon. After this stage begins, the star moves

16. Ibid., p. 18.

back towards the main sequence. After the exhaustion of helium, another giant phase begins. When the last of its fuels are exhausted, the star is thought to reach one of the final states described earlier. Again, none of these transitions have been observed (with the possible though uncertain exception of WZ Sagittae). We see simply a large collection of different kinds of objects, varying greatly in such properties as brightness, density, and temperature. Stellar evolution has attempted to put all these together into an evolutionary sequence; however, from here on I shall consider them as individual and independent objects, since no evolutionary relationship has been demonstrated. Leaving our discussion of stellar evolution, we shall proceed to examine the wonders and variety of the objects of God's creation.

WHITE DWARFS

White dwarfs are a fairly common type of star. This is determined from the fact that there is a relatively large number of them near the sun. They are too dim to see at great distances, so it is assumed that they have the same distribution elsewhere as they do near by. In some cases, both the mass and the diameter of a white dwarf have been determined, with the result that the density of these stars is found to be extremely great. The mass is found from the stars' gravitational influence upon other stars, that is, their companions in binary systems. Their actual size can be determined if their distance, brightness, and temperature are known. The actual measurements have been done on only three white dwarfs out of hundreds known. Astronomers have shown that the stars have a diameter about the same as the earth's, and masses comparable to that of the sun, giving them a density of about 15 tons per cubic inch. It is impossible for nuclear reactions to be happening here. Their radiation must simply be due to heat they had to begin with, either when they were created, or the heat left over when nuclear reactions ceased. The reason they can be so dense is apparent from the nature of the atoms which make them up. The electrons "in orbit" around the nuclei, as in the case of the solar system, are relatively far from the center of the atom, leaving much empty space. If the electrons were squeezed into the empty space by strong gravitational forces, a great deal of matter could be put in a small space. A white dwarf represents the limit to which matter may be squeezed in this way, and still remain atoms. However, matter can be squeezed even denser in some kinds of objects.

PULSARS

In 1967, when Cambridge was making a study of rapidly twinkling radio sources, using a radio telescope, an unexpected signal was detected. Pulses of radio waves were being received at extremely regular intervals of close to one second. After normal possibilities such as interference from manmade sources had been ruled out, the only alternative was that somewhere in the heavens there was some sort of object which could transmit radio signals with the regularity of a clock. The best explanation was that some spinning object was sending out a directional beam which regularly swept past the earth like a lighthouse beam. But an object which can spin in only one second cannot be too large before the speed of rotation exceeds the speed of light. It must be considerably smaller than the average star. In parallel with this, theoretical research was proceeding on objects called neutron stars. Until then they had never been seen. But once the curious radio signals were discovered, it was found that neutron stars would provide the best explanation. A neutron star is one in which matter has been squeezed even further than in a white dwarf, past the point where electrons are able to stay separate from the nucleus. They collapse into the nucleus and combine with protons to form neutrons. The whole star is one gigantic nucleus with no space at all between particles. A neutron star having the mass of the sun would take up a sphere only 12 miles in diameter. In a neutron star one cubic inch would weigh about 40 billion tons!

Since 1967 many other pulsars have been discovered. The fastest spinning is the one belonging to the Crab Nebula, the remnant of the supernova observed by the Chinese in A.D. 1054. This might indicate that a pulsar is what is left over after a supernova occurs. The Crab pulsar is spinning once every 33 milliseconds, or about 30 times per second. It appears that the energy lost by the pulsar as its spin slows—for a tiny decrease in the spin rate is observable—equals all the energy given off by the Crab Nebula, which is about 100,000 times the rate at which the sun radiates. The pulsar, in some as yet undetermined fashion, must be supplying all the energy which the nebula radiates.

An object only a few miles across, giving off 10^5 times as much energy as the sun, is more than slightly awesome. It is illustrative of the immense power of God, who created it. Perhaps in no better way is the greatness of the physical power at God's command displayed than in the astronomical objects which He has made. On earth we are already experiencing an energy shortage while using only one or two trillion watts, while the sun pours a million times that much power upon the surface of the earth constantly. This in turn is only one two-billionths of the power of the sun. Each pulsar supplies 100,000 times this much power, and in this galaxy alone there are at least 200 billion stars. Energy is being poured profligately into space at an inconceivable rate. This shrinks into insignificance compared to the universe, which is populated with billions of galaxies. All this energy is, in effect, going to waste. Doesn't this make it abundantly clear that God is able to supply all our needs far beyond anything we can ask or think?

PLANETARY NEBULAE

Another unusual object is the planetary nebula. This type of object really has nothing to do with planets, but derives its name from its planetary appearance when seen in a telescope. In reality, a planetary nebula is a spherically shaped shell of expanding gases which have been expelled from the surface of a star (figure 16). Though the stars themselves are too small to show a disk through a telescope, the gaseous shells are as much as a light year in diameter and can be seen as a ring around the star. The central star is always extremely hot, perhaps as a result of whatever violent event caused the shell to be expelled. Temperatures are typically $10^{5\circ}$ K. (200,000° F.), making them the hottest known stars. Though they are quite hot, they are not very bright, meaning that the star is small, sometimes as small as a white dwarf.

VARIABLE STARS

The most important class of unusual stars is the variables. As the name implies, variable stars change their brightness, either periodically or irregularly. There are many types of variables—regular, sporadic, and even novae and supernovae are included in this classification. Among the stars classed as variables there are those which do not actually vary in brightness themselves, but are caused to do so because they are eclipsed by other stars, just as the moon eclipses the sun. Among the regular variables are the Cepheids, the RR Lyrae variables, and the long period variables. The Cepheids are famous because they provided the means for the original estimates of intergalactic distances. The Magellanic Clouds are two irregularly shaped galaxies and among the closest to the Milky Way. None-

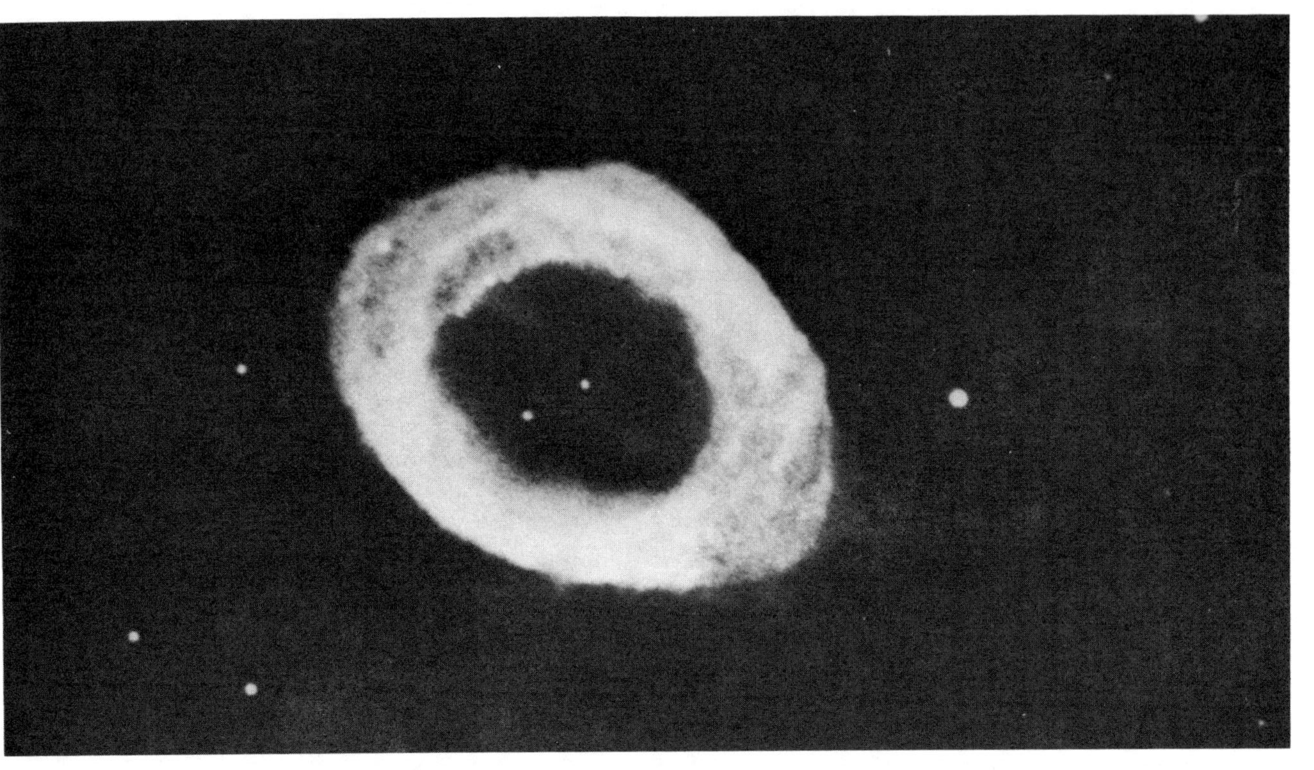

FIGURE 16.—The Ring Nebula. Lick Observatory Photograph.

theless, they are distant enough so that all the stars within them may safely be considered to be at the same distance from us. When Cepheid variables were discovered in the Magellanic clouds, it was observed that there was a direct relation between their brightness and the periods of their pulsations. Since all the stars were essentially at the same distance, the brightness differences could not be due to distance differences; they must be intrinsic. This means that the period of pulsations really does bear a relation to the brightness. Hence it was possible, once the scale had been worked out, to tell the actual brightness of a Cepheid variable if only the period could be measured. Once the actual brightness was known, one could measure the apparent brightness, and then calculate the distance from the difference. There is some uncertainty in the use of Cepheids for distance measurement, since the original formulation of the distance scale was based upon statistical methods; there are no Cepheids close enough to enable us to find their distances directly using parallax. But this uncertainty is not very large, and this method provided the first proof that other galaxies outside the Milky Way really existed. Cepheids are very bright, being yellow giants or supergiants, and can thus be seen at great distances. Their periods range from one to fifty days, and their light output varies by a factor of two or three from their brightest to their dimmest. Perhaps the most interesting fact about them is that their light variations are a result of real changes in the size of the stars. They expand and contract at speeds up to 12 miles per second. Polaris, the North Star, is a Cepheid, with a period of about four days.

RR Lyrae variables have also been used to measure distances. They are different from Cepheids in that all RR Lyrae variables have the same brightness. Their periods are shorter than those of the Cepheids, about .3 to .9 days. Thus when a star is recognized as an RR Lyrae variable from its short period, its brightness is immediately known and its distance is easily calculated.

There are many types of irregular variables. One of the most interesting types is called a flare star. A flare star is an M type star, cool and dim. But on occasion they can flare up in brightness for periods of a few minutes to half an hour. It is thought that the increase is due to a flare on the surface of the star, much like the solar flares that erupt on the sun from time to time. But since the M star is so much dimmer than the sun, a large flare can be much brighter in proportion to the total brightness of the star, and thus be more visible.

The most interesting of the irregular variables are the novae and supernovae. Both appear to be explosions involving whole stars and amazing increases in brightness. Within a few hours or a few days a nova can increase in brightness by over 100,000 times. It then begins to dim, rapidly at first, and then more slowly, until after a year or so it has returned to its pre-nova brightness. Meanwhile, a shell of gas has been blown off the star and has been rapidly expanding and can be seen growing in photographs. This cloud may be expanding as fast as 1,000 miles per second. Some stars appear to go through the nova stage repeatedly, with periods of a few years to perhaps a few thousand years.

The supernovae are the most fantastic showpieces of the universe, surpassed in brightness only by the famous quasars, and much more spectacular because of their changes in brightness. While a star is undergoing a supernova explosion it can outshine all the rest of the stars in its galaxy together. The brightest supernovae emit as much energy in one second as the sun does in three hundred years, completely dwarfing the energy output described for pulsars. It may remain at its brightest for about a week, decreasing to about half that in two months. When the event is over, only a small remnant of the original star remains. This may be the way in which pulsars are formed, but so far only two supernova remnants have been shown to be pulsars and the observational evidence is inconclusive.

No one knows what causes these tremendous explosions, though theories abound. The fact that they are so rare makes them difficult to study, and they remain somewhat of a mystery. It is estimated that in our galaxy a supernova occurs only once every three or four hundred years. However, they are bright enough to be seen easily in nearby galaxies, and are observable in even very distant ones. A total of over 50 supernovae have been observed if those in other galaxies are included.

The best known of all supernovae, of course, was the one observed on July 4, 1054, by the Chinese. It grew to be as bright as Venus and was visible during the day. In that location we now see the Crab Nebula, an expanding cloud of glowing gases, showing a faint green color in photographs. It is expanding at the rate of 800 miles per second.

In this chapter we have seen objects and events that cause us to stand in reverential awe of the One who created them. Truly in the heavens we have seen the glory of God, and in the firmament His handiwork. We have seen everything from the ultimately dense to the perfect vacuum, from the largest star to the smallest dwarf, from the brightest objects in the universe to the dimmest, and from the hottest to the coldest. Surely our God is a God of amazing talent and imagination, greatly to be reverenced, feared, worshiped, and loved. We have spent much time trying to show, in our own inadequate way, that God is glorified because the heavens prove the truth of His word. But in the end it is the heavens themselves which speak, showing His glory and revealing His eternal power and deity. And that is why He made them.

9 GALAXIES

A casual observation of the sky on a clear night reveals only bright points of light, mostly stars and a planet or two. In all only about 6,000 stars are visible to the unaided eye. Closer observation reveals there are occasional fuzzy patches and bright, indistinct regions. These are usually star clusters or star clouds, where the number of stars become increasingly faint until the eye can no longer distinguish individual stars. On a very dark night, far away from city lights, a faint band of light can be seen stretching across the sky—the Milky Way. This is our own galaxy, the one of which the sun is a tiny member. This faint band is really composed of uncounted thousands of stars which together give a faint glow to the sky but individually are almost invisible. This is all the ancients could have known of galaxies, for almost nothing outside the Milky Way is visible without a telescope.

In the southern hemisphere the Magellanic Clouds have been known for centuries, but it has only recently been realized that they are galaxies independent of the Milky Way, each containing billions of stars of its own. In the northern hemisphere, if you know just where to look and the sky is dark, you can see the center of the famous Andromeda Galaxy, a spiral galaxy much like our own.

The structure of our own galaxy being obscure, and that of other galaxies being virtually invisible, it is no wonder that there is no mention of galaxies in the Bible. There were still visible stars sufficient in number to show God's glory. They were a standard of comparison when one wanted to talk about inconceivably large numbers; there was no need for more. But today's instruments have opened the heavens. They have brought wonders to our eyes of which the ancients could never have dreamed, and which, even to our minds glutted with superlatives and "astronomical" numbers of our day, inspire such awe that our minds fail to comprehend. As our capacity to observe and understand grows, the power and majesty of God as revealed in the heavens grows even faster. The deeper we probe into space, the greater the wonders we see, from the standpoint of both beauty and power. Though galaxies are not mentioned in the Bible, they still show the glory of God and the truth of His word.

THE MILKY WAY

The study of galaxies begins with our own, the Milky Way, or, as it is called, simply the Galaxy. The band of light visible in the night sky is only a small portion of the entire galaxy. Most of it is forever obscured from our eyes by vast clouds of dust and gas which are found throughout the galaxy. With so little really visible, it is not surprising that until recently the entire universe was thought to consist of our own galaxy, with the earth occupying a favored position at the center. Nothing outside was known. It was not until 1924 that the existence of other galaxies than our own was finally proved.

The Milky Way belongs to a class of galaxies known as spirals, an example of which is shown in figure 17. At the center is the nucleus, a dense region of stars. Here the stars are so close together they cannot be seen individually. Projecting from the nucleus are the features which give the spiral its name, the spiral arms. There are usually two distinct arms in a galaxy, but often there are three or more. Sometimes the arms are broken, segmented, or forked, so that it cannot be said how many arms it really has. In the arms of the nearer galaxies the brighter stars can be photographed individually. The first Cepheids outside our own galaxy were identified in spiral arms of nearby galaxies, such as Andromeda. They proved that these other "nebulae" were really distant island universes like the Milky Way and not just a part of our own Galaxy. The Galaxy is about 100,000 light years across and contains 10^{11} stars, an unimaginable number. The solar system is 30,000 light years from the center, putting it near the edge of the Galaxy and in one of the spiral arms known as the Orion arm. Portions of two other arms have been identified, the

FIGURE 17.—The Andromeda Galaxy. Lick Observatory Photograph.

Perseus arm and the Sagittarius arm. The total structure of the Galaxy is not known, and even the local arms are known imperfectly.

Nebulae

But a galaxy is made up of more than just stars. A large part of any spiral galaxy is the clouds of gas and dust which are another of its distinguishing features. The ellipticals, which are the other major classification of galaxies, have little or none. If it were not for the matter between the stars, the interstellar matter, we would be able to see clear across the Galaxy. As it is, these clouds, though extremely tenuous, prevent us from seeing most of the Galaxy, obscuring stars farther away than about 6,000 light years. At its densest a gas cloud might have 1,000 to 10,000 atoms per cubic centimeter, compared to 2.6×10^{19} atoms per cubic centimeter of earth's atmosphere at sea level. Still, over a distance of thousands of light years, this amounts to a great deal of material, plenty to blot out any distant stars.

These clouds do not fall at random in the Galaxy but tend to concentrate in the inner edges of the spiral arms. They also tend to lie in the plane of the Galaxy, blocking our view of the rest of the Galaxy which falls in the same plane. If we look "upwards" or "downwards" (away from the plane of the Galaxy), the view is much clearer. It is through these thinner areas in the clouds that we are able to see other galaxies outside our own. The reason it was once thought that the earth was at the center of the Galaxy is that stars tend to fall off in number at the same rate, no matter what direction one looks. If, for instance, we were at the edge of the Galaxy, the number of stars should be less in the direction of the edge than in the direction of the center. We now know that this is only apparently the case, and that it is the dust clouds which make it appear that stars fall off at the same rate in all directions.

Another strange effect that dust has upon starlight is that it absorbs more blue light than it does red. This means that the light which succeeds in passing through the dust is redder than when it entered. Consequently, a distant star looks redder than it really is, and of a different spectral type. The farther away a star, the stronger is the effect. This adds a special complication to the determination of distances in the Galaxy, but corrections can be made.

The interstellar matter which we have roughly been referring to as clouds can be divided into two types of material—gas and dust. By far the majority of interstellar matter is in the form of gas, mostly hydrogen, with some helium, and traces of other elements. The dust, also called interstellar grains, composes only about one percent of the interstellar matter. Dust grains are extremely small, being probably only 1/30,000 to 1/50,000 of an inch in diameter. It is the grains of dust which actually do the obscuring of distant stars; the gas absorbs very little light. How, it may be asked, if the gigantic stars can be seen only as points of light, could we ever determine that interstellar grains are so small? It is not because they can be seen or measured directly, but by the effects they have upon the light passing through them. The reddening effect can take place only when the absorbing grains are of about the same size as the wavelength of the light which they are scattering, and the wavelength of visible light is very small.

These clouds are seen in photographs as either light or dark nebulae. The word *nebula* simply means cloud. A dark nebula is dark because the dust it contains absorbs the light from the stars behind it, creating the appearance of an area of sky devoid of stars. It was once thought that this was actually the case. However, it became obvious that the stars are only obscured.

These minute interstellar grains have a contribution to make to the cause of creationism. When one considers how grains might form from lone atoms wandering in space, it becomes apparent that it will take a very long time for these grains to accumulate much matter, since there are so few atoms to begin with. In fact, calculations show that if one starts with a minute amount of matter much smaller than a grain—and imagine that every time it strikes another atom they will stick together—then it will take at least three billion years for the grains to grow to the size we find them to be. If one uses a more realistic assumption, that only a certain fraction of those atoms which it strikes will actually stick, then the time required for the grain to grow to its present size is much longer than the age of the universe.[1] Further, there are processes which oppose the grainbuilding process during this time and tend to destroy the grains. At the very least this will slow down the growth further and make grain formation by this process extremely doubtful. For instance, another fast-moving atom or a photon of light might strike the grain and knock off a number of atoms. Or, since the most abundant atom in space is the hydrogen atom, it will be the most likely to strike the grain. These, if they

1. Harwit, *Astrophysical Concepts,* p. 394.

FIGURE 18.—The Pleiades. Lick Observatory Photograph.

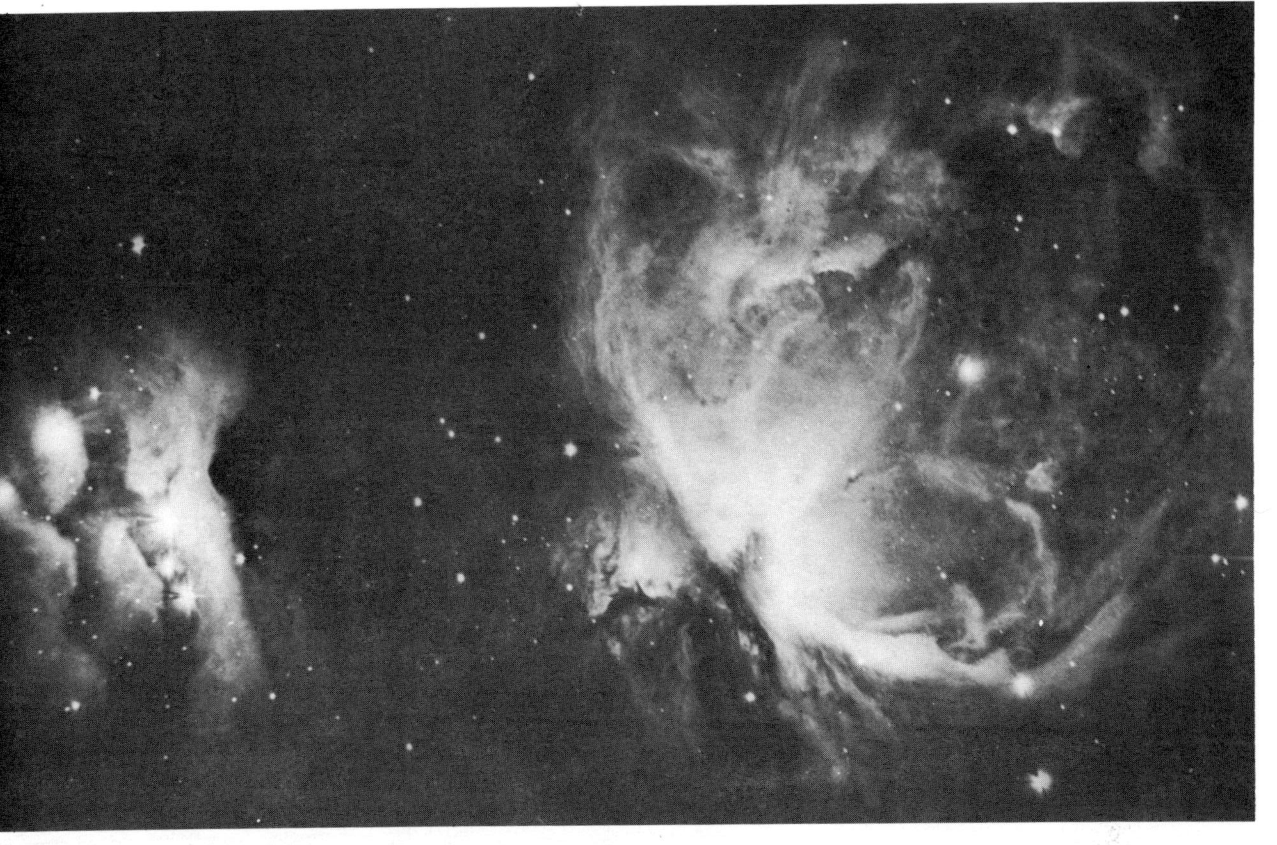

FIGURE 19.—The Orion Nebula. Lick Observatory Photograph.

did stick in the first place, would quickly boil off again, since the temperature, even in the coldness of space, is high enough to prevent them from "freezing" to the grain.

These arguments also apply to another class of interstellar matter, the interstellar molecules. In recent years radio telescopes have detected a growing number of complex molecules in the dust clouds of space, including water, carbon dioxide, and molecules as complex as formaldehyde. How can such complex molecules form in space, where their chance of meeting just the right atom to make that molecule is extremely small? To be sure, they are very rare compared to the molecules in the earth's atmosphere, but there still must be an extremely large number of them to be detected here on earth. For instance, in one cloud, ethyl alcohol, the kind used in alcoholic beverages, was found. In the one cloud alone there is enough alcohol to fill 10^{28} fifths of 100 proof.[2] This would fill a sphere 1,000 times the volume of the earth! Molecule formation and destruction is not a well-understood process, but it seems certain that so many complex molecules could not form by chance encounters of atoms. The reasonable alternative is that they were created as they are now.

The other type of nebula is a light nebula. As the name implies, instead of appearing as a dark patch with no stars, a light nebula is a light area, appearing to shine by its own light. There are three reasons a nebula can appear light. In one case, the dust cloud is not different from a dark nebula, but happens to fall near a bright star. The light of the star reflects off the dust and causes it to appear light. This is called a reflection nebula. An example is shown in figure 18, which is a photograph of the Pleiades star cluster.

The second reason that a nebula might appear light is because of the gas and not the dust. If a nebula falls near a hot star, some of the radiation from the star is absorbed by the atoms of gas, which then reradiate it at a different wavelength. This is called fluorescence and is the same principle involved in an ordinary fluorescent light bulb. An example of this is the most famous nebula of all, the Orion Nebula, figure 19. This is easily found in the winter sky as the middle "star" of Orion's sword.

The Crab Nebula is an example of the third means by which a nebula might appear bright. The Crab Nebula's light is what is called synchrotron radiation, a rather exotic process. Free electrons with

2. *Science News* 108 (1975), 257.

speeds close to that of light are spiraling around the magnetic field in the nebula. As they spiral, they give off radiation. These electrons are thought to be somehow emitted by the pulsar at the center of the nebula. This mode of radiation is fairly common among energetic celestial objects. Another object which commonly emits synchrotron radiation is a quasar.

We have in these objects a marvelous example of God's handiwork. In describing these objects it is easy to concentrate on the physical mechanisms involved in their giving of light and to treat the objects as textbook examples of these various mechanisms. But in doing this we tend to forget the objects themselves as seen entirely apart from any physics. Nebulae are objects of great beauty, subtle color, and awesome size. Like dark giants, they engulf whole groups of stars, rendering them invisible. Or they surround and amplify the tremendous light and glory of stars thousands of times brighter than the sun. Or they glow mysteriously with a dim light created by billions of invisible electrons spiraling in magnetic fields in the blackness of space. How fortunate we are that God chose to sprinkle the heavens with such beauty as this and to show His handiwork in so many marvelous ways. As we venture farther and farther into space, we are continually confronted with new objects, all beautiful in their own way and all pointing to the masterful skill of their Creator.

Star Clusters

Some of the most important components of the Galaxy are the star clusters. Many of the stars that make up the Galaxy reside in these clusters, and the clusters are distributed in an orderly way throughout the Galaxy. Clusters fall generally into two types—galactic clusters and globular clusters. Galactic (or open) clusters tend to fall in the regions of the spiral arms. The positions of these clusters, along with the clouds of interstellar matter, delineate the positions of the arms. Galactic clusters, having a relatively small number of stars, are not strongly bound together by their mutual gravitation. They are basically unstable, and after a few million to a few billion years, should they exist that long, they break apart into individual stars. The continued existence of these clusters, however, is not proof of a young universe, since astronomers maintain that such clusters are still in the process of forming.

The globular clusters tend to fall preferentially near the center of the Galaxy. One third of all known globular clusters (about 120 in all) fall in only two percent of the total area of the sky, near the constellation Sagittarius. This is believed to be the direction of the center of the Galaxy. Finding the distances to these clusters is a tricky matter. Even though some have variable stars whose brightness can be used to determine distances, there is the problem of the absorption of light by interstellar matter, making their actual brightnesses uncertain. The distances are found using the RR Lyrae variables mentioned earlier and vary from 15,000 to as much as 80,000 light years from us. The fact that they appear to be moving very rapidly and that they all tend to fall in the same region of sky suggests that they are in orbit around the massive nucleus of the Galaxy. This is one reason for believing the center to lie in the direction of Sagittarius.

Globular clusters have no gas or dust within them and hence star formation is impossible there. Added to this are the facts that on the HR diagram the turnoff point toward the giant region is well down the main sequence, and that they consist primarily of Population II stars, which are thought to be old anyway. This causes astronomers to believe that globular clusters are among the oldest things in existence. These observations taken together tend to indicate an old age for these clusters. There is no doubt that this conclusion is a reasonable one, considering how the evidence is stated. But there are problems.

One aspect of the study of globular clusters that raises some interesting questions concerning age is the subject of cluster dynamics. This is simply the study of the way that stars within the cluster move and how the structure of the cluster as a whole is affected. The pertinent number to describe the dynamics of a cluster is called the relaxation time. This may be described as the time between the formation of a cluster and the period when it reaches an unchanging state. This state is characterized by what is called the equipartition of energy. This simply means that, on the average, all stars within the cluster, no matter what their size, have about the same amount of energy. Thus large, massive stars will be moving slowly and will have about the same energy as a smaller, quickly moving star. Since massive stars move slowly, they will tend to settle down at the center of the cluster, while the smaller, faster stars will be farther away from the center. Thus a globular cluster in equilibrium will have a core with primarily heavy, slow stars and a halo with light quick stars. Clear?

The relaxation times for globular clusters are variously estimated at from 10^7 to 10^{13} years, depending upon whom you consult.[3] In the latter case, astronomers are in deep trouble, because this is a thousand times older than the universe, and many globular clusters are now observed to be in a state of equilibrium, at least in their core regions. This would mean that the globular clusters would have to have been created already in a state of equilibrium, since that state never could have been reached in the time they have existed. In practice, however, the lower limit of 10^7 years is usually used, and a relaxation time of 10^9 years is considered long.

In order to solve the problem of long relaxation times, astronomers postulate that the cluster core undergoes "violent relaxation," which means that the heavy stars in the center collapse to form extremely dense objects, perhaps even black holes.[4] This idea is encouraged by the fact that some globular clusters have recently been shown to be x-ray sources, and black holes ought to be an excellent source of x-rays. An interesting thing about this model is that eventually the entire core of the cluster should collapse into an infinitely dense hole, and that within only about 3 to 15 relaxation times.[5] Since for clusters with "short" relaxation times this period has already elapsed (if the universe is really old), there remains the question, whatever happened to all those collapsed globular clusters? Their absence is a mystery.[6]

In light of the above theories, an x-ray globular cluster should therefore be one which has a short relaxation time and has thus had its core collapse into a black hole. But there is one globular cluster x-ray source, called NGC 6712, which has no central condensation at all, a low central density, and a long relaxation time.[7] This is just the reverse of what is expected. Apparently the theory is incorrect. Cluster dynamics, however, is one area of intensive research of late, and we certainly have not heard the last word on the subject.

This is based upon globular clusters within our own galaxy. But when we begin to examine those in other galaxies, we find a different story. Andromeda's globular clusters have a larger abundance of heavy elements, about the same as in our sun, which is a Population I star. This makes them "young."[8] In the Magellanic Clouds the sit-

---

3. N. A. Bahcall and M. A. Hausman, *Astrophysical Journal* 213 (1977), 93; Harwit, *Astrophysical Concepts*, p. 94.
4. A. P. Lightman, *Astrophysical Journal* 221 (1978), 567.
5. A. P. Lightman, *Astrophysical Journal* 215 (1977), 914.
6. W. H. Press and S. A. Teukolsky, *Astrophysical Journal* 213 (1977), 183.
7. S. L. Shapiro, *Astrophysical Journal* 217 (1977), 281.
8. H. Shapley, *Galaxies* (Cambridge: Harvard University Press, 1972), p. 116.

uation is even more difficult. The globular clusters seem to be made primarily of bright, early stars, that is, young stars not more than a few million years old.[9] And yet astronomers believe that all globular clusters formed at about the same time.

There are other globular clusters which are near the Milky Way galaxy but which are moving extremely fast. They are moving so fast that they will not orbit the center of the Galaxy like other globular clusters, but will escape from the Galaxy entirely within a few million or billion years. But if this is so, how can it be that after billions of years they are still near our galaxy? At these speeds they should have escaped long ago. The obvious answer is that they have not been moving that fast for very long, and that they were created recently. Not only that, but their shape indicates that they have not been influenced by the gravity of the Milky Way. If they had ever been close to the Galaxy, it would have distorted their shape.[10] They are fairly close now, but they have not been much closer. This implies that the time they have been traveling at their high speeds has been very short indeed. They were thus created recently, but contain stars which apparently are billions of years old. An interesting combination. How reliable are astronomical ages, really?

There is one further thing which globular clusters have to say about their ages. Globular clusters contain hundreds of thousands of stars, each one of which, like the sun, should have its own solar wind. Now, the total amount of mass given off by the sun in its wind is not large, but when multiplied by 100,000 stars, and carried on over a period of millions or billions of years, it does indeed amount to a great deal of matter. One estimate is that in 10 million years a globular cluster with one million stars should have accumulated a mass of gas equal to 50 times the mass of the sun.[11] This should be an easily detectable amount. However, a survey of nearly 50 globular clusters, almost half of those known, has shown that there is no such buildup of gas.

Attempted explanations appeared immediately. Perhaps the gas was emitted at such a great speed that it did not accumulate in the clusters, but escaped entirely. In this case no buildup would be expected. Now some clusters are bound together more tightly than others, and it has been since shown that even though this might explain why gas

9. Ibid., pp. 40-47.
10. Harwit, *Astrophysical Concepts,* p. 43.
11. J. E. Hesser and S. J. Shawl, *Astrophysical Journal* 217 (1977), 143.

was not found in some of the clusters, those clusters which were more tightly bound should still retain the gas.[12] Another possibility is that since these clusters are apparently in orbit about the center of the Galaxy, they must periodically pass through the disk of the Galaxy. Perhaps at this time the gas is somehow swept out of the clusters, maybe by encounter with clouds of dust and gas in the galactic disk. However, the time given above, 10 million years, is about the amount of time between these encounters of the globular clusters with the galactic disk. The intracluster gas should build up to the 50 solar mass level between each encounter. Thus this explanation does no good.

Another possibility is that the Galaxy has surrounding it a halo which contains a thin gas of its own. If the cluster is moving fast enough through this gas, the pressure it produces may constantly sweep all the stellar wind gas out of the cluster, preventing any buildup. Again, however, calculations show that this mechanism would not be entirely effective. There should still be clusters which would be able to retain the gas.[13] There is no way to explain why such gas has not been detected, except that there has not been time since the creation of these clusters for such gas to build up. Globular clusters are young objects.

Radio Waves

We have seen a little of the structure of the Galaxy. It has a nucleus surrounded by spiral arms. The arms fall in the plane called the disk. The nucleus is thicker than the disk and is called the central bulge. Surrounding the entire galaxy is a spherical region called the halo, or corona. In the halo there is a thin haze of individual stars as well as the globular clusters. Much of the structure of the Galaxy has been determined without the aid of visible light. One major source of information is the radio waves that come from other parts of the Galaxy, for while much of the interstellar matter is opaque to visible light, it is transparent to radio waves of the right frequency. In fact, it is the clouds themselves which emit (and absorb) the radio waves, and which thus are used to outline the otherwise invisible portions of the Galaxy. The increased radio emission from the Sagit-

12. D. A. VandenBerg and D. J. Faulkner, *Astrophysical Journal* 218 (1977), 415.
13. Ibid.

tarius region is another reason for suspecting that it is in this direction that the center of the Galaxy lies.

It is actually the hydrogen in the clouds which produces the radio signals. It is characteristic of hydrogen to emit radio waves with a precise wavelength, 21 centimeters. (By contrast, the radio waves of the normal AM broadcast band have a wavelength of about half a mile.) All radio telescopes can actually do is discern that a signal is coming from a particular direction. In order to convert this into a picture of our Galaxy, the Doppler shifts are measured as well. One can thus tell how the clouds are moving with respect to us. This, combined with a model of how the Galaxy is rotating, indicates where the clouds are and how they are moving. If it is assumed that the clouds fall within the spiral arms, as they are observed to do elsewhere, the clouds thus outline the spiral arms of the Milky Way. The amount of information is still meager, and there is little agreement among the various investigators who have attempted to map the Milky Way. What is definitely known is that the Milky Way does possess a spiral structure, and that all maps have shown disconnected segments which appear to be parts of spiral arms.

But how do we know that the Galaxy is rotating? First, if it were not rotating, it would collapse under its own gravitation, just as the planets would collapse into the sun if they were not in orbit around it. There is also evidence of rotation in other spiral galaxies, for Doppler shifts of light from different portions of these galaxies indicate motion consistent with rotation. Finally, the rotation of the Galaxy in the neighborhood of the sun can actually be measured. The Doppler shifts of nearby stars indicate that they are all moving with respect to the sun in the way that would be expected if they are all rotating together around the center of the Galaxy.

GALAXY TYPES

This is about as far as we can go with a galaxy in which we are embedded. To further investigate the structure of galaxies requires looking to those outside our own, since they can be seen as a whole. We have talked about spirals so far because we believe that we are a part of one, and also because they have more apparent structure than other types and are thus more interesting. The elliptical galaxies are the second major classification of galaxies, and have very little visible structure. There is a third class, called irregulars—galaxies which cannot be made to fit into the other two classifications. The spirals

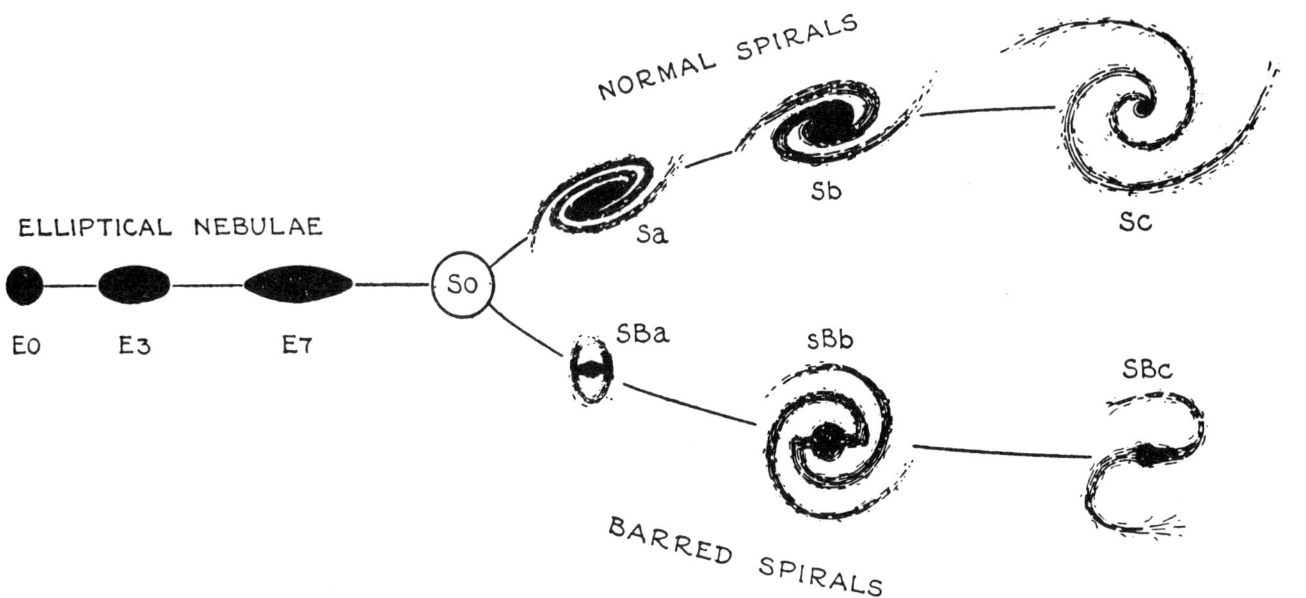

FIGURE 20.—The sequence of nebular types. Yerkes Observatory Photograph.

usually do not conform to the idealized structure of a nucleus with two symmetrical spiral arms emanating from them. Most spirals have arms with holes, forks, loops, or other strange features. There is a continuous range of shapes and sizes which, just like stars within the spectral classification, can be arranged in a line with properties gradually changing from one galaxy to the next in a smooth sequence. At the start of the sequence are the elliptical galaxies, which are circular in shape. They share many properties with globular clusters but are much larger. They are brighter at the center than at the edges, but do not have a well-defined nucleus like the spirals. Elliptical galaxies, like globular clusters, consist primarily of Population II stars and have little or no dust or gas.

As we progress along the galaxy sequence, the elliptical galaxies get flatter and flatter, until they are almost cigar shaped. At this point there is a transition from ellipticals to spirals. The nucleus becomes better defined and the fuzziness at the edges begins to show some structure. Further down the line the edges begin to look more and more like arms until, when we reach the extreme spiral end of the sequence, there are galaxies like that of figure 17. Not even part of the sequence are the irregular galaxies, which can be almost any shape. The Magellanic Clouds are irregular galaxies.

In the sequence of galaxy types I neglected to mention that about half way through there is a fork in the road. At the point where the ellipticals give way to spirals there is a division into two types of spirals—the normal ones discussed so far, and the barred spirals. A barred spiral differs from a normal one in that the arms, instead of starting at the nucleus, begin at the ends of a solid-looking bar of stars passing through the nucleus. Sometimes they begin from a ring which entirely circles the nucleus. It is not known how the bar shape can exist, but it appears to rotate almost as a solid bar instead of the normal differential rotation where the inner portions move more quickly than the outer portions.

This differential rotation presents a problem for astronomers if spiral galaxies are really very old. The fact that they appear as spirals at all suggests that in some manner they are being wound up. This is a simple result of the laws governing orbiting objects. By measuring the Doppler shift it is possible to tell that it takes a galaxy about 100 million years to turn once on its axis for a middle portion of an arm. Now, if a galaxy is about 10 billion years old, as astronomers believe, it should have turned about 100 times. However, in-

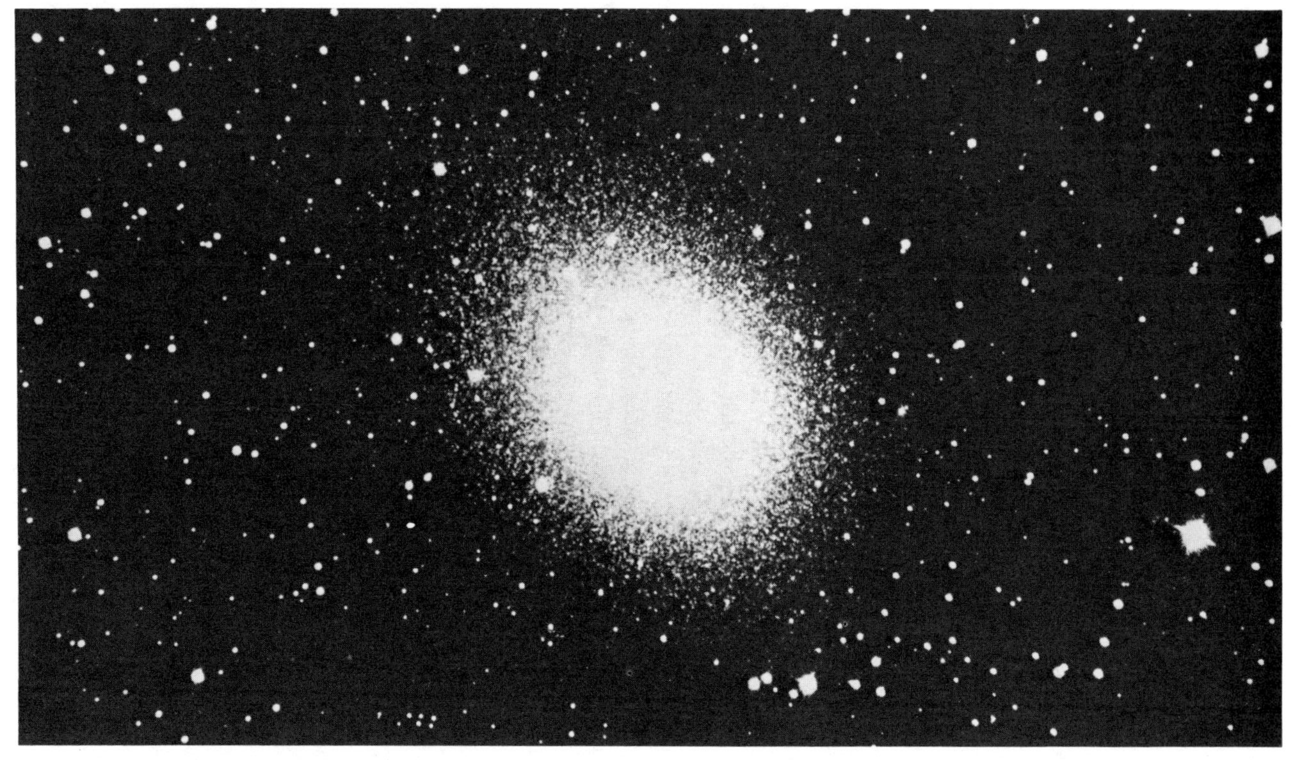

FIGURE 21.—Elliptical galaxy NGC 185. Yerkes Observatory Photograph.

stead of seeing the arms wrapped around the nucleus 100 times, at most one or two revolutions are seen. This suggests an upper limit for the age of the galaxy of 200 million years. This, of course, is considerably longer than the 10,000 years suggested by creationism, but recall that this is a maximum possible age. The real age could be anything less than this if we assume that galaxies could have been created with a spiral structure already. There are, of course, many theories as to why spiral arms appear as they do, but there is as yet no complete explanation.

The Size and Complexity of Galaxies

Galaxies range in size from the very small to the very large. Dwarf ellipticals may be only somewhat larger than a globular cluster in the Milky Way. In these dwarf galaxies there are more age problems for the evolutionary scientists. Galaxies possess relaxation times just as we discussed previously for globular clusters. Once again, the relaxation time is the time required for the galaxy to adjust itself so that no significant changes are taking place in its shape. Another way of saying this is that stars have been so disturbed by the gravitational effects of other stars that there no longer remains any hint of what their original orbits were. Observations of the dwarf galaxies indicate that they are relaxed. Calculations, on the other hand, indicate a relaxation time for dwarf galaxies of about 10^{13} years, again, 1,000 times the supposed age of the universe.[14] There is no alternative but that the galaxies were created already in the relaxed state.

The level of the galaxies is another fitting place to stop and admire God's handiwork. As we advance to each higher level of organization in the universe, God has been there first, arranging and creating. Whether we look at the smallest observable atom or the largest galaxies, we see beauty and order. At each progressively larger distance God has placed a signpost—the sun, another star, a galaxy—each larger and brighter, and, if possible, more beautiful than before. As P. J. E. Peebles points out, "In a sense the miracle is not that the universe contains irregularities like galaxies, but that the universe is as approximately uniform as it is."[15] He says that a universe with no irregularities is understandable, but that once an irregularity starts,

14. P. W. Hodge, *Galaxies and Cosmology* (New York: McGraw Hill, 1966), p. 124.

15. P. J. E. Peebles, *Physical Cosmology* (Princeton: Princeton University Press, 1971), p. 213.

it tends to get progressively worse. In the end matter should pile up in lumps much denser than galaxies. The fact that we have neither an empty universe nor one filled with dense lumps is testimony to the guiding hand of God in creation. A universe like ours does not simply happen by itself.

CLUSTERS OF GALAXIES

Galaxies are not loners. Like stars, galaxies tend to come in clusters. A cluster of galaxies may have as few as two or as many as thousands of members. At least half of all galaxies, and maybe all galaxies, are members of clusters. The Milky Way belongs to a relatively small cluster of galaxies called the Local Group. The most recent count indicates 21 members, but more are being discovered year by year. The Local Group contains both spirals and ellipticals as well as some dwarf galaxies, extremely faint and small. The size of the cluster is about 2.5 million light years, or roughly 25 times the diameter of the Milky Way. The best-known member, other than ourselves, is the Andromeda Galaxy, also known as M31. It is a spiral somewhat larger than the Milky Way. It is one of the farthest members from us in the Local Group, being about two million light years away. Doppler shifts indicate that it actually is approaching us at a speed of 128 kilometers per second. There is a hierarchy in the clustering of galaxies as there is for everything else. Andromeda, a member of the Local Group, has satellites of its own, two small elliptical galaxies. There is some indication that the Milky Way also has galaxies in orbit around it. The Milky Way and Andromeda galaxies are members of a small cluster of galaxies. There may be higher levels of organization as well, since clusters tend to cluster. A cluster of clusters of galaxies is called a supercluster. Some astronomers have even postulated super-superclusters, but it is impossible to tell as yet whether such things exist.

One of the most convincing available proofs of a young universe comes from the study of clusters of galaxies. It is apparent that the force holding a cluster of galaxies together is their mutual gravitation. The question naturally arises as to whether the clusters thus bound are stable or unstable, that is, have they always appeared and will they always appear as they do now? or will the cluster eventually break up with each member galaxy going its own way? If the cluster is gravitationally bound, then there is enough mass within it to produce gravitational forces sufficient to hold the cluster together. The reason the cluster needs to be held together is that the individual galaxies often have large velocities which would carry them out of the cluster in a short time (a few million years) were they not sufficiently restrained by the gravitational attraction of the other members. A simple analogy is a rocket sent from the earth into space. If the rocket is not moving very fast, it will reach a maximum height and then fall back to the earth. It may have just enough energy to put a satellite into orbit around the earth so that it remains in place permanently without escaping from the earth. But if we wish to send a rocket to the moon, we must give it a much higher initial speed, so that it escapes completely from the earth's pull. In deciding whether our moving rocket is bound to the earth or not, we must take two factors into account—the mass of the earth, which determines what the gravitational forces are, and the speed of the rocket.

Measuring the Speed of Clusters

When dealing with clusters of galaxies, scientists must have the same type of information. Computations are considerably more difficult because there are so many members to take into consideration. The speeds of the individual galaxies are easy to estimate from their Doppler shifts. In practice, the Doppler shifts give only the speeds of the galaxies in the line of sight, that is, the speeds at which they are moving directly towards us or away from us. The speeds at which they are moving from left or right must be estimated to give the entire speeds. But in large clusters it is enough to assume that the speeds in the various directions average about the same.

Measuring Cluster Mass: Three Methods

It is the masses which are difficult to determine and thus make the problem of determining the boundedness of clusters troublesome. There are a number of ways to do it, some more accurate than others. The internal rotation method uses the Doppler shifts to determine how fast the galaxy is spinning. The rate of spin varies from its inner to its outer parts as we have seen before. Using laws of orbital mechanics, it is possible to estimate the mass of the galaxy. This is the most accurate method, but it is difficult to apply and can be used for only the nearest of spiral galaxies. Galaxies farther away appear too small to make the required measurements, and most clusters of interest are too far away. Thus the best that this method can do is give an indication of the average masses of certain types of galaxies near to us.

The second method is the double-galaxy method. It uses the same method that enables astronomers to find the masses of double stars, but more assumptions are required and the results are less accurate. This is because for the double-star method the period of revolution of one star about the other can be easily measured, as can the orbit. For galaxies, however, the period of revolution is much too long to be measurable, and hence we cannot tell the shape of the orbit either. How can anything be done at all, then? Individual masses cannot be determined, but averages for various types can be, using statistical methods. The assumption which is required, and which we shall see in a few moments is probably correct, is that these pairs of galaxies are really in orbit about each other and not just appearing to be. If this is not true, the results of the double-galaxy method would be meaningless. This does have an advantage over the internal rotation method, since it can be used for elliptical galaxies. This is because it depends only upon the motions of the galaxy as a whole and not upon internal motions. Elliptical galaxies obviously do not have spiral arms in which such motions can be measured. Masses measured in this way agree tolerably well with those obtained by the internal rotation method.

The third method is to use the virial theorem. This theorem is too complex to give in detail here, but because of its importance to the discussion I shall try to give a general picture of it. In physics two kinds of energy are recognized—potential and kinetic. Kinetic energy is the familiar energy of motion: the faster something is moving, the more kinetic energy it has. The energy of motion is given by the familiar formula:

$$E = \tfrac{1}{2}MV^2.$$

Here M is the mass of the moving object and V is its speed. If the speed of the object is doubled, the energy is increased by four times, i.e., 2^2. The total kinetic energy of a cluster of galaxies is the total of the individual kinetic energies of each galaxy. The kinetic energy of each galaxy is determined by the formula above.

Potential energy is harder to understand. Potential energy can be thought of as energy stored in the gravitational fields of the galaxies. For example, if we imagine two stationary galaxies a certain distance apart, their mutual gravitation will cause them to begin moving towards each other. When they finally collide, they will be moving with a particular speed (V). The kinetic energy formula can then be used to determine what their energies are. This kinetic energy had to come from somewhere, for energy cannot appear out of nothing. Since it was the gravitational forces which brought about the motion, it is apparent that the energy was stored in the gravitational fields of the galaxies. It was potentially there and could appear as kinetic energy, or energy of motion, at a later time. Hence the name potential energy, which is abbreviated as PE. Now the virial theorem states that for a large number of objects which are gravitationally bound to each other, the total kinetic energy equals –½PE. Very simple, right? But how can there be negative energy? Saying that the potential energy is negative means that one has to *add* energy to the system to drive the objects apart and put them out of range of each other's gravitational forces. This state is said to possess zero energy, so they must have had negative energy before the energy was added to break up the system.

Now, while kinetic energy depends upon the masses and the speeds of the individual galaxies involved, the potential energy depends upon their masses and their positions, that is, the gravitational forces depend upon the distances between the galaxies. This should be obvious, since in our example the farther apart the stationary galaxies were placed, the faster they would be moving when they finally collided, and hence the more energy they would have. Now, if the masses are so difficult to measure individually, why don't astronomers just measure the speeds and positions of the galaxies involved and use these to find the total mass? The virial formula tells us how these quantities all relate. But remember, before one can use the virial theorem, he has to assume that the cluster of galaxies is stable. If he has incorrectly assumed that the cluster is stable, the wrong masses will result. This will be apparent when comparing the masses derived by using the virial theorem with those derived from the other two methods.

Discrepancies Among the Three Methods

When the masses are computed with these three methods, there is a large discrepancy among them. The first two methods agree rather well, implying that the assumption that the pairs of galaxies were in orbit around each other was a good one. But the masses given by the virial theorem are radically different, being from ten to 100 times higher than the masses determined by other methods. Now, the first two methods required rather few assumptions, basically that the laws of physics apply everywhere, and, in the case of the double-galaxy method, that they were in orbit around each other. The agreement between the first two methods implies the validity of the second assumption. The virial theorem method also makes this assumption, that the cluster is in a state of equilibrium. But doing so yields masses that are obviously wrong. This means that the assumption of equilibrium is wrong. The masses of the individual galaxies are not great enough to hold the member galaxies together. The actual speeds measured for galaxies in clusters range from zero to hundreds of miles per second. At this rate the clusters as we see them will be totally dispersed in about 10 million years. Ten million years may sound like a long time, but this is the time required for clusters to totally disperse, and they obviously have not done so yet. Thus the clusters must be less than 10 million years old.

Now, if the clusters of galaxies are less than 10 million years old, so are the stars within the galaxies, and any planets revolving around them. Astronomers in answer to this say that there are three possibilities: (1) there is more mass in the clusters than can be seen, and it is enough to cause the clusters to be bound; (2) all clusters are really breaking up; or (3) we do not understand physics on such a large scale. The conclusion which we reached, that all clusters are really breaking up, is almost universally rejected by astronomers, since they have already decided that the clusters are billions of years old. If this is the case, they obviously cannot be breaking up. Nor are astronomers about to change their minds on the age question. Possibility number three is seldom invoked, since to admit that we do not understand the physical laws by which the universe operates is to end all astronomy and most of physics, because once we allow this we cannot come to any conclusions about how things behave anywhere in the universe except here. All research is at an end.

Therefore astronomers postulate that somewhere in these clusters of galaxies is some "missing mass." They say that since the galaxies apparently are not massive enough to hold the clusters together, there must be some matter within the cluster which is invisible to us but which is real enough and massive enough to hold the cluster together. Since the galaxies have too little mass by a factor of from 10 to 100, there must be 10 to 100 times as much invisible mass as visible mass. This sounds unreasonable, as some admit. How could so much mass be invisible? To date there is little evidence of any missing mass.[16]

---

16. T. L. Swihart, *Astrophysics and Stellar Astronomy* (New York: John Wiley and Sons, 1968), p. 227.

Just like Oort's cloud of invisible comets, missing mass was invented for the sole purpose of saving a theory from the evidence.

A number of possible types of matter that should be invisible from earth have been proposed as candidates for residents of clusters of galaxies. But in most cases so far, someone has subsequently thought of a way of seeing it, and has looked for it without success. One of the more spectacular explanations is that there are black holes in the clusters. Now black holes can hold a great deal of matter and remain invisible themselves. But theory predicts they should have some visible effects. For instance, one likely candidate for a black hole in the Milky Way is called Cygnus X-1. The feature that makes this a likely candidate is that it produces x-ray radiation. This is thought to be a result of the intense heating that matter undergoes as it falls into a black hole. Certainly if there were 10 to 100 times as much matter in black holes in a cluster of galaxies as there is visible matter, there would be a considerable flux of x-rays. This does not seem to be present in the right amounts.

Now if there were black holes within the clusters, they could either reside within the galaxies themselves, or between the galaxies. If there were a few massive black holes scattered between the galaxies in the cluster, they would produce gravitational forces on the visible galaxies and distort their shapes from the nice, symmetrical shapes we are used to seeing. This is not observed. Could there, then, be a lot of small black holes within the galaxies themselves? Taking the Milky Way galaxy as an example, we find that 60 percent of all the mass known to exist in the galaxy is in a visible form. (The total mass is known from the dynamics of the visible stars.) The remaining 40 percent is probably in stars too faint to be seen or in gas clouds. But even if this 40 percent were in the form of black holes, and if every other galaxy had similar proportions of mass in black holes, it would not even double the mass thought to reside in galaxies. In fact, galaxies would have to be 90 to 99 percent black holes in order to cause clusters to be bound.

Again, recent evidence may have begun to change this picture. Some but not all clusters of galaxies contain a large central galaxy called a cD galaxy. This galaxy appears to be extremely massive and to have an extensive halo of dim stars. The theory is that these massive galaxies have stripped billions of stars from other galaxies in the cluster and now contain a substantial fraction of the cluster mass. It is hoped that the large mass of the single cD galaxy in a cluster will be enough to keep the cluster bound.[17] This is not certain as yet, and not all clusters contain cD galaxies. Astronomers are searching for large numbers of dim stars in other galaxies as well in hopes that all galaxies will turn out to be more massive than had been previously thought. In the case of three spiral galaxies, a halo of dim stars has actually been photographed.[18] Whether or not all galaxies have similar halos, and whether they will be massive enough to bind clusters of galaxies remain to be seen.

We have seen ways by which the age of a galaxy or the cluster in which it resides can be estimated. In all cases the ages are contradictory, ranging from thousands of times the maximum age of the universe to less than a few million years. This simply serves to show that all dating methods are entirely unreliable. Some systems (clusters of galaxies) are in a state in which they could exist for only a few million years, while other systems (dwarf galaxies) are in a state which it would take them trillions of years to reach. Clearly, the only way in which all these systems can coexist is for them to have been created recently in the states in which they now exist. Further, as we shall see in the next chapter, it is impossible for galaxies to form in the first place by any known natural process. Is it any wonder that creation provides a much better explanation?

MEASURING GREAT DISTANCES

In this chapter on galaxies we have at last broken away from the cramped confines of a single "crowded" galaxy and have passed through the suburbs of intergalactic space to the other urban centers of the universe—the other galaxies. Here the normal means to discerning distances become useless—distances are inconceivably large. New methods must be found, and because the more reliable methods used at close range are useless, measured distances become less and less dependable as we go farther and farther. How are such vast distances measured? For the very nearest galaxies some of the methods already discussed may be used with reasonable accuracy. Cepheid and RR Lyrae variables are the first to be used and the most accurate. They are useful in the galaxies of the Local Group and a few others nearby, but this is only a microscopic portion of the universe.

Novae might provide an accurate method of determining distances

17. P. Gorenstein and W. Tucker, "Rich Clusters of Galaxies," *Scientific American,* November, 1978, p. 110.
18. H. Spinrad, *et al., Astrophysical Journal* 225 (1978), 56.

to galaxies somewhat farther away than Local Group members, but as yet almost no use of them has been made due to their rarity and the difficulty in observing them. They are difficult to observe, since they usually occur near the nuclei of galaxies, where the stars are densest. For the Andromeda Galaxy, at least, there is a relationship between how bright the nova becomes and how long it takes to decay back to a dim star once more. Thus by measuring how long a nova takes to dim again, its real brightness can be calculated.

From here on out the distances become less and less reliable, because they depend more upon statistics than upon precise measurement of individual distance indicators. That is, they assume that what appears to be true on the average for a particular type of galaxy can be assumed to be true for any individual galaxy. This is not always a good assumption, for the characteristics of an individual galaxy are bound to differ from the average, but at these distances this is the only type of analysis that can be applied. An example of this method is the clouds of ionized hydrogen in spiral galaxies. (Ionized hydrogen consists of hydrogen atoms which have lost their electrons.) These clouds are, on the average, 800 light years in diameter for certain types of spiral galaxies. If there is a galaxy whose distance we want to obtain, and we observe in it an ionized hydrogen cloud, we can assume that this cloud also has a diameter of 800 light years. Comparing the apparent size of this cloud in a photograph with the "known" size of 800 light years, a distance can be obtained. But what if that particular cloud had a diameter of considerably less or more than 800 light years? The computed distance could be off by a large amount.

A similar statistical method involves the brightness of the brightest star in a galaxy. It is assumed that for most galaxies the brightest star is about the same brightness. Thus by comparing the observed brightness with the supposed real brightness, the distance to the galaxy is found.

The same assumptions are made when using the brightest galaxy in a cluster of galaxies to find the distance to the cluster. As we move farther and farther away, it is necessary to choose brighter and brighter objects as distance indicators. When dealing with clusters of galaxies, it must be assumed that the brightest galaxy in a cluster is always of the same intrinsic brightness. An object used in this way is called a standard candle. At these great distances there are sources of uncertainty other than the variation of characteristics from averages. One of the primary culprits is called a selection effect. An example of a selection effect is using the brightest galaxy in a cluster when we are examining extremely distant clusters, for under these circumstances we are likely to see only those clusters which have unusually bright galaxies. Hence one is likely to use for his standard candle, a candle which is not standard, and obviously incorrect distances will result.

It is easy to see that with all the assumptions which must be made, and the statistical manipulations which must be carried out, there will be large uncertainties in the distances of extremely distant objects. In fact, the cosmic distance scale is admittedly unreliable. This does not hold any great significance for the creationist, however, for even if the scale is off by a factor of two or more, the size of the universe is still immense. And one must still deal with the question that by now has certainly occurred to most readers, "If the universe is only 10,000 years old, how can light from distant galaxies, billions of light years away, have reached us yet on earth?" This is the subject of chapter 12.

We have reserved the most significant distance indicator of all to the last. Doppler shifts are indispensable to the astronomer. They enable him to measure the speeds at which distant objects are moving relative to the earth. As it turns out, all distant galaxies display only a redshift, not a blueshift, indicating that all distant objects are moving away from us. More remarkably, the redshifts increase with distance. If we could set up some kind of scale enabling us to tell the distance of an object only from a measurement of its redshift, the problem would be solved. This is the subject of our next chapter.

10 COSMOLOGY

To an astronomer, cosmology means the history and structure of the universe. Thus, for a Christian, cosmology is found in Genesis 1:1, Hebrews 11:3, Jeremiah 51:15, and other verses. But while the Bible gives a complete and simple history of the universe, it says very little about the structure. And at present, only the structure can be observed, the history being essentially invisible. Thus the Bible and astronomical observations taken together should give a complete picture of cosmology. Anything else is pure speculation. By this I mean that man's attempt to write the history of the universe without the help of God is totally vain. So little can be discerned of the history of the universe through observation that nearly everything astronomers say on the subject is merely theorizing.

No one was present at creation except the Creator Himself, so no man can make definitive statements about it except as revealed to him in the word of God. As far as the history of the universe is concerned, man has been observing for only a few hundred years, and only in the last 50 years or so has he had the ability to probe deeply into space, the realm of cosmology. How is it, then, that astronomers confidently relate the history of the universe over the last 10 to 20 billion years? To answer this we must see how they arrived at presently accepted cosmological models.

COSMOLOGICAL MODELS

Any science, and especially cosmology, may be roughly divided into two pursuits, observation, and theory, or model making. A model is a mathematical or mental structure used to fit all the observational evidence together into a coherent whole. Usually a model will make predictions, which can then be compared with new observations to determine how good the model is. A cosmological model, like all others, begins with a set of assumptions about the nature of the universe, and usually includes a set of mathematical equations embodying these assumptions. These equations are expressions of physical laws, the most important of which for cosmology is the description of gravity. When the scientist formulates his model, he decides how he wants his universe to behave by his selection of assumptions and equations. Once these assumptions are established, the mathematics which he uses is followed to its logical end. The solutions of the equations are the predictions of his model. The last step is to compare these predictions with actual observations. If the observations are not consistent with the predictions, the model must be revised or discarded.

We are now prepared to answer the question as to how the scientist makes definitive statements about the history of the universe. The statements he makes are the results of the solution of the mathematics which he used to describe his model. The assumptions he made were arbitrary in the sense that he chose those which made sense to him, be they correct or not. The reason there are so many cosmological models is that different astronomers feel that different assumptions better describe the universe as they see it. Thus the statements a scientist makes are a direct result of the assumptions he began with. These in turn were chosen according to his own likes or prejudices. The only evidence he normally has for his model is that there is no direct evidence against it. Often the evidence is quite general and is consistent with a number of different models. In fact, there is literally an infinite number of models which are more or less consistent with the evidence.

Model making proliferates in cosmology, perhaps more than in any other science, simply because there are so many possible models which can be made to be consistent with the evidence. It is therefore difficult to distinguish between models on the basis of observations. More and more it is becoming an endeavor of the mathematicians who are able to produce more and more complex models. In the process the models are becoming more and more divorced from reality. It is almost the accepted belief nowadays that if something can be described mathematically, then the mathematics is no longer simply a description of reality, but is reality itself. To many people it makes no difference whether the mathematics corresponds in any way with reality; the equations are things of beauty in themselves. If the universe by chance does not conform to the mathematics, that is the universe's problem. In fact, it is sometimes said that ours is only one of a number of possible universes, all of which may exist somewhere. After all, if man can describe them mathematically, then they must exist, must they not? Ours becomes simply one of a number of possible universes, and not necessarily the best, no matter what standards one uses. This presents a philosophical problem. Why are we in this one? Does it appear the way it does only because this is the only one in which we could exist and hence observe? As Christians we may be reassured by the knowledge that the all-wise God created our universe, and that in doing so He chose the best possible one for His purpose, and hence for us. We do indeed live in the best of all possible worlds. This is not to say that our own world does not suffer under the burden of sin, but that is the result of man's folly. When God created the universe, He did it perfectly.

You can begin to see what I meant by saying that anything beyond Genesis 1:1 is pure theorizing; it all depends upon the assumptions made by the scientist before he even begins. When an astronomer says that 15 billion years ago the universe began with a big bang, he is merely stating what his equations tell him, equations made up by him. Swihart says,

> The dearth of definitive observations results in a "Let's-wait-and-see" attitude, but it also encourages many persons to supplement the data with philosophical arguments. For example, one person might consider it "unthinkable" that the Universe can have a beginning or an end, while a second person might find it equally distasteful that the universe can be self-sustaining for an indefinite length of time. These two persons will find considerable disagreement over the relative merits of different cosmological theories regardless of the data. A statement to the effect that astronomers are on the verge of discovering the nature of the Universe has been uttered many times in recent decades. I do not believe that this threshold will ever be crossed. A theory may receive the consensus support of the experts (even this is difficult to imagine at present), but cosmology leans too heavily on the philosophical

attitude of the investigator for any one theory to be accepted with the same confidence that is given to other branches of physical theory.[1]

ASSUMPTIONS OF CURRENT MODELS

When a scientist makes a statement about the nature of the universe as a whole, therefore, he is simply stating his own philosophy. One element of philosophy that is common to every model is an utter and absolute rejection of the Creator as having any influence upon His own universe, either now or at any time in the past. This is never stated explicitly, of course, but it is implicitly assumed in the whole world of science, and has been increasingly so for decades. As the Apostle John said, "He was in the world, and the world was made through Him, and the world did not know Him" (John 1:10, NASB).

The most important physical assumption which is common to all models is that there have been unlimited amounts of time in the past during which the universe has developed to its present state. We have seen that this is not an extremely good assumption, but without it a great portion of modern science would cease to exist. Without billions of years there would be no cosmology, or evolution, or any of today's theories of origins. These theories of origins have all been devised to explain the universe, and to do so without God and special creation. They must have large amounts of time to allow things to develop by themselves. Hence, if men are to continue to ignore God, as the Bible assures us that they will, they must have large amounts of time, which they are determined to have at all costs.

There are other explicit assumptions which are common to nearly all cosmological models:

1) *Homogeneity*. This simply means that the universe is virtually the same everywhere, except for local irregularities such as galaxies.

2) *Isotropy*. Since the apparent expansion of the universe was discovered, it has been determined that all matter seems to be moving away from all other matter, at a rate which depends only upon distance; there is no preferred direction in space.

3) *Universality*. The same physical laws apply everywhere as they do here.

These assumptions sound fairly reasonable. In fact, without them it would be almost impossible to formulate any models at all, especially without the law of universality.

---

1. Swihart, *Astrophysics and Stellar Astronomy*, p. 245.

THE NEWTONIAN MODEL

Now let us look at some cosmological models. Since a law of gravity is essential to a cosmological theory, the first real model belongs to Isaac Newton, who first formulated a law of gravity. Doppler shifts, of course, had not yet been discovered, and Newton assumed that the universe was static, that is, it was neither expanding nor contracting. This assumption now appears to be incorrect. Besides this, the law of gravitation says that every bit of matter in the universe is attracted, though perhaps quite weakly, to every other bit. Thus if the universe started out as static, it would eventually begin to collapse. It would, that is, unless the universe were infinitely large so that there is no center for it to collapse to. But if

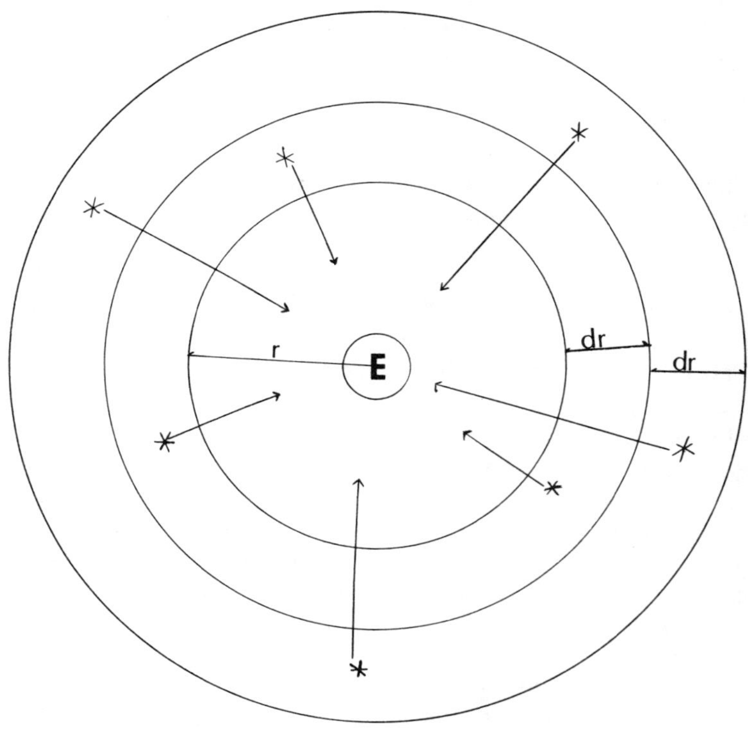

FIGURE 22.—Olber's Paradox.

the universe were infinitely large, we run into another problem, called Olber's paradox.

If the universe were infinite in extent and homogeneous so that every portion of space had the same distribution of stars, it can be shown that the amount of light reaching earth should be infinite, a result which does not appear correct. Imagine that the universe is divided into spherical shells with the earth at the center. (If the universe were infinitely large, one point is as good as another to choose for the center.) Each shell has the same thickness (figure 22). As we advance to each larger shell, it obviously contains more stars, which can thus give more light to the earth. But at the same time this shell is farther away and should make the stars appear dimmer. As it turns out, these effects just cancel each other, and the result is that each shell gives just the same amount of light to earth. But if the universe is infinitely large, there are an infinite number of these shells, and hence there should be an infinite amount of light reaching the earth. Since this is not the case, there is something wrong with the assumptions somewhere. This is Olber's paradox.

EINSTEIN'S THEORY

The next major step in the formation of cosmological models was not made until Einstein developed his famous general theory of relativity. Though he was not the originator of this idea, Einstein's theory popularized the concept of "curved" space which has confused many a student. In effect, he describes space with a complicated type of geometry totally unfamiliar to our way of thinking. Contrary to flat space which behaves like the geometry taught in high school, a triangle in curved space may have more or less than 180 degrees, or a circle's circumference may be more or less than pi times its diameter. In this theory the curvature is actually caused by the presence of matter, and anything moving nearby follows the curvature caused by the first matter. Thus a planet orbiting the sun is following the curved path prescribed for it by the curvature caused by the sun. Thus the general theory of relativity is a gravitational theory.

It can be charged that Einstein's theory falls into the trap of substituting the mathematics for the reality, as described earlier. In fact, it is because of this theory that the mathematics of cosmology is so complex and so far removed from the reality of everyday observation. General relativity is a difficult theory to test. There have, however, been repeated confirmations for certain predictions of the theory, such as the bending of light rays as they pass the sun. Rays of light supposedly bend along the curvature of space created by the sun just as a piece of matter does. Light, which is not normally expected to be possessed of gravity, thus follows the curvature of space, not the gravitational field. The general theory of relativity is an integral part of all cosmological models, and thus curved space is basic to all as well.

The first model that Einstein proposed for the universe on the basis of his theory was static, just as Newton's was. Einstein's equations, just like Newton's, say that all matter attracts all matter, and thus a static universe cannot continue to exist indefinitely. To counteract this, Einstein added another term to his equations, which added a repulsion to neutralize the gravitational attraction. This, he hoped, would allow the universe to be static. In reality, however, this added to the problem, for either the universe should contract as expected before, or it should expand because of the new repulsion term. A static universe was still not possible. At first this was regarded as a weak point in the theory. But then came the discovery which has changed man's concept of the universe.

The Expanding Universe Model

In 1912 Slipher first noticed that the spectra of nearly all galaxies show a redshift. This means that they are receding from us. It seemed that the fainter the galaxy was, the greater its redshift. In 1929 Hubble began to try to determine the distances to these galaxies by other means and to compare them with the redshifts. The remarkable result was that galaxies seemed to increase in their speeds of recession from us in proportion to their distances. For instance, if galaxy A is twice as far from us as galaxy B, it will be moving twice as fast. With the exception of quasars and certain other peculiar objects, this is true today as well, though with our superior equipment we can see many times as far as Hubble could.

The implication, then, is that the universe is growing continuously in size. This might be what Jeremiah meant when he said, "He hath made the earth by his power, he hath established the world by his wisdom, and hath stretched out the heavens by his discretion" (Jer. 10:12). Of course, any theories for the nature of the universe must account for this expansion. Now Einstein's model seemed more palatable, for it had predicted the expansion before it was discovered. Since that time, models using the general theory have proliferated.

Some have been bizarre, such as the one in which the entire universe has no matter in it but is still expanding. Then what is it that is expanding? Space itself. A more relevant question for all expanding models is, "What is it expanding from?"

If the universe is such and such a size now, they argue, then it must have been smaller in the past, since it is observed to be expanding. If we follow this far enough backward in time, the universe must have been very small, as small as we wish to make it by going back far enough. This leads to all sorts of problems which would not even come up if scientists were to realize that time can be pushed back only so far; they do not have an infinite amount of time to play with. If creation took place only a few thousand years ago, then pushing the expansion further back than that is bound to lead to false results. And so it does. To bring all the matter in the universe back to the same point requires 10 to 20 billion years. Astronomers postulate that at that time all the matter in the universe was at that one spot, and some explosion of unimaginable force blew it apart at near light-speeds. What was the matter like and how did it get there in the first place? And how did it come to be distributed as it is now? These are the basic questions that cosmological models try to answer, but the solutions continue to be elusive. With the entire universe the size of a pinpoint,* normal physical laws as we know them must have been drastically different. There is no way scientists can determine what conditions would be like under these circumstances. One could not even tell matter from energy. Yet astronomers continue to make confident assertions about just what went on during the first billionth of a second!

THE STEADY STATE THEORY

In rebuttal to these unacceptable conditions, some astronomers developed an alternative called the steady state theory. The cosmological models we have seen so far are called evolutionary models, because they deal with a changing universe. They are also called big bang theories to denote the original titanic explosion. The steady state theory is not an evolutionary one, that is, it does not regard the universe as changing drastically with time, as do the big bang theories, since the proponents of the steady state theory have added another assumption to the list. The principle of homogeneity, or the cosmo-

* Question: Why did the universe not become a black hole?

logical principle as it is also called, assumes that no matter where a person is in the universe, everything will appear approximately the same to him. The steady state theory adds what it calls the perfect cosmological principle. This states that no matter where a person is in the universe, and no matter what *time* he observes, all things will appear about the same.

How can things have appeared the same in the past or in the future as they do now, if the universe is expanding? Shouldn't things have been closer together in the past and won't they be farther apart in the future? The steady state theory solves this problem by assuming that matter is continuously created—out of nothing—in the space between the galaxies. This process is called continuous creation. As the galaxies spread apart the new matter forms at just the right rate in the newly created spaces between, so that new galaxies are formed to replace the receding ones. This preserves the appearance of the universe for all time.

The steady state theory is presently in a state of disfavor. There are a number of ways in which it may be tested, and so far all the tests indicate that the theory is not in agreement with observation. Its proponents occasionally come up with new revisions in an attempt to revive the theory, but the majority of astronomers still reject it. I have mentioned it not because of its viability but because of the philosophical implications. The rationalism of modern science has constantly been extending its realm, and as it does so it attempts to push God the Creator further and further out of the picture. It began with earthbound theories of evolution, geologic and biological. It grew to include the formation of the earth and solar system. In cosmology man has attempted to push God entirely out of the universe by assuming that the universe managed to evolve by itself from some initial state, the big bang. The big bang theories, however, were still faced with the origin of the big bang itself; it still seemed to require some sort of creation. In the steady state theory the final step has been taken to eradicate any vestige of God or creative acts from the universe. In this theory matter forms by itself, taking the creative act away from God. The universe stays the same over infinite periods of time, eliminating any need for any creative event. Satan has been hard at work to eliminate God from science, and in the steady state theory he has achieved the ultimate. Though the steady state theory appears to have suffered irreparable defeat when faced with the observational evidence, it stands as a warning to us of the lengths to which godless science will go to leave out the Creator.

We find that modern cosmological theories fall generally into two categories—evolutionary theories (big bang theories) and steady state theories. There are a number of variations within each type. The Christian can accept none of these on Scriptural grounds. Both assume large or infinite amounts of time, and both are designed to deny the Creator. The steady state theory might at first seem more distasteful, as it denies any specific creation event, while at least the big bang theory has a starting point. However, the big bang has the same defect.

THE BIG BANG

Some Christians believe what is called the gap theory. This states that between the first and second verses of Genesis there is an indefinite period of time. During this period the geologic ages of the earth occurred as geologists and biologists say. This is not the place to discuss the pros and cons of this theory as compared with the literal view adopted in this book. Rather, I mention it to say that even those people who endeavor to reconcile the time-table of the Bible with that accepted by modern science can in no way interpret the big bang as the creation event of Genesis chapter 1. This presents a challenge to the gap theorists to explain the evolutionary origin of the universe without accepting the big bang.

The major reason why the big bang cannot be accepted by either the literalists or the gap theorists is that the order of events as given in Genesis is entirely different from the one given in modern cosmologies. The theory states that stars began to form nearly 15 billion years ago, while the earth formed a mere 4.5 billion years ago. This contradicts the Biblical statement that the earth was formed on the first day and the stars on the fourth. Even the sun, according to the Bible, was formed after the earth, while evolutionary theory says they were formed at the same time from the same cloud of matter. It is also true that no astronomers would ever think of the big bang as the creation event of Genesis. The big bang was invented specifically for the purpose of doing away with the creation event. An astronomer would laugh at the naivety of anyone who chose to equate the two events.

Further, most astronomers do not believe that the big bang was the real beginning of anything, but was only one event in the infinitely old history of the universe. Having run the universe backwards to the point where all matter was together, they must somehow account for the existence of this matter by inventing some event which took place earlier. Where did the matter come from? Though admittedly the question does not even have a meaning (physical laws do not apply at the moment of smallest size, thus preventing anyone from using them to find out what went on before), it is now assumed that this matter was in such a compressed state only because some former universe contracted from a large size down to the singular state, and then expanded again in our time. Where did that universe come from? It came from a previous big bang billions upon billions of years earlier. A universe which undergoes such expansion and contraction is called a cyclic universe. Scientists thus avoid the question of the origin of matter by assuming that it has always existed. Can observation resolve the question of whether the universe is really cyclic or not? Will the universe ever contract again, and then start completely anew in another big bang? The reader can see how vital this question is to the big bang theory. Without it there is no explanation of the origin of the present universe, and creation of some sort is the only alternative. Creation implies a Creator, and the Creator is the one these theories have been developed to eliminate. Philosophically, if not physically, the universe must be cyclic in order for the rejection of God to be complete. Thus, while astronomers, like all scientists, are expected to be completely objective in their interpretation of the evidence, there is an undercurrent of hope, apparent in all literature on the subject, that the universe will indeed turn out to be cyclic.

THE UNIVERSE: BOUND OR UNBOUND?

What is the universe really doing? There is no way to tell. Just as a cluster of galaxies may be bound or unbound, depending upon how much matter there is in the cluster, so it is with the universe as a whole. One can examine the matter seen in the universe to determine if there is enough to produce the gravitational attraction needed to keep the universe from expanding forever. For the observational cosmologist this is one of the most important fields of study. So far there has been evidence for both sides.

Lately, however, the observations tend to show more and more clearly that the universe is open, that is, unbound, and will never contract again. The methods used to determine this are varied, and some are entirely dependent on assumptions about the state of the universe within seconds after the big bang itself. Thus, if the big bang never occurred, these conclusions are invalid, no matter what they predict. These methods include measurement of the amount of deuterium (heavy hydrogen) in the universe, which indicates that there is very little there. Assumptions about the big bang lead to the prediction that there should be a particular ratio of heavy hydrogen to normal hydrogen in the universe. From the observed amount of heavy hydrogen, there is not enough regular hydrogen to close the universe. There appears to be too little hydrogen by a factor of 25 to 30 to cause the universe to be bound.

In 1974 two astronomers, Gott and Gunn, decided that the expansion of the universe has been continuing at a constant rate for a long time and shows no signs of slowing down. If it is not slowing down, then it will never contract again. This, too, is based upon assumptions concerning the big bang.[2] To avoid these assumptions, one can simply measure how much matter there is in the universe, and ask whether or not this is enough to cause contraction. The result is that the observed matter is far from being enough. If we further assume that there really is enough missing mass in clusters of galaxies to cause them to be bound, adding even this much more matter to the universe is not enough to prevent infinite expansion. It is short by a factor of 10 to 20.[3] Further analysis of the expansion shows that the expansion may be accelerating instead of slowing down or remaining constant. This is just the reverse of what would be expected from the law of universal gravitation.[4]

The Christian may be expected to be as anxious to find that the universe is unbound as astronomers are to find it is bound; an unbound universe would necessitate some kind of creation. In fact, though, even though I would like to see the universe unbound, whether it is bound or not really makes no difference to the Christian. First, the universe will not last long enough to reach the state of contraction; God has promised us a new heaven and a new earth. But our philosophical system takes no note of whether the universe is bound or not. If the universe is unbound, as all evidence now seems to indicate, we find that again God is glorified in the things which He has created, since man's philosophy is given a severe blow. The universe, by its very nature, cries out that it was created, and that there is a Creator. However, nature does not present a complete revelation of God—

2. *Science News,* December 21, 28, 1974, p. 391.
3. *Science News,* May 3, 1975, p. 285.
4. *Scientific American,* December, 1975, p. 50.

this is available only through His word. It is not likely that even in the face of great amounts of astronomical evidence astronomers will admit creation and turn to God. They simply regard the necessity for creation as a puzzle.

BIZARRE THEORIES

The cyclic universe is still a problem. After the collapse of the previous universe, why should it expand again? The reexpansion is sometimes referred to as a bounce, but there is no known mechanism which should cause the universe to bounce back from a contraction.[5] In response to this, even more bizarre theories appear from time to time. One invokes the Heisenberg uncertainty principle, a well-known principle of modern physics. This states that there is a limit to how precisely one can measure things, although the limit is very small. Beneath this limit matter may appear from nothing and disappear, as long as the time of its existence is very small. In fact, it must disappear so quickly that it cannot be observed, thus making it unmeasurable. The reason for this is that energy (or matter) cannot be created or destroyed. Now some scientists have said that the very existence of the universe is a result of this principle which, by chance, has produced an unusually large amount of matter out of nothing. The reason why this does not violate the principle that matter cannot be created is that gravitational energy, as we explained earlier, is a negative energy. The negative energy from the attraction of all matter in the universe is supposed to just cancel the positive energy bound up in matter. Eventually this must disappear into the nothingness from which it came.[6] Such strange theories are usually not taken too seriously, but they show the extent to which people will go to avoid admitting a real creation.

THEORETICAL PROBLEMS

Besides observational problems for modern cosmological theories, they face formidable theoretical problems as well. These problems affect the evolutionary and steady state theories equally. The first problem is the formation of the galaxies. The issue is simple. In the case of the big bang, all the matter is flying apart at tremendous speeds. How, then, could substantial portions of matter come together to form galaxies? It is the same as exploding an atomic bomb

5. *Science News* 104 (1973), 390.
6. Ibid.

in a lumber yard and having the pieces fall together in the form of a house! The same problem exists in the steady state theory, for although there was no initial explosion, the matter which is spontaneously created finds itself already participating in the expansion, moving away from all other matter in the universe. Instead of an explosion pushing the matter apart, the steady state theory starts with an expanding universe which takes the matter along with it. Even if somehow seed galaxies (already existing concentrations of matter whose gravitation attracts nearby matter into them) are postulated, they still would not be able to attract matter at a rate sufficient to keep up with the expansion.[7]

A second problem common to both types of theory is the nonexistence of antimatter. Antimatter is the stuff of science fiction rocket engines and quasar theories. In reality it has been made in the laboratory a few particles at a time. Antimatter resembles normal matter in every way, except in reverse. Protons are negatively charged and electrons are positively charged. Every elementary particle known, including those which do not have an electric charge, has its antiparticle. The spectacular property of antimatter is that when a normal particle contacts its antiparticle, they totally destroy each other, and all the mass that made them up is released in the form of energy—gamma rays. No matter is left at all. The problem, both physical and philosophical, is that only real matter is known. There is, however, no reason to suppose that normal matter is to be preferred by an impartial universe, yet antimatter is conspicuously lacking as far as we know. If all matter were formed in the big bang, there should have been as much antimatter formed as matter, after which the two would have annihilated each other, leaving nothing at all.

The same problem arises in the steady state theory, for the spontaneously created particles could have been either matter or antimatter. When it all came together to form a galaxy, assuming it could, they would cancel each other at that time. Poof! no galaxy. Apparently nature has a preference for matter over antimatter. It is a puzzle. Now it is true that one cannot tell whether something is made of matter or antimatter just by observing the light which it emits. Therefore it has been proposed that some of the observed galaxies—half, to be exact—are really antimatter, preserving the ex-

7. Harwit, *Astrophysical Concepts,* pp. 468-470.

pected balance. This may postpone the solution of the problem philosophically, but not physically. The problem of why the matter and antimatter did not cancel each other when they were closer together (big bang) or when the galaxies formed (steady state) remains unsolved.

OBSERVATIONAL TESTS

We now come to the observational tests by which astronomers hope to distinguish between the individual models of the universe. Not only do they wish to be able to tell whether evolutionary or steady state models are correct, but hopefully which particular model is best. While I stated that a large number of models fit observations with more or less success, closer and closer attention to detail eliminates them one by one as each model makes a slightly different set of predictions about the nature of the universe. In fact, when all is said and done, *no* models fit the universe exactly as we see it—all are eliminated. We shall see how scientists get around this difficulty as we proceed.

Let us start by analyzing what we would expect to see if the big bang type of theory were true. If the universe had expanded from a single point, galaxies and all other material in the universe would start out close together and move progressively farther apart. Since light does not move infinitely fast but has a constant speed of 3×10^5 km/sec, it takes a certain amount of time to get to the earth from distant objects. Even at this fantastic speed, light from the nearest stars takes years to get here. Since by definition a light year is the distance light travels in a year at 3×10^5 km/sec, a galaxy a million light years distant could not be seen on earth until a million years after light left it. This means, assuming that the big bang is true, that when we look at galaxies or quasars millions or billions of light years away, we see them as they were millions or billions of years ago. But since this long ago all objects were closer together, we see distant objects as clustered closer together than nearby objects.

The steady state theory, on the other hand, says that things have always looked pretty much as they do now, and that in the past the galaxies averaged the same distance apart as they do now. This means that as we look at distant galaxies their spacing should be the same as in our own region of space. What is really seen? Unfortunately to distinguish between these two types of theories, we must go so far back in time that the matter which we wish to observe is too far away to be seen. Radio telescopes, on the other hand, are sensitive enough to detect radio sources at tremendous distances. It is by the use of radio telescopes that the observations must be made, and this requires some further explanation before we can give the results.

Radio Sources

Looking for radio sources has its own problems, since for most sources it is not known which objects the radio signals come from. Consequently, we do not know how far away the radio sources are or

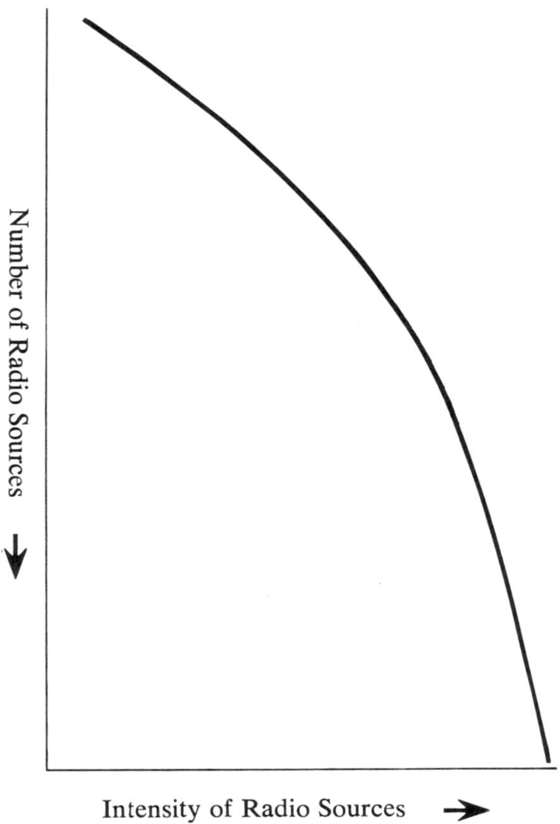

FIGURE 23.—The total number of radio sources increases with faintness.

how far apart to expect them to be. Assumptions must be made. The assumption is that the fainter a radio source is, the farther away it is. While this may seem like a bad assumption since, for example, some stars are millions of times brighter than others, it turns out to work correctly if we can also assume that the distribution of strengths of radio sources here is the same as the distribution at great distances. By this I mean that there is a certain range in the energy outputs of radio sources, there being, perhaps, twice as many sources at one strength as there are at another. If this same range applies everywhere, we can go ahead and make our comparison. The result is a plot of the number of radio sources versus their strength, as in figure 23. The interesting results are that there are too many distant sources for either the big bang or the steady state theories. Both are wrong, apparently.

It seems that astronomers will have to develop a different type of theory altogether. But, as the reader may have guessed, a way has been found to get around the evidence. Supporters of the big bang assume that somehow the radio sources have changed significantly in the past few billion years and that they were brighter in the past. If this were true, it would mean that those sources which are farther away (i.e., earlier in time) were stronger sources and could be seen more easily by the radio telescopes, implying that we could see more of them than would be expected. The steady state theory, on the other hand, cannot get around the observations so easily. They cannot appeal to changes in the strength of radio sources, known as source evolution, since such changes would be in violation of the perfect cosmological principle—things would have appeared different in the past. The evidence strongly implies that the steady state theory is incorrect. The introduction of source evolution does allow the big bang theory to be brought into conformity with the evidence. However, the assumption of evolution is introduced purely to save the big bang theory. Such ad hoc assumptions are usually frowned upon in the sciences, except, that is, when they are necessary to preserve a theory which everyone wants to keep. The fact remains that there is no evidence for source evolution. Like Oort's cloud of comets, its purpose is to shore up a failing theory.

An important point is that it is not known what types of objects are included in the radio counts. There are basically two types of objects which are known to be radio sources—radio galaxies and quasars. Not all galaxies emit a significant amount of radio signals, but there are certain strong emitters which are known as radio galaxies. Our own galaxy has a fairly weak radio emission from the vicinity of the nucleus, but this is too weak to be observed from distant galaxies. Quasars are the much publicized objects which appear to be emitting vast quantities of energy and to be at immense distances. Many are strong radio emitters. Only a few of the many radio sources counted in the experiment have been specifically identified with particular radio galaxies or quasars. Repeating the radio source count experiment using only those sources identified with particular objects gives results much different than before, results which are consistent with both the steady state and big bang theories. This difference is due to the fact that galaxies near enough to be seen, and hence identified as radio sources, are too close to show the condensing effect that would confirm the big bang. Only at greater distances can deviations from the local density of galaxies be discerned. When the source count experiment is done for only those sources identified with quasars, the results are different again. With increasing distance (faintness) the number of sources increases rapidly, implying that things were closer together in the past—far too close for either theory. It appears, then, that quasars may be responsible for deviations in density of more distant sources. What are quasars? How far away are they? No one is sure. And what of those unidentified sources which constitute the majority of the sources used in the original experiment? Are they galaxies or quasars, or both?

To the big bangers it makes little difference as far as proving or disproving their theory is concerned. Since they have adopted source evolution, they can make practically any distribution of quasars or radio galaxies fit into their theory by appropriate adjustments. The steady staters, though, point out that radio galaxies do fit their predictions and that it is the quasars which do not. Therefore they propose that quasars are not really distant after all. If they are not distant, their density makes no difference. All the counts mean is that there are more weak quasars than strong ones. The redshifts of the quasars which are used to determine their distances are thus in error for some unknown reason, and the steady state theory is preserved.

Controversy has been raging for years about the actual meaning of the radio source counts, and there is little likelihood that it will ever really be able to distinguish between the big bang and steady state theories unless the true nature of quasars is first determined. If it is demonstrated that quasars are distant objects and that their redshifts are indicative of distance, then the steady state theory is destroyed. If they turn out to be relatively local, the steady state theory may still have a chance.

Redshift Magnitudes

A second type of observational test to distinguish between models is the redshift-magnitude relation. As Hubble said, the farther away a galaxy is, the faster it appears to be moving away from us; the speed is proportional to the distance. Cosmological models predict that there will be deviations from this relation, and these deviations will be larger for farther galaxies. The way to use this is to use those galaxies whose distances are known and compare their redshift derived distances. The results, plotted in a graph of redshift versus distance, may be compared with theoretical predictions. The trouble with this is that the distances to most galaxies are found from their redshifts to begin with. This takes the form V = H x D where V is the velocity as determined from the redshift, D is the distance, and H is a constant called the Hubble constant in honor of the discoverer of the relationship. For nearby galaxies we can measure both the distance and the redshift, using methods described already. Using these data we can solve the equation to find H. Then for more distant galaxies whose distances cannot be measured with simple methods, the measured redshift and the Hubble constant are used to find the distance. But if the distance of a galaxy is determined from this equation, it has become a circular method. Since the distance is determined from H, we can never find the behavior of H from the distance.

What is really done is to make the same assumption that was made for radio source counts—that the fainter objects are the more distant ones. The distance is derived from the apparent magnitude, or brightness. The distances determined in this way are then used to calculate H for various distances. To say that the Hubble constant H varies with distance is the same as saying that there is a deviation from the linear relationship described above, and the Hubble constant is not really a constant. This deviation can be compared with the predictions of the various theories. The results are shown in the graph of figure 24, which is a redshift-magnitude diagram. In this graph the magnitudes of galaxies are plotted against their redshift, which is equivalent to distance. The curves represent the predictions of various theories, and the dots are the observations. The steady

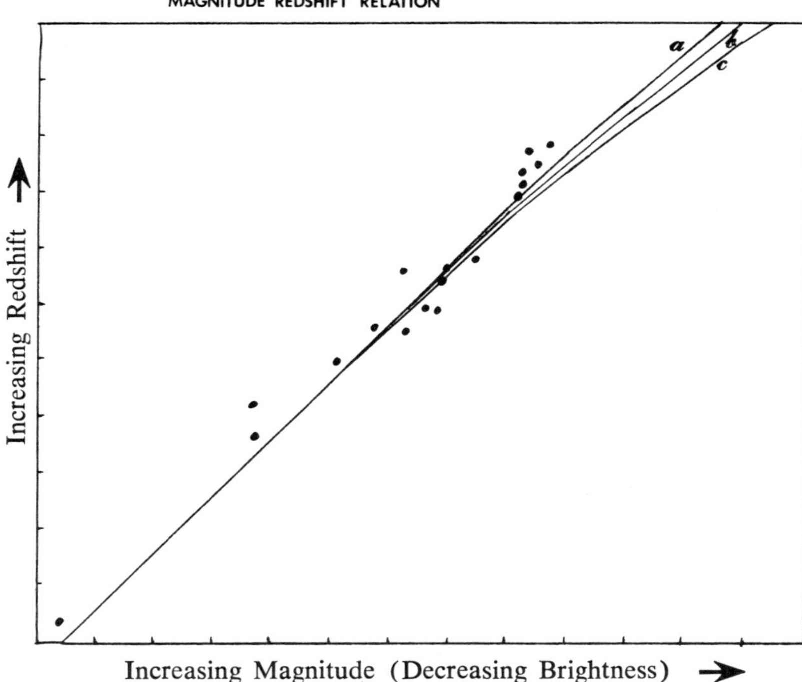

FIGURE 24.—The magnitude-redshift diagram shows that as the distance increases (i.e., the sources get dimmer), the redshift increases proportionally.

state model is not supported by the evidence. As may be expected, there are not enough observations at large distances to give a definite choice among the other alternatives.

Helium Abundance

Another observational test is based upon the amount of helium in the universe. This is a particular case of a more general problem in cosmology, the abundances of the elements. Any theory which invokes natural laws to explain the origin of all things must be able to explain why we see the elements we do and in the correct amounts. Hydrogen is by far the most abundant element, helium is second, and all the rest are rare by comparison, comprising about one percent of all matter. The big bang theories make definite predictions about the abundance of helium. Many different lines of evidence indicate that there is one helium atom for every eleven hydrogen atoms.[8] We have seen that helium is believed to form from hydrogen in the interiors of stars. Could the helium observed in the universe have come from this source? Even if we assume that the universe is 10 billion years old and that all stars have been patiently making helium all that time, there still would not be as much helium in the universe as is observed. There would be only one helium atom for every 160 hydrogen atoms, less than one tenth the actual amount. This is strong evidence against the steady state theory, for even though it assumes an infinite past during which helium may have been created, the matter in the universe is moving apart quickly enough to "dilute" all that helium, and the observed amount would still be much less than what is seen.

Though this observation hurts the steady state theory badly, the big bangers have another recourse—the big bang itself. Since this much helium could not have been formed in stars, it must have been formed in the major energetic event in the theory—the initial explosion. Conditions in that explosion can be juggled to give the amount of helium actually observed, more or less—one helium for every twelve hydrogens, or 27 percent by weight. This would be consistent with theory but for one unusual type of object. There are certain B type stars which have an underabundance of helium, almost 100 times smaller than the abundance in the rest of the universe.[9]

Here, then, is the problem. The observed helium abundance is so high that there is no way to explain it, unless one assumes that it was all formed at one time in the big bang; stars could never have made so much. However, if we allow that helium was made in the big bang, then it must be present in the same proportions everywhere, in all types of stars. There is no known way in which only certain B type stars could have gotten rid of all their helium. This means that the helium could not have existed in the material from which those stars formed. The helium, therefore, could not have formed in the big bang. But then where was it formed? Theory has trouble telling us. The only alternative is that all things were created as they are. God gave some objects more helium and some less, apportioned to each one as He willed.

---

8. D. W. Sciama, *Modern Cosmology* (Cambridge: Cambridge University Press, 1971), pp. 150-153.
9. Ibid.

LINGERING QUESTIONS

There are many other possible tests to distinguish between the cosmological models, but for these tests the results are disappointing at present. There is never quite enough evidence to tell anything significant. Cosmology, of course, is a great deal more complicated than I have presented here, and for any objection one might present there is one way or another of getting around it, with more and more complicated assumptions and mathematics. Many astronomers have basically made up their minds that the big bang was real and that only the details have to be worked out. Those details are very uncertain.

Why have I spent so much time discussing models of the universe which leave God out, and which we therefore believe are entirely wrong? First, the modern Christian should be acquainted with these ideas, as they are becoming more and more part of our daily lives and conversations. Developments in cosmology, because of their philosophical nature, are emotionally charged issues, and the Christian should be able to discuss them knowledgeably. Second, it is even more important that he know what philosophical ideas lie behind these theories, and what their consequences are for the Christian faith. I hope to have shown that, because of the assumptions which lie behind these theories, the theories cannot be correct. They leave the Creator out of His creation. Without a proper understanding of God's role in the origin of the universe, astronomers will never arrive at a knowledge of the truth.

The Christian need not feel that his faith is threatened when he reads of a "proof" for a large age for the universe or of evidence for the big bang. He can now see that these proofs are a result of mathematical equations based upon incorrect axioms. Finally, I have attempted to show the weak condition of all modern theories by pointing out that actual observational evidence does not support any of them. Instead, they are shored up by revision after revision based upon unverifiable assumptions, such as radio source evolution. Cosmology thus far has failed, and will continue to do so until it gives God His rightful place.

It would be legitimate for an astronomer to challenge us at this point by saying, "If we are all wrong, how does the Christian explain all these observations using the assumptions he derives from the Bible? Does it tell why there is an overabundance of radio sources? Does it explain why the universe is expanding?" I confess that for most of these and related questions I have no answer. The Bible does not give any details, but the simplicity of the creation account leaves us with the impression that God feels these things are hardly worth the trouble of explaining them. Perhaps these things are obvious, or perhaps we are not to know. Our best answer is to demonstrate that theories not based upon uniformitarian assumptions are better able to explain the facts than are conventional theories. In any case, the purpose of this book is not to make idle speculations, but to cause the reader to see that after all man's attempts have failed, God's word stands true. Perhaps a Christian explanation lies in the future, to come from among the ranks of creationists who have only recently begun to realize the potential for explaining nature with Biblical presuppositions. I hope so.

11 OF GALAXIES, QUASARS, AND REDSHIFTS

THE DISCOVERY OF QUASARS

Astronomy has become considerably more exciting in the last few years with the discovery of new objects. It was with a great deal of surprise that M. Schmidt discovered in 1962 that an object which had previously been thought to be a star turned out to have some unusual properties. He examined the spectrum of the "star" because it had previously been identified as a radio source. The spectrum revealed that the object had a large redshift. The redshift was interpreted, using Hubble's law, and indicated a distance of 1.5 billion light years. The strange object, known as 3C273, suddenly became the most distant object known. It was not long before other quasars were discovered, some possessing redshifts even greater than that of 3C273.

The implication of the great distances involved is that objects which are so far away and yet still visible must be exceedingly bright indeed, brighter than whole galaxies. What could be so bright? We still don't know. Some quasars turned out to be variable, having periods as short as one day. This implies that their size is no more than one "light day," or about 10 to 20 billion miles across. While this sounds large, it is on the order of the size of the solar system. An object this small which could produce the energy output of an entire galaxy is almost beyond belief.

Quasar is short for "quasi-stellar radio source." Quasars are so named because on a photograph they look exactly like stars, and they can sometimes be identified by their radio emissions. Later it was discovered that there is a class of radio quiet quasar-like objects, called blue stellar objects, or BSOs. All these as well as other variations on the same theme are now lumped together and called quasars. All have very large redshifts compared to other celestial objects, except for the most distant galaxies. As described in the last chapter, it is these quasars which cause radio source counts not to fit any cosmological models. When we add to the fact that it is their apparent distance which makes their brightness so hard to account for, it becomes evident that it is vital to find the real distances to quasars, which will tell us the real meaning of their redshifts.

Some astronomers have been contending for years that quasars must really be closer to us than they seem, simply because there is no known way they could produce enough energy to be seen at such fantastic distances. Others, supporters of the steady state theory, also argued for close quasars in order to save their theory from the radio source counts. However, attempts to explain the redshifts as other than cosmological (caused by great distance) have consistently failed. Occasionally other observations of quasars indicate that they are far away. The situation was and still is unresolved.

THE REDSHIFT CONTROVERSY

Then in 1966 an astronomer named Arp, who was compiling a catalog of peculiar galaxies, noticed that quasars in general seemed to lie unusually close to certain types of peculiar galaxies, almost as if they were in some way connected to them. Since these particular galaxies were not nearly as distant as the quasars were believed to be, it was thought by him to be an indication that quasars were actually nearby. The redshift would have to be explained by some means other than their speed. Thus began an interesting and often heated dispute, which has become known as the redshift controversy. This name comes from the fact that some astronomers maintain that the quasars' redshifts are caused by their high recessional speeds at their large distances, while others say that the redshifts are caused by a different mechanism. As time passed, the accepted interpretation of the redshift began to lose its credibility among some astronomers.

Quasars were not the only companions to these peculiar galaxies. Further analysis revealed a consistent pattern; a giant elliptical galaxy would be at the center of a line of elliptical galaxies and quasars. The best example of this is called M87, which is a giant elliptical galaxy and is also a radio source. The remarkable feature of M87 is its two jets of gas blown out in opposite directions and pointing along the line of galaxies. The implication is that these other elliptical galaxies were blown out from the apparent explosion in M87.

Wondering if this were really the case, and if it might be a general occurrence, Arp investigated a number of other bright E galaxies and found that 11 out of 13 were also members of similar chains. The ejection process involved, Arp thought, might be a general method of galaxy formation. Now two interesting facts emerge. First, while one would expect that all the galaxies in a given chain would be at about the same distance from us, their redshifts indicate otherwise. If redshifts are really indicative of distance, the galaxies in the chain are all at different distances. This shows that redshifts are not a reliable indicator of distance. Second, if the observed redshifts are indicative of velocities, these chains of galaxies are not stable, since all the members are moving at different speeds and are thus moving rapidly away from each other. Within a time of 100 million years a chain would be completely dispersed, just as the clusters of galaxies mentioned earlier. Yet theory says these galaxies are 10 billion years old.

This beginning led to considerable research into the nature of quasars, galaxies, and redshifts. If quasars, like the galaxies in the chains, are ejected from giant galaxies in explosions and thus are not really distant, one would expect to find quasars nearby to galaxies and not randomly distributed. On the other hand, if they are really distant, it is reasonable to expect to find them near clusters of galaxies. In the latter case, their redshifts would be the same as the redshifts of the galaxies in the clusters, since they would really be indicative of distance. Arp maintains that when one looks at distant clusters of galaxies no quasars are found. Quasars must thus be dim, since they are not seen at the great distances of those clusters. Instead he finds that quasars are not randomly distributed but fall in the same regions of sky as the brightest known galaxies. The brightest galaxies, of course, are the nearest ones. This implies that quasars are physically associated with galaxies, and that they are intrinsically dim, since they are not seen near distant galaxies. Furthermore, quasars fall in pairs with a bright galaxy halfway between, as if they had been ejected in opposite directions at the same time. A large number of quasar pairs are lined up across M31, the Andromeda Galaxy, which is one of the nearest and brightest galaxies.

Taken together, this evidence implies that quasars may actually be local objects, ejected by galaxies in some sort of explosion. This means, first, that they do not need to be exceedingly bright and so their energy generation is not a problem. Second, and more important, it means that redshifts, of quasars at least, are not distance indicators. What about redshifts in general? It turns out that quasars are not the only example of discordant redshifts; there are many others.

A small galaxy orbiting a large one is called a companion galaxy. Many large galaxies possess one or more companions; Andromeda has two. Arp thought that if some galaxies are formed by explosions in larger galaxies, then perhaps this is true of all companion galaxies. What he found when he examined 19 known companion galaxies was that 13 of them have higher redshifts than the galaxies whose companions they are. Statistically, one would expect the Doppler shifts to be evenly divided between those larger and those smaller than the major galaxies. The sample is not large, but the implication is again that perhaps redshifts are not indicative of distance.

Arp feels that ejection of one galaxy from another's nucleus is a common occurrence. The ejected galaxy would be expected to be smaller than the galaxy from which it came. He suggests that the ejected galaxies are small, compact, and bright objects when ejected. As they move away from their "parent" they expand into more normal galaxies. The small compact objects would be the quasars and would possess an extreme surplus of redshift. As the objects expand, the surplus decreases, until it vanishes when the galaxy reaches normalcy. If this hypothesis is true, it might be possible to occasionally find a small galaxy embedded in a larger one. This is found in an entire class of galaxies called "spiral with companions on the end of arms." The existence of this type of galaxy tends to confirm Arp's hypothesis.

If two galaxies appear to be close together, perhaps even companions, but have different redshifts, astronomers usually call this a chance association; they only appear close, while the galaxy with the greater redshift is really much farther away. However, if examples could be found where the galaxies were actually connected, it would virtually prove them to be at the same distance. One example is NGC 722, which has two faint companions attached to it by luminous filaments. The companions, however, have redshifts indicating they are moving away from us 17,000 kilometers per second faster than NGC 772. Can these redshifts really be caused by the companions' greater distance?

Astronomy journals are full of articles on this subject, both pro and con. The fact remains that the examples just given cannot be dismissed, but are extremely significant. This is true because (1) quasars may not be distant objects after all, in which case their redshifts are not at all important in determining the structure of the universe, and (2) redshifts themselves for all types of objects are called into question.

There are still other examples of unusual redshifts. One astronomer studied a total of 550 galaxies and found that spiral galaxies tend to show larger redshifts than ellipticals at the same distance.[1] In the Virgo cluster, a large cluster of galaxies, the redshifts of the galaxies increase smoothly from ellipticals through spirals.[2] Even in our own solar system, when Pioneer 6 passed behind the sun it showed a Doppler shift which could not be explained by any known effects.[3] And some binary stars, both of which must, of course, be at the same distance, show differing redshifts.[4]

With so many examples of unexplained redshifts there is serious doubt as to whether any reliance may be placed upon redshifts at all, either as a distance indicator or as a velocity indicator. All the thought that has gone into the big bang theory is useless if Hubble's relationship fails, and Hubble's relationship is based entirely upon the increasing of redshifts with fainter and fainter objects.

Let us now return to our radio source counts. It may be recalled that these radio sources are either radio galaxies, quasars, or unidentified. (There are other types such as supernova remnants, but these are not significant to the subject of cosmology.) It is assumed that the unidentified sources are also radio galaxies or quasars. Now if we eliminate the quasars because their redshifts are not indicative of distance as well as the unknown sources because many of them must be quasars, we are left with only radio galaxies. A radio source survey using only radio galaxies gives the astonishing result that the observations are in perfect accord with a *static, non-evolutionary* universe![5] This is a universe which is not expanding and in which

1. T. Jaakkola, *Nature* 243 (1971), 531.
2. DeVaucouleurs, *Nature* 236 (1972), 166.
3. Merat, *Astronomy and Astrophysics* 30 (1974), 167.
4. Kuhi, *Astronomy and Astrophysics* 32 (1974), 111.
5. Sciama, *Modern Cosmology*, pp. 85, 89.

sources do not change with time. Some think this is a result of the fact that we cannot see galaxies far enough away to observe the deviations predicted by cosmological theories. But how far does one have to be able to see? We can already perform the test as far away as we can see anything at all (assuming quasars to be local), the visible edge of the universe. Where else can we go to see the predicted deviations?

The real source of the redshifts remains a problem. If the universe is static, why do more distant (i.e., fainter) objects have a larger redshift? There are theories which try to explain redshift as being caused by phenomena other than speed. One type is called the tired light theory. Tired light theories try to explain redshifts as due not to velocity but to distance. While varying in detail, they generally state that the farther a photon of light travels the more energy it loses. Red light has less energy than blue, and hence light which loses energy appears redder. The galaxies with greater redshifts may indeed be farther away, preserving the distance-redshift relationship, but the redshift is not due to speed.

Some events have occurred recently which lend support to an alternate interpretation to the accepted one. Three astronomers, Karoji, Nottlae, and Vigier, have tested the redshift-distance relation by using faint radio galaxies. What they thought at first from their observations was that there is a different distance-redshift relation in different areas of sky. This would be in violation of the assumption of isotropy discussed in the previous chapter. However, they discovered that this was not the case. Instead, they found that light from distant galaxies was more redshifted when it has passed through a cluster of galaxies on the way to earth. "If this is true," Vigier writes, "the idea of universal expansion itself is in deep trouble, and one would have to come back . . . to the static . . . model proposed initially by Einstein himself."[6]

Let us review. The evidence given by Arp is important because it indicates that redshifts may not be trustworthy and that quasars may not be as distant as has been thought. He himself, however, still believes in a great age for the universe, even if not for individual associations of galaxies. The strings of galaxies have lifetimes quite short compared to the accepted age of the universe, but could still be millions of years old. In fact, ages of at least this long are necessary

6. *Science News,* November 1, 1975, p. 277.

if galaxies and quasars are really ejected from giant galaxies, for they appear at distances of thousands and millions of light years from the "parent" galaxy. It would have taken them millions of years at their present speeds to have covered this distance. (Of course, their speeds may have been different in the past, in contrast to the uniformitarian assumptions of astronomers.) Creationists would have to examine this evidence closely in the light of what is known of the Biblical date of creation. We will talk about this more in the next chapter.

IMPLICATIONS FOR UNIVERSAL EXPANSION

Arp's evidence does not prove that galaxies or quasars are ejected from giant galaxies, but casts doubt on the redshift as evidence of a universal expansion. When doubtful quasars are eliminated, the remaining radio sources are consistent with a static universe. The existence of any redshift at all thus remains unexplained. Recent evidence indicates that redshifts may not be due to universal expansion but to some other cause.

Why would God create a redshift which increases with distance when He must know that men would interpret it as evidence of a universal expansion? Recall the discussion of Olber's paradox in an earlier chapter. The sky is not so bright as to burn us up because of the redshift, since redshifted light is light with less energy. If the light from farther away is consistently less energetic, it will not be able to burn us up. It may well be that God created the universe large enough to show His might and glory, and then made the redshift so we would not be burned up by it.

What are the consequences of a static universe to astronomers? The expansion of the universe has been almost completely accepted by astronomers as proof of an evolutionary universe changing according to natural laws. The big bangers can point to the instant of explosion and say it is the beginning of the universe as we know it and push all the philosophical questions about the origin of matter beyond this beginning and say that they cannot be answered further. The steady staters, to account for the existence of matter at all, must postulate continuous creation. However, if their perfect cosmological principle is to be retained, and the universe has the same density now as it always has, then it *must* be expanding to make room for the new matter. Otherwise the whole universe would fill up.

If the expansion of the universe proves to be incorrect, steady staters are obviously wrong. The big bang theory is also wrong, because the initial explosion did not occur. A static universe would mean disposing of all cosmological theories developed in the last 50 years. This alone is enough to upset any scientists, for radical changes to accepted dogma are, despite scientists' reputed objectivity, received only with reluctance if at all. But even more than this they are faced anew with the problem of creation. If there was no big bang and no continuous creation, where did everything come from? It is true that galaxy formation is easier to account for in a static universe, but the very existence of the matter from which they formed is not. If matter was spontaneously created, why isn't the universe full? The universe cannot simply have existed forever as it is now, for even nuclear burning in stars does not have an infinite lifetime. The only solution would be creation *ex nihilo* by the Lord God Himself.

What has been presented, of course, is just one possibility among many. The evidence definitely shows problems with the accepted evolutionary theories, but it is still possible that the universe is expanding and was created in the process of doing so. This would in no way contradict the Bible or the concept of a recent creation.

The heavens declare the glory of God in an amazingly real way. The very existence and nature of the universe absolutely require an all powerful God. However, even if evolutionary concepts are overthrown, man is still stubborn, and he will still not accept this incomplete revelation in nature as proof of God's reality or, more especially, of the person and work of Jesus Christ. It is up to us as Christians to bear witness to that fact.

12 PROBLEMS OF TIME

One day is with the Lord as a thousand years, and a thousand years as one day (II Pet. 3:8).

Creation is an extremely difficult fact to prove. What, then, have we accomplished in this book, and can we expect any more progress in the future? I have given numerous examples of evidence which demonstrate that the universe is not as old as we are commonly led to believe. Usually it has been in the form of an upper limit for the age of the universe, often in the millions of years. If these assertions are true—and I believe they are—the 10-billion-year-old universe of the scientists is in serious trouble, but we are still a long way from proving a 10,000-year-old universe. If upper limits of this sort are all we can produce, the outcome of any conflict between creation and evolution can be based only upon subjective interpretations of the evidence. Remember, we are combating a philosophy, not a body of objective facts proving evolution. "For we wrestle not against flesh and blood, but against principalities, against powers, against the rulers of the darkness of this world, against spiritual wickedness in the high places." We are fighting the interpretation of the facts, and the world's interpretation is based upon a rejection of God. It is no wonder that we have difficulty communicating creationist views and, in fact, can seldom even attract the attention of evolutionary scientists. And if we can succeed in showing that the universe is less than billions of years old, scientists will most likely come up with a different interpretation of the evidence, enabling them to keep their billions of years.

QUESTIONS ABOUT A YOUNG UNIVERSE

Is it likely, then, that creationists will find some evidence that really points to 10,000 years rather than a vague "less than 10 million"? If we are to do so, it will most likely be within our own solar system or within the solar neighborhood. The reason for this is somewhat intuitive but has a sound physical background. Various objects have natural characteristic time scales. To see time periods on the order of 10,000 years we must look at objects with time scales of about that length. Objects with time scales of millions of years cannot show the "resolution" necessary to reveal something only 10,000 years long. Conversely, objects with extremely short time scales can have changed enough in 10,000 years so as not to show any effects of what happened that long ago. Think of it this way: we are not likely to find any short time scale (10^4 years) events in a distant galaxy, because everything about a galaxy naturally has a longer time scale than that. It takes a galaxy hundreds of thousands of years to rotate and 10 million years to escape from a cluster. The "expansion time" of the universe is billions of years. To try to see evidence of an event of short duration in these slow phenomena is like trying to see a single grain of sand in a seashore miles away.

On the other hand, within the solar system things happen much more quickly. The revolution of the planets around the sun takes from a fraction of a year to a few hundred years. Comets' periods may be in the thousands of years. We are looking at the details, so to speak. If creation 10,000 years ago affected the orbit of a comet, it might be that after these years, which are only a few years to a comet, it may still show the effects of the influence. Nearby stars may demonstrate the same influence. The rotational periods of some binary stars are in the hundreds or thousands of years. Light travel time from nearby stars to us is from a few years to a few thousand years. As yet it is not even clear what to look for, but if we are to see direct evidence for a 10,000-year-old universe, it will probably come from objects of approximately that natural time scale.

The reader has undoubtedly been asking two important questions which I have saved until now. One is, "If the universe is so young, why do we see objects which have characteristic times in the millions of years?" How can long-period objects exist in a short-period universe? For instance, if a galaxy has gone through only two or three percent of its first revolution, doesn't it seem that God has misled us with the very existence of these characteristically long-time-scale objects? The second question is, "If all these galaxies are millions of light years away, doesn't the light take millions of years to get here? And if so, how can we see them now? If the universe is 10,000 years old, we should not be able yet to see anything farther away than 10,000 light years."

Long-Period Objects

These are extremely important questions which Christians must face directly. Their faith in a recent creation may hinge upon the answers. Since the first question deals more with a feeling that things simply don't fit, I feel safe in answering it in a "suppose" kind of way. Suppose you were creating a universe for people on earth to see. The purpose of this universe is to be for signs and seasons and days and years. You want people on earth to know that the universe is infinite in extent. How can you do it? You must make the sun to give light and heat to the earth; can you fill the universe with others like it? A universe composed only of individual stars distributed evenly throughout all space would not appear very large, for even the brightest stars can be seen only to a limited distance. Beyond that would be a blur (ignoring Olber's paradox).

If the stars were arranged into dense clumps so that their combined brightness contributed to the brightness of the clump, it could be seen to much greater distances than individual stars. These clumps, of course, are the galaxies. These can be seen at immense distances. If we desire to have the same physical laws apply everywhere in the universe (which cannot be proved either way), this galaxy would have to possess the total mass of all its constituent stars and would have to rotate to keep all the stars from collapsing. The characteristic time scale of the galaxy turns out to be hundreds of millions of years.

If you want your galaxies to be conspicuous at even greater distances, you might consider clumping a bunch of galaxies together. This of necessity must be larger still than the individual galaxies which make it up, and hence has a longer characteristic time. When I talk about the characteristic time of a cluster of galaxies, I mean either the time it would have taken the cluster to expand to its present size if the galaxies had started out quite close together, or the time it would take them at their present speeds to disperse the cluster completely.

In either case the time is on the order of 10 million years. But there is no reason to believe that God would have started them all out at the same place, and it is obvious that they have not yet dispersed. Hence they can be younger than their characteristic time scale. Returning to our suppose argument, if you were creating a cluster of galaxies, would you make all the component galaxies start out at a point? No, since it would be too small to be seen from earth. Would you create them already dispersed? No, since they would not be recognizable as clusters, nor would they be evidence to the earthlings of the youth of the universe. From this simple argument it sounds reasonable that God would have created not only the clusters of galaxies but the entire universe in a full-blown, completed state, in good order and already in operation. The fact that it takes a galaxy 250 million years to rotate does not necessarily mean that it has been doing so for that period of time. Spirals may have been created already wound up. The fact that a young universe can contain objects which have an apparent age greater than 10,000 years should not upset us. But if it does, recall that the evolutionary universe of billions of years also contains such objects; dwarf galaxies behave as if they were trillions of years old.

Distances in Light Years

The question concerning the speed of light is more difficult. The fact that the speed of light can be measured accurately and its behavior described mathematically means that our answer must be correspondingly more physical and precise than our "suppose" argument. There is no doubt that there really are objects greater than 10,000 light years away. Ten thousand light years still leaves us well within the Milky Way Galaxy, and other galaxies are thousands of times farther away than this. No arguments or revisions of the distance scale can change this basic fact. To retain a recent creation we must explain how light traveled farther than 10,000 light years in less than 10,000 years.

Some Christians maintain that since by this reasoning we could never even know that other galaxies existed, God made special provision for us so that man could see them, by creating the universe with the appearance of having been running for a long time. This much I agree with. But they then say that this includes the light from distant objects as well, that is, the light from astronomical objects was created en route to earth already, never having really been at the object from which it is supposed to have come. If we see an event in a distant galaxy, for example, a supernova, the light from that supernova was actually created fairly near the earth and was never really at the supernova. In fact, the supernova would have to have happened before the beginning of the universe! It never really happened. This is the conclusion we are forced to if we assume that light was created en route to earth instead of actually having originated at the luminous object. If the events never really happened, maybe the galaxies don't even exist, only their light. Maybe God is fooling us into believing there is something there when there really isn't.

Obviously we must reject this hypothesis. First, God would not deceive us in this way; it is contrary to His nature. Second, the light coming from these distant objects carries a great deal of information, the same type we have seen that comes from stars. It tells us the elements present, the types of stars in the galaxy, and so forth. How could this information exist if there is nothing there, or if the light has never really been at the object? There must be another way.

One possibility was hinted at when I said above that we must explain how light could travel more than 10,000 light years in 10,000 years. This implies a higher speed for light in the past. Now the speed of light is known as one of the fundamental constants of nature; it is believed to be constant everywhere in the universe and at all times. There are other such constants, one of which is the gravitational constant. It is this constant, called G, which determines how strong the gravitational force between two objects is. There is growing evidence, however, that this "constant" might not really be constant after all. Thomas Van Flandern has concluded from the motions of the moon in its orbit that the gravitational constant is indeed decreasing and hence gravitational forces between massive objects is getting weaker. He bases this upon the fact that the moon appears to be slowing in its orbit around the earth more quickly than can be explained by tidal effects. This is due to the moon's moving farther away from the earth, which may be a result of a change in the gravitational constant.[1] This is very small and difficult to measure, but if true, it shows that at least one of the "constants" of nature is not really constant.

Could the speed of light have varied in the past? To be honest, there is little or no evidence for a change in the speed of light. In the past century or two many measurements of the speed of light have

1. *Science News* 106 (1974), 116.

been made, and there is a slight tendency towards higher values in the past. But the deviations from the presently accepted value are always near the value of the margin of error in the experiment, causing the reality of the change to be uncertain. Still, it is interesting to consider the possibility that in the past the speed of light was considerably higher than it is now, and near the time of creation was extremely high. This would have enabled light from distant galaxies to reach the earth in its history. As time passed, the speed would have decreased until it reached its present value. A theory like this would have immense effects in other areas and might be testable. However, no serious theory for a variation in the speed of light exists.

For those who like more exotic explanations, there is the theory of Moon and Spencer. They suggest that space is flat, not curved, as far as the matter it contains is concerned. But light would travel in a different type of space, called Riemannian space, which *is* curved. The curvature of space for light could be so great that light's real travel distance is shorter than the physical distance between us and the emitting object. In fact, light from an infinite distance could take as little as 16 years to reach the earth, and light from nearer distances would take less time still. This would produce no observable effects for distances on the scale of the solar system, but the effect would grow with distance.[2]

Was Adam able to see stars in the sky on the day he was created? Genesis 1:14-19 implies that he could. Were these but the closest stars, while the other, more distant stars winked on one by one as their light reached the earth? Had light, traveling at fantastic speeds, already reached the earth from the most distant parts of the universe by the sixth day of creation? Or did God perhaps after all create light from distant parts of the universe already en route to earth? Perhaps none of the suggestions given above are correct. But the purpose of this chapter was simply to demonstrate that it is neither impossible nor unreasonable to believe that the universe is 10,000 years old, in spite of its great size. One's faith in the word of God need not be threatened by apparent light travel times. Hopefully this will be a fruitful area of research by Christians, and eventually a coherent Christian cosmology will emerge, not based upon the assumption that God does not exist, but that He is the Creator and has had providential care of the universe from its beginning until now.

---

2. Moon and Spencer, *Journal of the American Optical Society* 43 (1953), 635.

13 LIFE

And the Lord God formed man of the dust of the ground, and breathed into his nostrils the breath of life; and man became a living soul (Gen. 2:7).

LIFE ON OTHER PLANETS

Is man alone in the universe? Is there no one else, perhaps on some other planet, who shares man's intelligence? Is there any kind of life anywhere else? Formerly such speculations were left to science fiction writers; in recent years astronomers have turned their attention to this question. The sudden acceptance of, and in fact preoccupation with, possible life on other planets within the scientific community is partially the result of man's technical skills. He is now actually able to visit other planets for the first time in history. The possibility of arriving only to be greeted by other intelligent beings or, as astronomers consider it, the much more realistic possibility of encountering harmful microorganisms, has forced scientists into considering the possibility that such things really exist.

This is not the only reason for the great surge of interest in extraterrestrial life, however. There are more philosophical reasons. Man himself is a reason. Since scientists believe that life on earth evolved from nonliving things, they ask why this should not happen elsewhere also. In fact, if it has not happened elsewhere, it makes the earth a unique place in the universe, and man a unique being. Uniqueness is not a nice word to a scientist, who deals in generalities. If it turns out that man is the only intelligent creature in the universe, it raises several serious questions about the origin of man and hence about a Creator. This, as has been stressed all through this book, is a subject which sinful man will avoid at all costs. He will not acknowledge his Creator. It is for this reason that the theory of evolution was developed, and it is for this reason that the theory of evolution must be extended to other planets as well.

Thus, for philosophical reasons alone, life on other planets is viewed as a virtual certainty. All we need to do is look hard enough, and in the right places, and we shall find it (unless it finds us first). We have come full circle from the days when even intelligent astronomers believed there to be life on every celestial body, including the sun, through the skeptical years when anyone considering the possibility of life elsewhere was a dangerous fanatic, to the present day, when scientists expect to find life under every moonrock. Complex formulas have been developed purporting to give the probability of finding intelligent creatures in a particular place in the universe. We have even sent signals into space, hoping to communicate with beings which we are not sure exist, or who we are not sure could hear us if they did exist.

How is the Christian to deal with all this? Is there any validity to the assumptions of astronomers (called exobiologists) who search for extraterrestrial life? Should Christians expect to find life on other planets, and what are our reasons for our answer? What does a Scriptural view of the universe cause us to deduce about exobiology?

DEFINING LIFE

The place to begin is with a discussion of life itself. What is life? The average person should have no difficulty identifying things around him which are alive. Living things move, grow, and eat. There are a few objects where a decision would depend upon definition. Is a seed alive? What about a virus? Though these objects might inspire a debate about semantics, there is nonetheless complete agreement that even these objects are products or precursors of life; we should not expect to find either viruses or seeds on a planet where no life exists. This brings up the question, what types of life might we expect to find on other planets? Would we even recognize it if we saw it? On earth life is based upon compounds which are formed by the element carbon. What if elsewhere it is based upon some other element? We obviously must establish some definition for life, something that would apply under all circumstances.

To the exobiologist life is something that evolves. According to the theory of organic evolution, it does so through a process of mutation and natural selection. This means that life reproduces and, in doing so, changes. The creatures which do not possess beneficial changes die, leaving only creatures possessing beneficial changes. In this way life is thought to progress from the simple to the complex. Based upon this assumption, then, our definition of life must include the ability to reproduce. It also involves the mutation of that life form in the process of reproduction. In order to reproduce, something must grow by consuming nutrients, which it assimilates into its body. This summarizes the working definition of life among exobiologists.

IS THERE LIFE ON MARS?

In all the universe, man or his artifacts have touched only three bodies besides the earth—the moon, Venus, and Mars. It was not really expected that life would be found on the moon, and none was. Nevertheless, the first astronauts who walked on its surface were kept in isolation chambers for some time after their return, for fear that somehow they had picked up some moon organism which might prove harmful to mankind. The Soviets apparently anticipated that the conditions on Venus were not conducive to life, for their probes did not even look for it, or at least no search was reported. Mars? From the beginning of man's imaginings about extraterrestrial life Mars has been the prime candidate. It is the most earth-like planet; it is one of the nearest. Surely life must have evolved on Mars.

To find out, a number of experiments were included on the two Viking landers which set down on Mars's surface in the summer of 1976. Each lander contained five different types of instruments to search for life. The first, of course, was the two cameras. But the cameras showed no signs of life whatever, only the dry, rocky, desolate Martian surface. Of the other four devices, only one, the gas chromatograph/mass spectrometer, searched directly for organic molecules. The other three all searched for evidence of metabolic products given off by microscopic life forms in the soil.

Since life on earth is based upon the element carbon, and since even molecules in space (detected by radiotelescopes) and in meteorites often contain carbon compounds, it was decided to look for organic (carbon-containing) compounds on Mars as a sign of life. The gas chromatograph/mass spectrometer aboard each lander tested two soil samples for organic molecules. The soil samples were first heated to 500° C. to break up complex molecules, and then the fragments were analyzed to see what they were. The results? The only organic molecules detected belonged to cleaning solvents used to clean the landers before they left the earth! This extremely sensitive experiment, which could have detected concentrations of organic materials 100 to 1,000 times lower than in the desert soils of the earth, found nothing else.[1]

The first of the metabolic experiments was the gas-exchange experiment. In this experiment, small amounts of a nutrient solution were added to soil samples in the hope that this would encourage any microorganisms to grow and reproduce. The gases which they gave off as waste products would be analyzed by the gas chromatograph. When the solution was added to the soil, large amounts of oxygen and carbon dioxide were released. This event, however, was quite brief. If the gases had been given off by living organisms, it would be more likely that the release of metabolic products would be gradual and long-lived. The observed reactions were undoubtedly the result of a chemically reactive soil and not life.

The labeled-release experiment was similar to the gas-exchange experiment, but the nutrient was made up of molecules containing radioactive carbon 14. As the microbes consumed the nutrient, it was reasoned, they would give off waste products containing the radioactive carbon. Detectors would tell if any gases in the chamber contained the radioactive carbon. If so, it would be evidence of the metabolic processes of the microorganisms. As in the earlier experiment, large amounts of gas were released immediately, and they did indeed contain the tagged radioactive molecules. Again, as before, the reaction was brief. Surely this was the result of some chemical reaction of the soil, which converted the formic acid in the nutrient into carbon dioxide.

The pyrolitic experiment tried to reproduce the actual conditions on the Martian surface. Rather than inject a radioactively tagged nutrient into the soil, it introduced radioactively tagged carbon dioxide and carbon monoxide into the soil chamber in place of Mars's natural gases. The soil was illuminated with artificial sunlight, and

1. Norman H. Horowitz, *Scientific American* 237 (November, 1977), 52.

later the soil was analyzed to see if any microorganisms had ingested any of the radioactive carbon. This was done by first ridding the chamber of the radioactive gas, and then changing any organic compounds in the soil into carbon dioxide, using heat and chemical reactions. If this carbon dioxide was radioactive, it meant that the carbon dioxide in the air had been changed into other organic compounds by microorganisms in the soil. Or did it?

Seven of the nine tests gave positive results. Was there, then, life on Mars after all? Many scientists who had been hoping to find life there maintained, and some still maintain, that this is evidence for life on Mars, despite the evidence of the other experiments. Norman Horowitz, writing in *Scientific American,* says that this also must be interpreted nonbiologically. Some of the soil samples were heated to 175° C. for three hours before the experiment was begun, and while this did reduce the amount of radioactive carbon dioxide produced, it did not stop the production altogether. These conditions would be enough to kill any earth microorganisms, so presumably they should also kill any Martian microorganisms, since they would be accustomed to living at even lower temperatures. While it might take rather exotic chemistry to explain the results of this experiment, there is very probably no life on Mars.[2]

THE NATURE OF THE SEARCH

The above working definition of life, as epitomized by the experiments aboard the Viking probes, is based upon evolutionary presuppositions, and deals with a chemical or physical aspect of living beings as we imagine them. But it obviously does not encompass the quality of life as we understand it from a Christian viewpoint. The Bible tells us much about life, but it is not a kind understood by the non-Christian. Life has a source and the source is Jesus Christ. "For as the Father hath life in himself; so hath he given to the Son to have life in himself" (John 5:26). "It is the spirit that quickeneth; the flesh profiteth nothing: the words that I speak unto you, they are spirit, and they are life" (John 6:63). And Jesus Himself said, "I am the way, the truth, and the life" (John 14:6). Someone might argue that this is not the type of life we should be discussing; scientists are searching for purely physical life. But I feel that even physically speaking this objection is invalid. The life that scientists are searching for on other planets is the kind described by the above verses. What

2. Ibid.

I mean is that all life comes from the Creator who is life. Nothing which has life has it without God. ". . . he giveth to all life, and breath, and all things" (Acts 17:25). ". . . the spirit giveth life . . ." (II Cor. 3:6). In the first chapter of Genesis we see God create living things, and in the verse which begins this chapter God breathed the breath of life into a body of clay and it became a living being. The existence not only of spiritual life but of physical life depends upon the life giving act of God.

What, then, are scientists looking for when they send space probes to other planets, or when they send radio signals into empty space? They are seeking life, which, if it exists, must have been created by God. But armed with his own definition man is doomed to fail. Consider that the only life we know for sure exists outside the earth is God Himself and the angelic beings which He created. These beings, if examined in the light of man's definition, are not even alive at all! The very author of life does not metabolize, or reproduce, or grow. Jesus Christ is the same yesterday, today, and forever. This life, the life possessed by God and by those to whom He has given life, is found only by the revelation of God, not by man's seeking. The history of religion on earth is a history of man's striving to reach out to God (with the exception of Christianity and Judaism). Man's search for extraterrestrial life is simply another man-made religion. In this case, however, it is not so much a search for God as a search for evidence to justify man's theories. Man is worshiping himself and his own knowledge and abilities.

BIBLICAL CONSIDERATIONS

But are we missing the point? If God did create physical life on other planets, we should reasonably be able to communicate with it, or at least find and identify it. The whole discussion, then, comes down to this: Did God actually create physical life elsewhere in the universe, and if so, what kind? If God did choose to create life on other planets, what kind would it be? Scientists are looking for anything remotely resembling life, from invisible microorganisms to super-intelligent beings. But would we expect God to create a planet populated by nothing but bacteria? Can we even answer the question, why did God create life at all? Without going off on a tangent, it may be said that He created first and foremost to bring glory to Himself. He did this on earth by creating man in His own image. The rest of life on earth is for man's benefit (Gen. 1:28, 29; 9:2; Ps.

8:6; etc.). Besides this, life on earth is so complex and so varied, that the pattern of life on earth, just like the rest of nature as it says in Romans 1:20, shows God's eternal power and Godhead. Would we expect from the nature of God as we know it from the Bible that He would create a planet elsewhere possessing life which was less beautiful, less complex, or less varied? I think not. Now generalizing from a single example, the earth, is not a safe practice, statistically speaking. But the earth is more than a statistic. We have a spiritual principle given to us in that God created an intelligent being in His own image, and that all other life on the planet is subject to that being because of the dominion given him by God.

In the light of this principle, is it likely that God created life elsewhere which is not intelligent, not made in the likeness of God, but only some lowly bacteria or swampy slime? God creates for a purpose, not haphazardly, hence this question must be answered no. The only alternative which seems consistent with our Biblical principle is that if God created life on other planets, it must be intelligent and also made, according to one criterion or another, in the likeness of God. Now before we start imagining a universe peopled with beings like ourselves, we must consider the ramifications of such a hypothesis.

God is love, and because He loved the world He sent His Son to die for the sins of the world. Jesus Christ is now in heaven making intercession for us with the Father. When this Second Person of the Trinity took on Himself the nature of a man, He was changed—not temporarily but permanently. He still bears on His hands the marks of the nails that held Him to the cross. If there are other intelligent civilizations on other planets, perhaps infinitely many, or perhaps but one other, are we to assume that they also were sinful and that to obtain their redemption the Son of God also visited their planets? The idea seems absurd. If there are a large number of other planets, Jesus must be busy dying constantly for them on one planet after another, instead of being in heaven making intercession on our behalf. But it says in Hebrews 9:27, 28, "And as it is appointed unto men once to die, but after this the judgment: so Christ was once offered to bear the sins of many. . . ." Christ died but once in the past and will never die again. "Knowing that Christ being raised from the dead dieth no more" (Rom. 6:9). Apparently in the entire universe, if there is life elsewhere, only one civilization strayed from the Lord and required salvation—ours.

The alternatives are narrowing. On Scriptural grounds it seems safe to say that if there is physical life elsewhere in the universe, it is intelligent and has never sinned. Is such a thing possible? Possible, perhaps. But does it seem reasonable that if the universe is filled with life, that only once would one of the planets fall into sin? The very angels themselves sinned (II Pet. 2:4) who had seen God face to face. Can one expect that mere flesh and blood (no matter what shape or color) could long resist the same temptation? If there are other intelligent beings, they are not yet in heaven, where we are told we will be perfect. Eventually, it seems, someone somewhere in one of these other civilizations would submit to temptation and the redemption story would have to be repeated. There is a final consideration. When the Lord reigns in the new Jerusalem, He will live with men and we shall be His people (Rev. 21:1-3). Would He forget all His other intelligent races? The new Jerusalem will be on earth, and God will live here. There isn't enough room on earth for many other civilizations to live here with us. If God did create other races on other planets, He must have done it only to abandon them later. This is not the way our Lord works. The Scripture says nothing about life on other planets, and every argument that can be made on the basis of Scriptural revelation suggests that we are the only intelligent race of creatures God has created, excluding angels. At the beginning of this book we saw that the heavens and the lights in them were created for signs and seasons and days and years; nothing was said about life. We are thus led to believe that scientists are doomed to failure in their search for life.

WHY CHRISTIANS JOIN THE SEARCH

Now that it has been shown that the Christian need not be surprised not to find life on other planets, we should analyze why he should ask the question in the first place. Scientists look for life on other planets to support their evolutionary, man-centered theories. But why should a Christian look for life elsewhere? Often it is for the same reason, though perhaps he doesn't know it. Today every person hears so much about life on other planets that he comes to believe it is there just because he is so conditioned. The Christian is usually not aware of what thinking is behind these statements.

But even more often one hears it said, "The universe is so large, it just seems there must be life out there somewhere." Christians are just as apt to say this as others, sometimes for the same reasons and sometimes for different ones. One reason is probabilities. If there is life on earth, it seems the chances are that in such a large universe there must be other life also. But probability presupposes that there is some mathematical way of describing the likelihood of finding life. We know that while God does not deal in probabilities in this way, evolutionists do. They say the entire development of life was by chance, and that if it can happen here, it can happen elsewhere also. Clearly, arguing about probability is arguing from the evolutionary point of view and is unacceptable to a Christian.

The second way it is often expressed by the Christian is, "Why would God make such a large universe and put only one populated planet in it?" But the reasons for the existence of the universe have already been examined; its purpose is for signs and to show the glory of God. And the universe must be just as it is to accomplish these purposes; if God created the earth in the manner and for the purposes we have seen, then the nature of the observed universe follows almost automatically. No life elsewhere need even enter the picture. God could easily create an immense universe for the benefit of one small planet—it is within the range of His abilities. To require that God fill the universe just because it is large is limiting His sovereignty. I have not totally eliminated the possibility that God has created life elsewhere, but I have shown that the usual reason for thinking there is life elsewhere is based upon the evolutionary patterns of thought, and that extraterrestrial life is not taught by God's word and may be in contradiction to it.

ORGANIC MOLECULES

When the first man set foot upon the moon, he stepped onto sterile soil. No life ever flourished there, nor will it ever do so in the future. Scientists who had been hoping against hope to find some indication of life there shrugged their shoulders and said, "We shall look elsewhere." The next place they chose was Mars. Mars is the only other place in the solar system besides earth where any life of an earthly nature could be expected to survive. I believe that in spite of this, and in spite of the anomalous results returned so far by the Viking probes, the soil of Mars will be found as sterile as that of the moon. Failing to find life on Mars, scientists will next search outside the solar system, looking for life on planets surrounding distant stars (if they even exist), the nearest of which could never be reached in our lifetime.

Though it would seem that a search for life has been put beyond our reach almost forever, scientists have found something to excite their interest even within the solar system—organic molecules. In meteorites which have landed on earth, and even in a very few lunar samples, molecules which on earth are associated with life have been discovered, including amino acids, the building blocks of life. A great fuss indeed has been made over the experiment in which such molecules were made in a laboratory by passing an electric current through ordinary gases such as ammonia, methane, and water. This has long been touted as evidence that lifelike molecules appear spontaneously and that life must thus evolve everywhere. The organic molecules in meteorites must have formed in a similar way, they say. But all this experiment really shows is that the organic molecules found in meteorites did not necessarily form from life at all and are no indicator of life. Nor need it disconcert us that such molecules form easily under some circumstances. Is it not natural for God to have formed us from the simple molecules easily formed in nature? If it were extremely difficult for such molecules to form, man would have a difficult time metabolizing food into the appropriate molecules within his body. Adam was formed from the dust of the earth. It should not be surprising, therefore, that the same things from which man was formed can also be found in the dust of the earth, or of the moon. It still takes an act of God to create life.

There are a number of different kinds of complex molecules which have been found in space, including alcohol, which is normally a waste product of living organisms. There are other organic molecules as well, and some scientists have been so bold as to suggest that, when the earth formed, it incorporated such molecules into itself and that from these, life formed. This is simply an illustration of the imaginative powers of men who desire to find life everywhere, and jump at every straw to prove that life evolved. I shall not give all the reasons why this is not a reasonable suggestion, but shall simply say that it is unnecessary. It has already been found that complex molecules could conceivably be formed by a lightning stroke under the right circumstances. Interstellar molecules need not be invoked. To do so is an indication of the state of man's mind and his desire to encourage himself into believing in evolution.

THE PATTERN OF SEARCH

Scientists, in the effort to estimate the probability of finding life on some other planet, usually follow a pattern in which they first estimate the probability of finding the right kinds of stars and then ascertain that those stars have planets, that those planets are hospitable, and finally that life has evolved. Let us follow this reasoning for a while and see where it leads. Near what kind of star could life exist? Many scientists start out by assuming that they should look at stars of the same type as the sun, but this is not necessarily reasonable. Any star which could supply heat to its planets should not be ruled out. Assumptions, however, of the time it takes for life to evolve lead them to consider only stars with long lifetimes. This means that the brightest stars are excluded, since lifetimes are in the millions and not billions of years. The majority of stars are less massive than the sun and have theoretically longer lifetimes. Most stars should be considered possible candidates. So far this is little different from the argument that since there are so many billions of stars, there must be life somewhere. All that has really been said to this point is that there are lots and lots of stars.

Well, then, how many of those stars have planets? One of the nearest stars to earth, Barnard's star, has long been thought to be possessed of a planetary system. These planets have not been seen; it would be impossible to see even the largest planet of the nearest star because of the great distances involved. Instead, the motions of Barnard's star have been carefully observed, and it has been seen to wobble as if there were some planets in orbit around it. In fact, it has been stated that there are two planets, one slightly larger than the other and both about the size of Jupiter.[3] Since one of the nearest stars seems to have planets, it is said, planets must be an extremely common occurrence in the universe. Recently, however, a more precise examination of photographs of 55 years in the life of Barnard's star shows no wobble at all.[4] There are no planets after all. Barnard's star, the great hope and shining example, has failed to come through. Of the one or two other stars around which planets have been thought to orbit, the uncertainties in the measurements are even greater than in the case of Barnard's star. Thus we find little or no evidence for any planets outside our solar system. Nor are we likely ever to find any by direct observation because of the difficulties involved.

Guesses as to the abundance of planets based upon theories of star formation are less certain still. A person may propose as many or as

3. Hartmann, *Moons and Planets,* p. 372.
4. *Science News* 104 (1973), 372.

few planets as he likes, depending, as we have seen, upon what assumptions he starts out with. It is useless to make definite statements on the basis of unproven theories. Still, one astronomer estimates that from one to 50 percent of all stars possess planets.[5]

Of these planets, how many would be expected to be habitable? The planet must be neither too hot (too close to its star) nor too cold (too far away). Most planets in our solar system are either too hot or too cold and, if other solar systems exist, it is reasonable to expect the same situation. There must be enough sunlight to produce photosynthesis, or its equivalent, and the light must have the right spectrum. For photosynthesis as we know it, the star would have to be approximately solar.

It is already apparent, though, that to guess the number of habitable planets is utterly impossible. There is simply no way to estimate the number of stars which might have planets, and the percentage of those planets which would be habitable. Any attempt to give actual numbers is a result of someone's wild imagination. Yet numbers have been assigned. One author suggests that five percent of all stars have habitable planets (but not necessarily inhabited), while other estimates range from one in a million to one in ten planets actually being inhabited by some kind of life.[6] Even under evolutionary assumptions these estimates are optimistic in the extreme. If we take one percent as a middle-of-the-road figure, then in our galaxy alone, out of about 2×10^{11} stars there will be 2×10^{9} inhabited planets. On evolutionary principles it must be assumed that those which contain intelligent life (a term difficult to define) would be smaller in number, perhaps, again, only one percent, or 2×10^{7} planets in the Galaxy possessing intelligent life. This corresponds to an average distance between civilizations of about 150 light years. Could life be detected if it were really there?

THREE TYPES OF TESTS

There are three basic ways to determine if life exists on nearby planets. First, an astronaut could go to different stars and search for life-bearing planets. Second, "people" from those planets could come visit us. Third, we could receive some kind of signal from them across the many light years. The first alternative is out of the question. Though the technological advances which lie in the future may

5. Hartmann, *Moons and Planets,* p. 373.
6. Ibid., p. 388.

be incredible, they will all be limited to the most fundamental limitation of nature—the speed of light. In our own time men have traveled to the moon, reaching speeds of 25,000 miles per hour. This is only .003 percent of the speed of light. At this rate it would take over 100,000 years to travel to the nearest star. Even if a spaceship could be built to travel 1,000 times faster, it would still take 100 years to reach the nearest star, and twice that long for a round trip. The chances of that one star having inhabited planets are pretty slim. If the ultimate could be built, a spaceship which could travel at the speed of light, it would have to examine every star within 150 light years to have a good chance of finding intelligent life. This would still take thousands of years. Obviously, going on a search for extraterrestrial life is not a practical idea.

Well, then, have we been visited by other creatures? The recent spate of UFO sightings and an incredible glut of books about such visitations notwithstanding, the answer must be negative. I do not intend to enter a discussion of UFOs; there are plenty of books on the subject already. Instead, I quote from *The Cosmic Connection* by Carl Sagan, perhaps the world's most outspoken proponent of extraterrestrial life. He first dismisses UFOs on the basis of probabilities; he apparently takes little stock in such sightings. Then, in regard to myths (which some say are actually about ancient alien visitation) or to artifacts (which some say were left here by ancient astronauts), he says, "There is only one category of legend that would be convincing: When information is contained in the legend that could not possibly have been generated by the civilization that created the legend. . . . Also convincing would be a certain class of artifact. If an artifact of technology were passed on from ancient civilization—an artifact that is far beyond the technological capabilities of the originating civilization—we would have an interesting *prima facie* case for extraterrestrial visitation. . . . To the best of my knowledge, there are no such legends and no such artifacts."[7]

Then, commenting on the cave paintings and other ancient drawings which some have imagined to be pictures of astronauts from other planets, he says, "In fact, the expectation that extraterrestrial astronauts would look precisely like American or Soviet astronauts, down to their space suits and eyeballs, is probably less credible than the idea of visitation itself. . . . These artifacts are, in fact, psycho-

7. C. Sagan, *The Cosmic Connection* (New York: Dell Publishing Co., Inc., 1973), p. 205.

logical projective tests. People can see in them what they wish."[8] If Carl Sagan, the most outspoken of exobiologists, rejects visitation from other planets, I need add nothing more.

This leaves the third possibility, that we might receive signals of some sort from another civilization. These would in all probability be in the form of electromagnetic radiation, that is, the familiar components of the spectrum. More exotic methods have been proposed, such as gravitational waves and tachyons (particles that move faster than light), but so far there is no evidence that either of these exists. Besides, there is no way of communicating in these modes. This leaves us with the old standby—light. This might be either in the form of radio signals, or infrared, or even visible light. The latter two would take too much energy to use as signals; no really intelligent society would waste so much energy on such an unproductive enterprise. Radio waves seem to offer the only reasonable medium for communication. In the past some groups have actually tried "listening" to some stars with radio telescopes, hoping to hear these signals. At present there is a project under consideration in the United States to spend considerable time and money on just this subject. So far nothing has been observed, but really very few stars have been examined. To listen to every possible star would take hundreds of years and cost billions of dollars. Amazingly enough, there is one particular radio telescope, the Arecibo telescope in Puerto Rico, which could actually communicate with another its own size anywhere in the Milky Way Galaxy. On some occasions it has actually been used for such an attempt. Again, there are only negative results.

So, on Scriptural grounds we should not expect to find physical life on any other planets in the universe. Even on evolutionary grounds life which we could detect would be quite scarce. Communication by radio is the only reasonable alternative, and if for no other reason than the limitation of our resources, we should not expect ever to detect any civilization which did exist. As the astronauts who have seen the earth from outer space have observed, the earth seems to be such a small, frail ball, all alone in space, that we can all be considered passengers on spaceship earth. Let us strive to concern ourselves with the business of our own spaceship, and, particularly as Christians, with the spreading of the gospel to our fellow travelers. The genuine extraterrestrial life, the heavenly beings, already know it.

---

8. Ibid., pp. 206-207.

APPENDIX

Scientific notation is designed to make the writing of extremely large or small numbers easier. A number expressed in scientific notation consists of a number times 10 to a power. This power is called an exponent. For example, in the number 4×10^5, the five above the 10 is the exponent. The exponent tells us that 10 is multiplied by itself five times. This is the same as a one followed by five zeroes. Thus $10^5 = 10 \times 10 \times 10 \times 10 \times 10 = 100{,}000$, and $4 \times 10^5 = 4 \times 10 \times 10 \times 10 \times 10 \times 10 = 400{,}000$. This is a much more compact way of writing large numbers. Ten billion is written simply as 10^{10} (10,000,000,000), and so on.

The same method can be used to express small numbers by using negative exponents. A number with a negative exponent is the *inverse* of what the number would have been without the negative sign. For example, $10^{-2} = 1/10^2 = 1/100 = .01$. 4×10^{-5} becomes $4 \times 1/10^5 = 4 \times .00001 = .00004$.

SCRIPTURE INDEX

Genesis

1—2, 100, 197
1:1—188, 190
1:1, 2—99, 197
1:2—100
1:14-18—62
1:14-19—224
1:16—80, 125
1:18—80
1:28, 29—230
2:7—225
5—3
9:2—230
10—3
15—125
15:5—125
37—125

Exodus

20:11—3, 98

Numbers

10:10—64
24:17—126
28:11—64

Joshua

10:12-14—82-83

Judges

5:20—125

II Kings

1:6—33
17:30—33
20:11—84
23:5—33

II Chronicles

32:31—84

Job

9:9—126
26:7—19
26:10—19
38:7—126
38:12—81

Psalms

8:6—230-31
19:1-3—2
49:7—6
104:19—62
139:14—18
147:4—124
148:3—80

Isaiah

9:2—126
13:9, 10—81
13:10—82
14:13—126
40:22—19
46:1—32
65:11—32

Jeremiah

10:12—194
51:15—98, 188

Ezekiel

32:7—81

Daniel

2:27—33

Joel

2:10—81
2:31—65, 81

Amos

5:25, 26—33

Habakkuk

2:14—18

Matthew

2:1, 2, 9, 10—127
24:29—65, 81
27:45—85

Luke

3—3

John

1:10—191
5:26—229
6:63—229
14:6—229

Acts

2:19, 20—81
7:43—33
14:17—22
17:25—230

Romans

1:20—1, 2, 23, 231
5:8—6
6:9—231
13:12—37

I Corinthians

6:14—37
15—23

II Corinthians

3:6—230
4:4—94

Galatians

1:6, 7—101

Ephesians

2:6—37

Hebrews

9:27, 28—231
11:3—97, 188

II Peter

1:19—37
2:4—232
3:8—219

Jude

13—32

Revelation

6:12—81
8:8—49
12:4—32
21:1-3—232

SUBJECT INDEX

Major references appear in boldface type.

Abraham, 125
Absolute ages, 67, 75
Accretion, 77, 78, 103-23 passim
Adam, 153, 224, 234
Adams, 57
Adar, 64
Age: of universe, 2-8, 187, 191, 195, 216, 219-24; of earth, 23-30; of Mars, 42-43, 45-46; of solar system, 45, 50, 55, 57, 59-61, 98, 100, 106-07, 111-12, 114; of Jupiter, 52; of moon, 66-76 passim; of sun, 88, 91, 93-94, 152; of stars, 136-37, 138, 143, 144-45, 151, 153; of globular clusters, 170-73; of galaxies, 176-78, 213; of clusters of galaxies, 179-80, 183, 185, 216-17
Albedo, 37-38
Alcohol, 234
Allende meteorite, 121
Amino acids, 234
Amorites, 82-83
Andromeda Galaxy, 161, 162, 163, 171, 179, 186, 214
Angel, destroying, 32
Angels, 128, 230, 232
Angular momentum, 112-14, 139
Antarctica, 27
Antilepton, 92
Antimatter, 201-02
Antiparticle, 89, 92, 201
Apollo 12, 68
Apollo 16, 71
Apollo 17, 71
Apollo group, 49-50, 72, 117
Apollo program, 66-68
Arcturus, 126
Arecibo telescope, 238
Argon, 36, 93, 120. *See also* Potassium-argon method
Aristotle, 130
Arizona meteorite crater, 50
Arontius Phinneus, 27
Arp, 212-14, 216, 217
A stars, 132, 139
Asteroids, 33, 48-50, 72, 74, 104, 110, 111, 115-16, 117-18
Astrology, 33
Astronomical unit, 22, 47

Astronomy, 1
Atoms, 13; size of, 9
Aurorae, 95
Australia, 26, 27
Axis: of earth, 20, 22, 80; of Uranus, 56, 108-10; of sun, 107-08

Babylon, 33, 84
Barnard's star, 129, 235
Barnes, Dr. Thomas, 28-30
Barred spirals, 176
Beryllium, 119
Bethe, Hans, 89
Bethlehem, star of, 126-28
Big bang theories, 195-209 passim, 215, 217-18
Binary stars, 129, 130, 154, 215, 220
Black hole, 139-40, 171, 184
Blue light, 164, 216
Blueshift, 16, 187
Blue stellar objects, 212
Bode's law, 47-48, 58, 110
Boron, 119
Bounce, 200
Bound universe, 198-99
Brightness of stars, 132; as measure of distance, 186-87
BSO, 212
B stars, 134, 138, 139, 208

Calendar, Jewish, 64
Callisto, 52
Canals, Martian, 39, 40, 41
Carbon, 139, 153, 226-27, 228
Carbon 14, 95, 228
Catastrophism, 23, 44, 49, 58, 74-75
cD galaxy, 184-85
Cell, size of, 10
Central bulge, 173
Cepheids, 156-58, 162, 185
Ceres, 47-48
Channels (on Mars), winding, 42, 43
Chemical composition: of rocks, 25; of earth and moon, 77-78; of planets, 116-21
Chiun, 33
Christian assumptions, 4-8. *See also* Creationism
Chromatograph, 227-28
Chromosphere, 85-87
Chryse, 45
Church, outmoded dogmas of the, 6
Clouds on planets, 38, 39, 52, 55
Cluster mass, measuring, 180-83
Clusters, 133, 139, 147-50, 153, 169-73; of galaxies, 10, 179-85, 186-87, 221-22
Cocoon nebulae, 102
Columbus, 19
Comets, 31, 32, **58-61**, 72, 115, 117, 127-28, 220
Companion galaxy, 214
Conjunction of two planets, 128
Continental drifts, 26-27
Continuous creation, 99, 196, 217, 218
Contraction: of Jupiter, 51-52; of sun, 87-88, 91, 103; of stars, 138-41; of universe, 198, 199, 200
Corona, 66, 86, 87, 173
Cosmic abundance, 116, 118
Cosmic Connection, The (Sagan), 237
Cosmic rays, 27-28, 53
Cosmological principle, 195-96
Cosmology, 11, **188-210**, 215-16
Crab Nebula, 155, 159, 168
Cratering rate, 43, 73-76
Craters: on Mars, 41, 43; on Mars's satellites, 45, 46; on the moon, 67, 68, 72-77; Arizona, 50
Creation, continuous. *See* Continuous creation
Creationism, 44, 45, 56, 67-68, 71-72, 73, 76-77, 79, 87, 91, 95, 98-99, 100, 105, 112, 113, 135, 147, 150, 153, 165-68, 185, 187, 217, 219, 220
Crucifixion, 85
Crust (of moon), 68-69, 71, 72
"Curved" space, 193-94, 224
Cyclic universe, 198, 200
Cygnus X-1, 184

Dark areas (Mars), 39, 41
Dark nebula, 165

Daughter elements, 24-25, 68
David, 1-2, 32
Davis, Raymond, 93-94
Day of Atonement, 64
Day of the Lord, 65, 66, 81
Day star, 32, 37
Decay rates, 24, 30
Deimos, 44-45, 111
Deuterium, 89, 119, 199
Disk, 102, 103, 173
Distance, measuring great, 130, 158, 170, 185-87, 206, 213, 214, 215
Doppler shift, 16-17, 174, 176, 179, 180, 187, 192, 214, 215
Double-galaxy method, 181, 182-83
Dust, interplanetary, 60-61
Dwarf galaxies, 178, 185, 222
Dynamics, cluster, 170-71
Dynamo theory, 28-29, 36, 38, 69

Earth, 10, **18-30**, 33, 34, 42, 77-78, 108, 120; shape and position of the, 19-23; age of the, 23-30
Eccentricity, 111
Eclipses, 65-66, 81-82, 85, 86, 87
Ecliptic plane, 20, 22
Ecliptic planetary orbits, 102, 107, 109, 115
Eddy, John, 95
Einstein's theory, 89, 193-94, 216
Electromagnetic radiation, 11, 238
Electron, 13, 92, 155, 168-69
Elliptical galaxies, 164, 174, 176, 177, 181, 212-13, 215
Energy, 11, 13-16, 155-56, 181-82; from Jupiter, 51-52, 87; of the sun, 85-94; negative, 182, 200; levels, 16
Envelope, 139
Equipartition of energy, 170-71
Eratosthenes, 19
Evening star, 34, 37
Evolution, stellar, 42, 95, 102, 134-54
Evolutionary theories. *See* Big bang theories
Evolutionist assumptions, 3-4, 42, 76, 88, 95, 100, 150-52, 191, 227, 229, 233, 236
Exobiology, 226-27. *See also* Life
Expanding universe, 194-95, 199, 201, 216, 217-18
Exponent, 239
Extraterrestrial life, 225-38. *See also* Intelligent life theory

Feast of Tabernacles, 64, 65
Fission, 77
Flare star, 158
Flood, 26
Fluorescence, 168
Formation, modern theories of solar system, 101-23
Fractionation, 121
Frequency, 11, 16
Funkhouser, 25
Fusion. *See* Nuclear fusion in sun

Gad, 32
Galactic clusters, 133, 169
Galaxies, 10, **161-87**, 212-18, 221; formation of, 200-01, 213, 218
Galaxy, the. *See* Milky Way
Galileo, 6, 53
Gamma rays, 201
Ganymede, 52
Gap theory, 99-100, 197
Gas chromatograph, 227-28
Gas-exchange experiment, 228
Gauss, Karl, 30
Genesis 1, interpretations of, 99-100, 197
Geocentricity, disproof of, 6-7
Giant stars, 133, 143, 147, 152, 154
Globular clusters, 133-34, 169-73, 176
Gott, 199
Grains, interstellar, 165-68
Gravitational constant, 223
Gravitational contraction: of Jupiter, 51-52; of the sun, 87-88, 91; of stars, 138-41
Gravitational potential energy, 87
Gravitational waves, 238
Gravity, 3, 19, 57, 59, 69, 104, 105-06, 108, 111, 115, 179-80, 181-82, 189, 192, 193-94, 198-99, 200, 223
Greenhouse effect, 55
Ground ice sapping, 43

Gulliver's Travels (Swift), 44
Gunn, 199

Half-life, 50
Halley's comet, 59, 60, 115
Halo, 87, 173; of dim stars, 184-85
Harwit, Martin, 128, 134, 136, 137
Hawaii, 25, 42
Heat flow (moon), 70, 72
Heisenberg uncertainty principle, 200
Helium, 13, 23-24, 36, 88, 89, 92, 93-94, 103, 118, 119, 133, 139, 153-54, 165, 207-08
Helmholtz, Herman von, 87, 91
Herschel, Sir John, 87
Herschel, Sir William, 56
Hertzsprung-Russell diagram, 141-50, 153, 170
Hezekiah, 84-85
Hiryama families, 117
Homogeneity, 191, 195
Horoscope, 33
Horowitz, Norman, 229
Hualalai, 25
Hubble, 194, 206
Hubble constant, 206, 215
Hydrogen, 13, 15, 52, 88-91, 92, 93-94, 103, 116, 118, 119, 133, 137, 138, 139, 141, 146, 150, 165, 174, 186, 199, 208
Hydrostatic equilibrium, 88

Icarus, 50
"Ice age, little," 95
Ice sapping, 43
Immensity of universe, 9-11, 187
Inclination, 111, 116
Infrared, 238; stars, 102
Intelligent life theory, 39-40, 125. *See also* Life
Internal rotation method, 180, 182-83
Interplanetary dust, 60-61
Interstellar matter, 135-38 passim, 144, 164-68, 169, 170, 173
Interstellar molecules, 168
Io, 52-53, 55
Ion, 13, 114
Ionized hydrogen, 186
Irons, 49
Irregularities, 178-79
Irregulars (galaxies), 174, 176
Irregular variables, 158-59
Isaiah, 19, 84
Isotopic ratios, 120-21
Isotropy, 191, 216
Israel, 82-83

Jesus Christ, 6, 32, 37, 126, 127-28, 229, 231; resurrection of, 23, 37; crucifixion of, 85
Jet streams, 117
Job, 19
Joseph, 125
Joshua, 82-84
Jovian planets, 34, 116, 118
Jupiter, 32, 33, 34, 47, **51-53**, 55, 59, 87, 111-12, 115

Kant, 102
Karoji, 216
Kepler, Johannes, 44
Kinetic energy, 181-82
Krypton, 120
K stars, 132

Labeled-release experiment, 228
Laplace, 102
Leaching, 25, 26
Lead, 24, 25. *See also* Uranium-lead dating
Leptons, 92
Leverrier, 57
Life, 225-38. *See also* Intelligent life theory
Light, 202, 238; energy, 13-16; speed of, 202, 222-24, 237
Light nebula, 168
Lithium, 13, 119, 144, 145
"Little ice age," 95
Local Group, 10, 179, 185
Long-period comets, 59-60, 115
Long-period objects, 220-22
Long-period variables, 156
Love, God's, 5-6, 231
Lowell, Percival, 40, 57
Lucifer, 126
Lunar highlands, 67

M31, 179, 214. *See also* Andromeda
M87, 213
Magellanic clouds, 156-58, 161, 171-72, 176
Magma, 27, 36, 68
Magnesium sulphate, 49
Magnetic fields, 27-30, 36, 38, 53, 55, 69, 139; of the sun, 113, 114-15
Magnetic reversals, 29
Magnetopause, 53
Main sequence stars, 132, 139, 140, 141-50 passim, 153, 154
Man, 225-26
Maria, 36, 67, 71, 72, 73
Mariner 4, 40-41
Mariner 6, 41
Mariner 7, 41
Mariner 9, 41, 43, 45, 73
Mariner 10, 34, 36, 38, 73
Mars, 32, 33, 34, **39-47**, 73, 111, 227-29, 233
Mascons, 69
Mass: of stars, 130, 132; measuring cluster, 180-83
Mass-luminosity relation, 146
Mass spectrometer, 47, 227-28
Mauna Loa, 42
Maunder, E. W., 94
Meni, 32
Mercury, 32, 33, **34-36**, 73
Mestel, L., 122
Meteorites, 25-26, 49, 50, 69, 71, 72, 73, 88, 119, 121, 234
Meteors, 32, 45, 68, 70, 73
Meteor showers, 117
Milky Way, 10, 161, **162-74**, 179, 184
"Missing mass," 183-84
Models: of solar system formation, 101-23; cosmological, 189-209
Molecules, organic, 233-34
Moloch, 33
Moon, 10, 31, 32, 37, 38, **62-79**, 82, 83-84, 87, 105, 120, 223, 227, 233
Moon (and Spencer), 224
Moonquakes, 70
Moonrocks, 25-26, 67-68, 77
Moreaux, Abbe, 40
Morning star, 32, 34, 37, 126
Moses, 125
Mountains (Mars), 41-42
M stars, 132, 158
Mutation, 227

Natural selection, 227
Naughton, 25
Nebo, 32
Nebuchadnezzar, 32
Nebula, solar, 100, 102, 103, 106-08, 114, 115, 116-17, 123
Nebulae, 122, 164-69; sequence of, 175
Nebular hypothesis, 102-23 passim
Neon, 36, 55, 119-20
Neptune, 33, 34, 44, **57**, 58, 110
Nereid, 57
Nergal, 32
Neutrino, 92-94, 152
Neutron, 13, 89, 120, 155
Neutron star, 30, 139, 155
New Mars, The (Hartmann, Odell), 43-44
New moon to the Jews, importance of, 64-65
Newton, Sir Isaac, 19, 57, 192-93
Ney, 61
NGC 722, 214-15
NGC 6712, 171
Nisan, 65
Noah, 26
Noble gases, 36, 119-20
North Star, 22, 158
Nottlae, 216
Nova, 127, 156, 159, 186
Nuclear burning of hydrogen, 89-91. *See also* Nuclear fusion in sun; Nuclear reactions in stars
Nuclear fusion in sun, 91-94
Nuclear reactions in stars, 135, 136, 137, 139, 146, 150-52, 218

Olber's paradox, 192-93, 221
Olympus Mons, 41-42
Oort cloud, 59, 115, 184
Open clusters, 133, 169
Orbits: of electrons, 13-16; of planets, 22, 107, 108-11, 122; of Mars, 42; of Mars's satellites, 45; synchro-

nous, 45; of Uranus, Nereid, and Neptune, 57; of Pluto, 58; of comets, 59, 115, 117; of satellites around the moon, 69; of the moon, 78; of planetary satellites, 110-12; of asteroids, 115-16, 117
Organic molecules, 233-34
Origin and Destiny of the Earth's Magnetic Field (Barnes), 29
Orion, 126
Orion arm, 162
Orion nebula, 167, 168
OSO-5, 61
O stars, 132, 134, 139, 143, 144
Oterma, 115

Pallas, 48, 115-16
Parallax, 130, 131
Parent element, 24-25
Passover, 65, 85
Paul, 22
Peebles, P. J. E., 178-79
Pentecost, 65
Perfect cosmological principle, 196, 204, 217
Perseus arm, 164
Phobos, 44-45, 46-47, 111
Phoebe, 110
Photosphere, 85, 87
Photosynthesis, 236
Piazzi, 47
Pioneer 6, 215
Pioneer 10, 52, 53
Pioneer 11, 52-53
Placet, 26
Planetary Geology (Short), 61, 74
Planetary nebula, 138, 140, 156
Planetesimals, 72-78 passim, 103-04, 105, 109, 115
Planets, 22, 32, 33-34, 73, 74, 76-77, 102, 104, 106-07, 108-11, 235-36; chemical composition of, 116-21
Plate tectonics. *See* Continental drift
Pleiades, 126, 133, 166, 168
Pluto, 10, 33, 34, **57-58**, 78
Polar caps, Martian, 39, 40, 41, 43, 46
Polaris, 158
Population I stars, 133, 134, 135-38, 171
Population II stars, 133, 135-38, 170, 176
Positron, 89, 92
Potassium-argon method, 25, 45-46, 67, 68
Potential energy, 181-82
Poynting-Robertson effect, 60
Pressure waves (P waves), 70
Probability, 233
Proton, 13, 89, 155
Proton-proton chain, 89, 90, 92, 93
Protoplanets, 105-06, 118
Protostar, 139, 144-47
Proto-sun, 102
Pulsars, 155-56, 159, 169
Pulsations: solar, 151-52; of Cepheids, 158
P waves, 70
Pyrolitic experiment, 228-29

Quasars, 17, 159, 169, 204-05, 211-17

Radiation: from Jupiter, 53; from Saturn, 55; synchrotron, 168-69
Radio galaxies, 204-05, 215, 216
Radiometric methods of dating, 23-26, 67-68
Radio signals, 155, 238; from Jupiter, 51-52
Radio sources, 203-06, 212, 215, 217
Radio waves (Galaxy), 173-74
Radon, 120
Rays: from moon craters, 75; bending of light, 194
Reddening effect, 164-65
Red giant, 138, 139, 140, 141, 146, 147, 152, 153
Red light, 164, 216
Redshift, 17, 187, 194, 205, 211, 212-17; magnitudes, 206-07
Red spot (Jupiter), 51
Reflection nebula, 168
Regolith, 68
Relative ages, 43, 67, 75
Relativity, 193-94
Relaxation time, 170-71, 178
Remnant magnetism, 29
Rephan, 33

Reproduction, 227
Resonance, 108
Retrograde motion, 38, 57, 58, 108-12
Riemannian space, 224
Ring Nebula, 157
"Rings" (sun), 117
Ring system: of Saturn, 53, 78, 106; of Uranus, 56, 78
Roche limit, 78, 105-06, 117, 119
Rotation, planetary, 108-11
RR Lyrae variables, 156-58, 170, 185
Rubidium-strontium dating, 67, 68
Russian space probes, 38, 227

Sagan, Carl, 237-38
Sagittarius, 170, 173-74; arm, 164
Salt method of dating, 23
Satan, 126
Satellites, 110-12; of Mars, 44-45, 46-47, 111; of Jupiter, 52-53, 111-12; of Saturn, 53, 55; of Neptune, 57, 58; of Uranus, 109-10. *See also* Moon
Saturn, 32, 33, 34, **53-55**, 78, 106
Schiaparelli, 40
Schmidt, M., 211
Schwartzschild radius, 140
Schwassmann-Wachmann comet, 115
Schyrl, Anton Maria, 44
Scientific notation, 239
Scriptural references to heavenly objects, 32-33, 37, 62, 65, 80-85, 98, 124-28, 188
Sea-floor spreading, 26
Seasons, cause of, 22-23, 80-81
Secchi, Father, 40
Seed galaxies, 201
Selection effect, 187
Severny, Andrei B., 152
Shear waves (S waves), 70
Shooting stars, 31, 32, 50, 117
Short, Dr. Nicholas, 61, 74, 75
Short-period comets, 59-60, 115
Siberia, 50
Signs: in the moon, 65-66; in the sun, 81-85
Silicates, 104-05
Sisera, 126
Six-day creation, 2-3, 98, 99
Slipher, 194
Solar system, 10, 13, **31-61**; formation of the, 97-123
Solar wind, 36, 53, 58, 69, 114, 118, 119, 172
Source evolution, 204, 205
Space program, 76-77. *See also* Apollo; Mariner; Pioneer; Viking; Russian space probes
Spallation reactions, 119, 151
Sparrow, 61
Spectral classification of stars, 130
Spectral lines, 11-17
Spectroscope, 13
Spencer, 224
Spiral galaxies, 162, 164, 174-78, 186, 215, 222
Spiritual interpretations of Genesis 1, 99-100
Sporer, Gustav, 94
Standard candle, 186-87
Stars, 10, 15-16, 122, **124-60**, 235. *See also* Galaxies
Static universe, 215, 217-18
Steady state theory, 195-97, 201-08 passim, 212, 217-18
Stellar associations, 133, 134
Stellar evolution. *See* Evolution, stellar
Stellar populations, 133
Stephen, 33
Stones, 49
Stony irons, 49
Strontium. *See* Rubidium-strontium dating
Sun, 32, 37, 42, 64, 65-66, **80-96**, 103, 106, 107-08, 112-15, 117, 118, 119, 151-52
Sundial, 84
Sunspots, 94-95
Superclusters, 10-11, 179
Supergiant stars, 133, 138, 143
Superior planets, 39
Supernova, 121, 127, 135, 137, 139, 155, 156, 159, 223
S waves, 70
Swift, Jonathan, 44-45
Synchronous orbits, 45

Synchrotron radiation, 168-69
Syrtis Major, 41

Tachyons, 238
Technetium, 151
Terminator, 19
Terrestrial planets, 34, 116, 118
Theories of solar system formation, modern, 101-23
Thermodynamics, second law of, 118
Thermokarst, 43
Thorium, 23-24
3C273, 211
Tidal effects, 105-06, 223
Tilt: of earth, 22, 80-81; of Uranus, 56, 108-10; of the sun, 107-08
Time, problems of, 219-24. *See also* Age
Tired light theory, 216
Tishri, 64
Titan, 55
Titius, 47
Tombaugh, Clyde, 57
Triton, 57, 58, 110
Trojans, 116, 117
T Tauri stars, 118-19, 144-46
Turnoff point, 148-49, 150, 153, 170

UFOs, 237
Unbound universe, 198-99
Uniformitarianism, 23, 26, 43-44, 49, 55, 68, 71, 73-74, 95-96, 114, 217
Uniqueness, 226
Universality, 191
Universe: age of, 2-8, 187, 191, 195, 216, 219-24; immensity of, 9-11, 187; expanding, 194-95, 199, 201, 216, 217-18; bound or unbound, 198-99; static, 215, 217-18
Uranium, 25
Uranium-lead dating, 67, 68
Uranus, 33, 34, 44, **55-56**, 57, 78, 108-10
Ussher, Bishop, 3, 30

Van Allen radiation belts, 27, 53
Van Flandern, Thomas, 223
Variable stars, 127, 156-59, 170
Venera 9, 38
Venus, 32, 33, 34, **37-39**, 55, 108, 227
Vigier, 216
Viking I, 45-46, 227-29
Viking II, 46, 227-29
Virgo cluster, 215
Virial theorem, 181-82, 183
Volcanism (moon), 68-72
Volcanoes (Mars), 41-42, 43

Water (Mars), 42, 43, 46
Wavelength, 11, 12, 16, 174
White dwarfs, 133, 140, 143, 152, 154, 155
White stars, 16
WZ Sagittae, 154

Xenon, 36, 120
X-rays, 171, 184

Zodiacal light, 60-61